Praise for *Shattered*

Laura Stearns' unwavering commitment to personal and collective healing radiates from every page of this unflinch̲ː̲ ̲ ̲ ̲ ̲ ̲tle book. Unflinching in that it names n̲ ̲ ̲ ̲ ̲ ̲ ̲ ̲ ̲ ̲ ̲ ̲uried far too long. Gentle in that it is, a̲ ̲ ̲ ̲ ̲ ̲ ̲ ̲ ̲ ̲ ̲ ̲ ̲ffirming struggle to become whole. St̲ ̲ ̲ ̲ ̲ ̲ ̲ ̲ ̲ ̲ ̲ ̲ ̲story of abuse and survival; skillful exp̲ ̲ ̲ ̲ ̲ ̲ ̲ ̲ ̲ ̲ ̲ ̲ sexual and emotional trauma; and the det̲ ̲ ̲ ̲ ̲ ̲ ̲efforts of Children's Theatre survivors to demand accountability and reparation. *Shattered* is, more than anything else, a call to action.

-Ricardo Levins Morales, Artist and social justice organizer

Laura Stearns' honesty and candor in addressing sexual assault of children teaches us, sensitizes us, motivates us, and guides us to build a world that is safer for children. Her willingness to shine a light on every corner of this dark time, and her demand for institutional accountability, offers hope for healing and tools that can diminish access and opportunity for future harm. Stearns' desire to become bigger than her abuse, and the uncompromising support from other victims, has given her the gift of vision and deep understanding. She offers promising solutions, community healing, hope and healing for other victims, and greater awareness for everyone who knows and loves them. The entire world should read this memoir.

-Patty Wetterling, child advocate, speaker, author, hopeologist and chair of the National Center for Missing and Exploited Children

Powerfully written, the reader is filled with rage at the denial and betrayal of a powerful institution, and the callousness of those who could have but did nothing after the sexual abuse of youth in their care was known. It's a story of the ups and downs of legal processing of these cases, especially civil efforts to obtain justice and how it often duplicates the betrayal and abuse of the original outrage.

It's a powerful account of a survivor's journal from the youth it is happening to, the adult who carried the pain flowing from the abuse, to the adult who overcomes; indeed, excels in recovery. If Laura can turn the horror of her experience into helping others, certainly, we who read this memoir can ask what we can do to put an end to this all too frequent story. The essence of privilege is to know one has it and do nothing.

-Jon R. Conte, Ph.D., University of Washington, Seattle, WA

Laura Stearns memoir is a written journey of how vulnerability and talent could strengthen a sexual predator's instinct in the highly competitive world of Children's Theatre. The chronology is engrossing with accurate descriptions of a child's naivete as she is both physically and emotionally exploited. The author is riveting in her description of the intentional blindness to the abuse which was so commonplace by the Children's Theatre Company hierarchy. She is also compelling and insightful in providing an important perspective of the necessity of being a successful actor while carrying the fearful burden of a prey.

-Sharon W. Cooper M.D., Forensic Pediatrician, International Consultant on Child Sexual Exploitation, expert witness, author, and editor of Medical, Legal, and Social Science Aspects of Child Sexual Exploitation

Shattered is a book that's waited to be written and read for over 30 years. What Laura Stearns has accomplished is nothing short of a marvel: a moving, heartbreaking, enraging, suspenseful page turner that illuminates the worst of crimes—the decades long run of child rape and other sexual abuse at Minneapolis' Children's Theatre Company—and details the conspiracy that covered it up and protected the perpetrators for far too long. It's about the ruination of childhood, the loss of innocence, institutional culpability, justice and a kind of healing. Deftly told, intimate, unblinking and necessary.

-Jeffrey Hatcher, playwright and screenwriter

SHATTERED

**CALUMET
EDITIONS**

Minneapolis

FIRST EDITION July 2022
Shattered: Exposing the Open Secret of the Children's Theatre Company
Copyright © 2022 by Laura Stearns.
All rights reserved.

For information, write to Calumet Editions,
6800 France Avenue South, Suite 370, Edina, MN 55435

Printed in the United States of America.
10 9 8 7 6 5 4 3 2 1
ISBN: 978-1-950743-90-2

Cover and interior design: Gary Lindberg

SHATTERED

Exposing the Open Secret of the Children's Theatre Scandal

Laura Stearns

A Memoir of Harm and Healing

CALUMET EDITIONS
Minneapolis

Table of Contents

For those who couldn't speak

Foreword
by Cordelia Anderson, MA

The topic of this book is not an easy one, but Laura Stearns manages to address child sexual abuse with humor, compassion and laser focus. Her story is a poignant account of her history of being sexually assaulted as a child. If you're ambivalent about reading this for any reason, rest assured that Laura's writing serves as a floatation device to carry the reader over a tumultuous tale. She offers insights through a unique lens to someone who lived through it and has found her voice to express it.

Laura clearly describes that her story is not only about her individual sexual assaults but is also about a highly celebrated organization—Children's Theatre Company in Minneapolis, Minnesota—which housed multiple individuals who perpetrated against numerous children. How can this happen with such frequency? What is the organizational responsibility? How do individuals, organizations and communities heal? What has changed for the individuals victimized, the community and the organization since the 1980s?

Whether we are aware of it or not, we likely all know someone who has sexually victimized someone or been victimized. Whether we're aware of it or not, we can all be part of healing and prevention. For those who have been sexually victimized as children, it is 110 percent understandable that they would want or need to pack it all away—hoping it will stay buried—and just move on with life. I met Laura at a point in her adult life when that coping skill no longer worked for her. She was ready to be public and to take further action to address the harm done to her and others. Once Laura reached this point, she filled the spaces in her being that were weighted down, silencing the trauma, and became a force for her own healing and compassionate, authentic justice. Laura's book offers reader insights not only into her story but also to the much broader dynamics of child sexual abuse, systemic trauma and organizational accountability.

Before your journey begins with Laura, there are a few challenges to conventional wisdom and questions I'd like to offer for your consideration:

~ Limits of "If you see something, say something" ~

This sounds simple and straightforward but is far from it when it comes to child sexual abuse. If something is particularly challenging or shocking, a common response of those who are informed about it directly or indirectly is to not see what they saw, to not hear what they heard and to put off taking action. There are many possible reasons for this, including:

- It's too confusing.

- It's too painful.

- It's too scary.

- It doesn't easily fit with their life narrative.

- It's easier to protect the perpetrator or the organization through which it occurred than those that are being harmed by it.

- It's easy to be blinded by the prestige or power of a charismatic or powerful leader or by an organization or institution.

- It's hard to see that an organization or an individual that does so much good can also do so much harm.

Hearing or seeing about such things can be like being hit by a stun gun—immobilizing. A person wants to run in the other direction and desperately wants it not to be real. A natural response is to minimize what one saw or heard or to accommodate the one who perpetrated the harm, often by blaming those victimized or anything and everyone else besides those who perpetrated it. If someone is assertive enough to confront the one who perpetrated, those who perpetrated are likely to respond with a dizzying, emotionally blinding series of strikes such as:

- How could you think that?
- What is wrong with you?
- If it was so bad, why didn't you say or do something earlier?
- Think of the trouble I—or this family/organization—will get in if you keep at this.
- Do you really want to destroy me or this organization?

How many of us have the words, skills and strength to speak up and out when we see or know of someone's harmful, problematic sexual behaviors—much less criminal sexual behaviors? I, for one, am brilliant at comeback lines, fifteen minutes after I'm out of a difficult situation. Way too often, despite extensive training, I'm so dumbfounded that I freeze up.

Think of what it is like for a child who is manipulated and victimized by someone they know, admire and trust.

~ Limits of "Just say no" ~

Those who sexually perpetrate against children are skilled at making the child think they are complicit. Acts of sexual harm, abuse, exploitation and violence are intermixed with emotional abuse, manipulation and other controls. The touch and attention often begin as something that is okay or wanted and then changes to something confusing and then harmful.

The line of when to say "no" is not always clear. It is hard to say "no" when scared or confused. It is hard to say "no" when you have a history of not being able to do so. It is hard to say "no" when the person you are trying to say "no" to has more power than you. It is hard to say "no" when you are trying to act as if you are not as terrified as you are. It's hard to say "no" if you are under the influence. It is hard to say "no" when you like the person but don't like what they are doing. It is hard to say "no" when part of the attention of touch feels good. It is hard to say "no" when you feel like you've caused or allowed the person to go to this point. It's hard to say "no" when you are in a traumatic emotional freeze. It's hard to say "no" when you think you are head over heels but, in reality, are in over your head.

There is a reason for "age of consent" laws—age and stage of development make a difference. An adult has the responsibility to act like an adult. An older or more powerful child/youth can manipulate a younger one. There is also a reason for "position of authority" laws. When one person has a position of authority over another, it means they have a different type of power and/or control over them. The person with the position of authority needs to recognize that and take responsibility for the power, privilege and authority they have. They need to recognize the impact their behavior and choices have on others. They don't need to blame their behavior and choices on those they are meant to guide, nurture and protect.

It is challenging for adults to sort all this through. Think of what it is like for a child who is being sexually victimized by someone they know, admire and trust.

~ Challenge the staying power of the "Dangerous Stranger" myth ~

Those who perpetrate acts of sexual abuse and exploitation against children may be adults or other youth. They are most often male but can also be female. What's the common thread?

In most cases, the person who perpetrates child sexual abuse selects children they have access to; that they know. Yet we consciously or unconsciously hang on to the belief that those who do this are monstrous strangers that are easy to identify. They are obviously creepy and oozing the yuck factor. Yes, there are people who pick unknown children to perpetrate against, but that is far less common. Why is it more comfortable to hang on to the notion that those who commit sexual crimes against children are monstrous, dangerous strangers?

- It seems easier to educate children to watch out for those they don't know, who might try to hurt them, than those they do know.

- It's easier to pass laws and establish organizational policies against "the other"—those we deem obviously (to us) dangerous.

- It is very challenging to acknowledge that someone can be a gifted teacher, director, coach, priest, father, mentor, politician, entertainer, etc. AND be someone who chooses to use that power, privilege and authority to sexually abuse, exploit and violate.

That's hard for adults to come to grips with. Think of what it is like for a child who is being victimized by someone they know, admire and trust.

~ Why children don't report right away when someone sexually assaults them ~

The reality is that it really is quite amazing that children ever do tell, given the barriers to them doing so are so steep. They may be protecting the person perpetrating against them. They may be protecting the family or organization. They may be protecting others that love them or who admire the person perpetrating. They may fear being blamed or may blame themselves. They may fear not being believed. They may not understand that what is happening to them was not their choice—that they were tricked and manipulated. They may not understand that they really weren't "special"—but rather, one of many. They may want to stop the sexually abusive, exploitive behavior but not want the person doing it or the family or organization to go away. They may not want others to find out, much less for it to be a highly visible public case.

Given all the barriers to tell, think of what it is like for a child who does tell or sees others do so, and their worst fears come true.

~ Address whose responsibility preventing child sexual abuse really is ~

It is not up to children to protect themselves. Rather than focusing primarily on what children need to do in order not to be victimized or on reporting once they are, prevention efforts need to focus on teaching people and systems not to behave in sexually harmful, exploitive and violent ways. Education and training need to go beyond identifying indicators a child may have been sexually victimized and focus on recognizing sexually and emotionally harmful behaviors and how to intervene.

Prevention includes learning to name boundary violations early and intervening rather than waiting until behaviors are obviously a reportable criminal offense. This includes restorative and transformative justice efforts that offer other ways to address the harm done and for individuals and organizations to take accountability. Prevention is not only about individual responsibility but rather what organizations and institutions need to do to create safe spaces for children. Prevention is not only about reporting after harm is done but about attending to the conditions and norms in place that allow sexual abuse to occur in the first place. It's not only about attending to why one person perpetrates but understanding why so many do. To prevent child sexual abuse, efforts need to address systemic and cultural changes that allow for the sexual abuse of children.

Prevention also involves policies and practices to address not only current safety and prevention measures but also historical trauma—compassionate and just ways to deal with those harmed in years and decades past.

For prevention to take hold, the leadership of voices of experience—those who lived these truths—are foundational. A movement is needed that doesn't accept that a given percentage of boys and girls will be sexually abused by age eighteen but rather believes that it shouldn't happen to any child and is not inevitable.

Think of the changes around breast cancer. There was a time—not too long ago—when there was individual and cultural discomfort with saying the word "breast" or even acknowledging in non-derogatory ways that we have them. Those who had breast cancer suffered in silence. Those who loved and supported them kept the secret. Now, the frequency and range of breast cancer are widely understood and easily talked about. Early identification and treatment have vastly improved. People march en mass to both acknowledge those living with breast cancer and who have died from it. The marches recognize the ripple effects of harm, first and foremost, to those living with cancer, but also to all of those who love and care about them and to all who work to treat and end it. The pink movement demands more money for treatment and research. The goal is ultimately to end breast cancer, not only to find better ways to treat those suffering from it. For prevention of child sexual abuse and exploitation, such a movement is building, but there is much more work to be done.

~ Why now ~

One of the challenges for those coming forward with historic sexual abuse—perpetrated decades earlier—is that they will be asked, "why now?" Why couldn't you continue to keep it quiet? Why bring all the pain up again now? Why now, after those who did the acts are gone or have gone on with their lives, and the organization has worked so hard to bury that history and move on? Why now? For many, the answer is because they finally have the capability and support to do so. Their silence is no longer containable. They need those that perpetrated to be held accountable and the acknowledgement of the decades of harm done to them. They have had to live with the trauma and the horrific reality of what happened every day, every week, every year, and they no longer want to carry that alone.

~ Perspective ~

I am writing this forward as someone with expertise from a forty-three-year career dedicated to a wide variety of ways to prevent child sexual abuse and exploitation. I started in this field in the 1970s when there were few of us interested in doing the work. There were no conferences, classes or research journals dedicated to the topic. My work teaching sexuality led me to work with women coming out of correctional systems who had been prostituted and others who were sexually abused. I had opportunities to counsel those victimized and those who committed sex offenses. I also had a job advocating for children whose cases were going through court. This was well before services like Children's Advocacy Centers or training for forensic interviewing of children. Looking back, I knew so little.

Now I would need to have completely different credentials to do what I was doing. Now there is easy access to such information. Then, I learned from every other professional I could and from listening very carefully to those harmed and to those who did the harm. I learned from my own life experiences. I made many mistakes but was also passionate about needing things to change.

In 1977, I had the opportunity to develop a child sexual abuse prevention program in the Hennepin County Attorney's Office in Minnesota. We knew enough to know there were few other models and that we had to go up against the inaccurate "Dangerous Stranger" models. We didn't want to scare children away from people or touch, but rather to help them and adults to distinguish between behaviors like touch that were helpful versus harmful. Through this, I had the opportunity to work with Illusion Theater in Minneapolis. I knew nothing about theater, and they knew nothing about child sexual abuse, but as part of this effort, we co-wrote a play called *TOUCH*. In 1980 the program received funding and support to move out of the Hennepin County Attorney's Office to Illusion Theater, where I became the newly launched Director of Prevention Program. We also received funding from a former federal agency, NCCAN— The National Center on Child Abuse and Neglect. The grant was for us to develop a new play, *No Easy Answers for Adolescents*, and to provide technical assistance to other funded prevention efforts across the country. I worked at Illusion Theater until 1992, when I launched Sensibilities, my own training and consultation business.

Most importantly, for purposes of this foreword, my life and life's work are complexly interwoven with these cases out of the Children's Theatre Company (CTC). By way of a few examples, I was asked by those investigating the case if I could help by talking to some of the children who were being victimized there. The catch was that in order not to compromise the investigation, I couldn't tell those I worked with at Illusion Theater nor the man I then lived with who worked as an assistant to the executive director at CTC.

It was known not only to key staff and board at CTC but also to the broader community that an investigation had been underway for some time. The fact that it was underway for some time fed the faulty thinking that there wasn't really any substance behind the "rumors" and reports. The challenge with the investigation, beyond the fact that it involved such a prestigious organization, was that the children victimized were so traumatized and/or protective of the organization that they wouldn't or couldn't talk.

Also, around that time, there was increasing local and national attention to child sexual abuse. In 1984, I was a lead issue expert with local television studio WCCO, working on and off camera on Project Abuse—a two-week intensive media series on child sexual abuse and its prevention statewide. Illusion Theater's plays *TOUCH* and *No Easy Answers* aired as did a documentary, a parent's educational program, and public service announcements. Project Abuse also included a helpline staffed by trained volunteers.

When the arrest of John Clark Donahue, the founder of CTC, happened in 1984, it was major national news. This was at the same time as other nationally visible cases like the McMartin Preschool Case in California. Child sexual abuse was in the news, as were debates about the best ways to interview children and how to prevent it from happening.

Decades later, I was approached by some of the survivors from CTC who wanted some outside support for those that had been victimized. Part of my work since the mid-1990s included doing restorative justice efforts such as circles as part of prevention and healing. We discussed this as an option, and I served as a circle keeper for some of the adults who had been victimized by various people at CTC. We also included other adults who had been there as children and hadn't been directly victimized but had been profoundly affected. The circle offered a chance to address the harms done in the same space and to listen to each person's experience in a compassionate and safe way. I've done many circles over the

years, but this was one of the most profound. While what is said
in circles is confidential, I can say in general that the participants
were so gifted at expressing their truths that I regularly experienced
goosebumps at the sheer compassion and insights expressed. Their
courage was palpable.

~ The Power of Laura and Her Book ~

This book is a key resource in the movement to end child sexual abuse
and exploitation. Laura's ability to tell you this amazing story allows
the reader the benefit of her insights. She is also a gifted speaker and
has worked with an unbridled passion for learning all she could, not
only about herself but also about the broader issues of trauma and
needs for systemic change. Her book helps readers to understand
the incredible role and complexities of organizational responsibility
and accountability to effectively address past harms and prevent
future ones. It is the leadership and passion of individuals like Laura
who helped make my decision to retire easier. Prevention needs
new leaders with a wide range of perspectives and lived experiences.
Prevention also needs people to care about this issue and to do
what they can whether they've been directly affected or not. This
book can serve as a much-needed spark in professional and personal
understanding and action. The book is a gift from the author that
we are the fortunate beneficiaries of. My sincere hope is that reading
it ignites a spark of positive possibilities and hope.

destructive threads into the picture that can't be removed and forever altering the person.

Young children have no defenses, and adolescents believe they know everything. All of them are vulnerable and malleable. Abuse of children often goes unnoticed, and the damage can go so deep the impact is unrecognizable as a wound. A child's response to abuse is often wrong-sized—inappropriate to the level of harm. Children, for example, might put huge compresses on tiny scratches or small bandages on gaping wounds because they lack the ability to understand the complexity of the damage.

As stories go, mine is horrific compared to some but tame in comparison to others. I didn't grow up in a war zone; I wasn't a runaway teen who was trafficked or beaten by an abusive parent. My life was quiet—in many respects, too quiet. Much of the trauma I experienced wasn't spoken out loud for decades. The abuse was hidden or ignored. The people who could have stopped it looked away.

I'm telling my story not because it's the most tragic but because I'm willing to say things that are often unsaid. Perhaps, because I dodged a greater level of harm than those less fortunate, I can speak out loudly now.

At age ten, after being sexually assaulted for the first time, I thought the bleeding between my legs meant I'd become a woman. I didn't ask for help or process it in a healthy way. I didn't even know there was something to process. Something had shifted. I stopped seeing myself as a child. I began to engage with the world as if I were a grown-up. I was sexualized before I even knew what that meant. I had no idea I'd suffered something that would haunt me for decades.

In the early 1980s, I spent four-and-a-half formative teenage years in an environment run by a so-called artistic guru, John Clark Donahue, lauded for his artistry and unconventional way of educating young people in theater. The institution he created, the Children's Theatre Company and School (CTC), was a cultural gem in my hometown of Minneapolis, Minnesota. It was known worldwide as a premier theater producing high-quality productions for children and families, using child actors who had honed their skills under Donahue's tutelage. He was considered a genius by many and surrounded himself with brilliant professional artists who helped make his vision—presenting classic children's literature as theater *by* and *for* children—come to life.

He was also a pedophile.

While Donahue charmed the public, the culture he created attracted other child predators and gave them a safe haven. Donahue's pedagogical methods removed the barriers that separated children and adults and allowed his young students to explore and discover their artistry in uncommon ways. The removal of those barriers, however, also left the students vulnerable to him and the growing nest of perpetrators. Those who enabled Donahue's criminal behavior fostered an environment that normalized the sexualization of children. It was there that I met a company actor and teacher named Jason McLean.

McLean raped me when I was fifteen.

Years later, during the summer of 2015, I'd been running from the truth of my abuse for more than three decades and was emotionally exhausted. Then I was also confronted with my past in a way that was impossible to ignore. I finally decided to face my demons and release the weight of shame I'd been carrying. I filed a civil lawsuit under the Minnesota Child Victims Act against McLean for raping me and against CTC for harboring and protecting him. That decision profoundly changed me.

Had I been the only one harmed there, I wouldn't have brought a suit against CTC or publicly revealed what had happened to me. The main reason I sued was that I knew there were over a hundred children who had endured similar atrocities at CTC, some of them suffering abuses far worse than mine. I believed I was ready to go into a courtroom if it meant the larger truth about what happened there could finally be revealed.

The situation at CTC was multifaceted and complex. Even trauma therapists have a hard time wrapping their heads around it. My lawyer, Jeff Anderson, said he had never in his entire career seen anything like it, and this guy took down the Catholic Archdiocese.

Cases like mine are rare. According to statistics from the Rape, Abuse and Incest National Network (RAINN), of the rapes that occur today in the United States, less than a third are reported to authorities. Of those reported cases, only about 15 percent lead to an arrest, and only half of those lead to a conviction. The number of cases that aren't concluded with a plea deal and go to trial is tiny. In civil court, it's even fewer.

I was raped four times between the ages of ten and nineteen by four different people. The vile residue of those experiences has permeated my bones. Shame is a silent poison that has no DNA of its own—it's symbiotic and lives off its host. It altered me. I didn't realize just how much until I found my way out of the shadows of fear and isolation and finally recognized that I was living half the life I could be living.

Trauma can blur hindsight, making it no longer twenty-twenty. It can be like looking through the wrong end of a blurry telescope. You don't know what the hell you're looking at. Some memories are clear; others are fragmented. They can be obscured by emotions that don't seem to jive. *Why am I so sad when I smell sautéed mushrooms? Why do I cry when something unexpected comes at my face?* Looking back can be arduous in the best of circumstances, but trauma complicates everything.

I've battled depression, anxiety, insomnia, night paralysis, stomach problems, control issues, passive-aggressive and compulsive behaviors, suicidal ideation, and an aversion to sexual intimacy. I've tried many things to purge mental obstacles and heal the emotional wounds that kept me from living a full life—self-help books, spiritual direction, therapy, Twelve Steps, Landmark Forum. These tactics had some effect, but they didn't have the strength to pull me from the deep hole I was in.

What finally catapulted me out of guilt and shame was the act of breaking my silence. I've found nothing more powerful than speaking the truth to blast away that wall separating me from my inner strength. It hasn't solved all my problems, but standing firmly in what's true frees me from the shackles of shame and allows me to use the therapeutic tools that were handed to me. It's hard to fight a battle with one hand tied behind your back.

Healing happens in waves for me. If I had waited until I was done, I'd never have written this book. Though I'm grateful for the truth-telling platform provided by the Child Victims Act, there's an aspect of writing my story that's still supremely difficult. I'm not interested in telling someone's story for them or hurting anyone. Navigating that desire is tricky. I'm not sure I'd be doing this if my parents were still alive—it would have been difficult for them to know the ugly truths I'm revealing in this book. They were abundantly proud of me for exposing a child predator and the institution that protected him, but they came from a generation that kept their dirty laundry tucked away. I didn't want to force them into a light that would hurt them more than it would help me.

I have similar concerns about my children. They may choose to read this book. My heart wants to soften the blow, so they aren't negatively impacted by the brutal details of their mother's abuse. But I can't soften the truth. I'm going to say it. They're of a generation that's taking on the difficult questions of our society, and they're committed to their pursuit of personal awareness and cultural responsibility. They're adults, and I trust they'll take care of themselves as they read it.

As I am writing this book, my ex-husband of twenty-seven years and I have very little communication. There's no malice between us, but there is pain. I don't want to cause more. I don't know how to tell this true story without including elements of our life together, nor do I want to erase him, but I will avoid sharing any details that don't contribute meaningfully to the story. It may feel like an incomplete picture of an important person in my life, and it is, but I'm not willing to invade his privacy unnecessarily.

I'm immensely grateful for the love and support my husband showed me over the years. Though my marriage ended, there were times of great joy, so much laughter, appreciation for nature, satisfaction in co-parenting, and a respect for the gifts each of us brought to our family unit. Ultimately, there was love. Our partnership would not have lasted as long as it did without that. The difficulties of traversing a long-term marriage while carrying the weight of abuse from childhood is very complicated. But this book is not about a marriage.

I've also tried to tread lightly where CTC victims are concerned by telling the story as I lived it. I won't expose someone's name and trauma experience who isn't ready to make that information public. If I use someone's name, it's intentional. Many victims and eyewitnesses have given me permission to mention their names and/or their personal accounts. The identities of some perpetrators and enablers are part of the public record, so I will not be shy about sharing their names. I use pseudonyms in the case of two of my abusers as a measure of self-protection and to avoid controversies that could arise from this exercise in truth-telling.

This book is an intimate look at how the threads of harm have colored my life and how I've taken them up with the purpose and intention to weave a different pattern. Of course, I've also had some wonderful things happen along the way. I've found great satisfaction in some of my work, have had many gratifying friendships, and have two amazing children I wouldn't trade for anything—and I'm so grateful my boys have a strong relationship with a father who loves them so deeply. I'm sharing the ugly parts of my personal narrative to be useful and to help heal parts of me, so I have more brain space for the beautiful things in my life.

Incredible people have blessed me with their wisdom over the past decades. I've read books that have given me clarity for living a healthier life. At times, I've had to hear things repeatedly and in different ways to understand a concept—I'm stubborn that way. Throughout this book, I pass on some of the wisdom that was passed to me, gems that have been around a lot longer than I have, but hopefully, I'll communicate these things from a new perspective that's accessible and fresh.

Some of the information shared in this book is hard to absorb; it's a painfully serious subject. I'll make it as accessible as I can, walking the reader through it with a light heart and a steady hand to hold. I feel compelled to tend to those who have experienced sexual trauma with a different kind of energy and attention, especially someone who was abused as a child. Seeing them, acknowledging them, and recognizing the difficulties of being present to the truths in this book is important to me. So, if at times you feel like I'm not talking directly to you, I'm probably not. But I encourage you to listen anyway because being trauma-informed is something we should all learn how to do and practice.

During a Twelve Step meeting, I once heard a woman refer to her desire to become "right-sized." That term has stuck with me. Compassion for others is a beautiful quality in a human being, but it can be distorted into an overblown sense of responsibility. Not wanting to be a bother is a thoughtful way to be, but it can get oversized to the point of self-harm. Self-love is important for healthy self-care but can be diminished and show up as self-neglect. My mission to become right-sized is at the heart of my journey.

Quite a few years back, I started seeing rocks with engraved words on them at gift stores. They were nothing special, just smooth and nondescript, embellished with one inspirational word, like "peace" and "love." At the time, the word that was constantly on my mind was "balance." I bought the rock with "balance" on it and carried it in my pocket for years, rubbing my thumb across the etching during stressful moments. Unlike those faddish Pet Rocks from the 1970s, my balance rock actually brought me comfort. Like my desire to be right-sized, I strive for balance, and that rock in my pocket was certainly worth the money I spent on it. I needed the reminder on a daily basis. I gave the rock away years ago to someone who was struggling to find their own balance. They needed the reminder more than me at the time.

As I age, I'm getting better at not knowing what's going to happen next. I'm trying to embrace the beauty of the process, practice patience, and witness with awe the evolution of my life. I'm learning to appreciate plants growing, watching buds develop and not just wanting them to be fully open. My kids were my first real teachers of this because they made me slow down—to sit on the floor and be present in their process. I learned to appreciate the gift of discovery. I saw the world through new eyes—theirs.

Being a parent is one of the most precious gifts. I'm grateful for the structure of parenting because I needed to step outside of myself to be the best mother I could be. I was so damaged, I needed to be bigger than I was, better than the sum of my parts, or I was going to fail miserably.

One tidbit of wisdom arrived in the form of a greeting card that resides on my refrigerator. It reads, "A wise woman once said, 'F*ck this shit,' and she lived happily ever after." The card has a sparkly gold background, and I love it more than I can say. The mantra fits me well. I'm in my fifties, and like many women my age, I just don't want to deal with the bullshit anymore. Being a woman in this society (no matter what age we are) carries the weight of antiquated norms and mores, which become very tiresome after decades. *My opinions are my own; stop trying to confiscate them. You don't need to explain things to me that I already have mastery over. I'm a woman, not a girl.*

The point is, I want to be appreciated for who I am today. I want to live in the moment, prepare for the future and not look back. But sometimes, we must look back to leave the past behind and move forward.

Breaking my silence about sexual abuse has been transformative. Silence can be deadly, and I hope to help others find the courage to speak the unspeakable things that have happened to them. I hold my tapestry up to the light so others can see what's possible when someone is willing to walk forward in spite of fear.

don't think I'm ignoring certain realities, there are some facts we all need to understand:

- Cisgender women are not the only ones who are sexually assaulted.
- Boys are as vulnerable to sexual exploitation as girls.
- Not all men are bad.
- Women can be sexual predators too.
- Sexual violence knows no boundaries and affects all cultures, ages, genders, sexual orientations and identities.

If I write something that sounds contradictory or appears to exclude someone or ignore their experience, that isn't my intention. I want to be an example of someone who's accountable for the things I do and say, but unfortunately, I may make mistakes. I will do my best, however, to speak the truth as I see it and do no harm to anyone who has already been wounded.

As a reader of this book, you are most likely a person who:

- Has survived sexual trauma.
- Likes to read compelling stories and has heard good things about this one.
- Thinks they may be a victim of sexual harm (it's not always obvious) and is looking for clarity.
- Is friends with or loves someone who is a survivor of sexual trauma and wants to better understand and support them.
- Works professionally with or on behalf of trauma survivors and is looking for useful information.
- Thought this was a different book and are disappointed.

For those in the last category, before you put this book down, consider this. According to statistics, people who didn't experience some form of trauma as a child—neglect, abuse or sexual harm— are 100 percent likely to be friends with, work with or are in a relationship with someone who did have such a terrible experience. Keep reading, and you will gain an understanding of what's going on inside them. It might make it easier for you to be in a relationship with them, whether casual or intimate.

There is a lot of literature on the subject of trauma, but one book, in particular, is astonishingly powerful: *The Body Keeps the Score* by Bessel Van Der Kolk, M.D. This work has revolutionized the way trauma is understood and addressed. It helped me understand how the energy around trauma lives in the victim's body long after abuse occurs, how the brain works hard to balance itself, how trauma can distort a victim's ability to cope, and the different ways the destructive effects of trauma can be treated. That book took a long time for me to read because I kept seeing elements of myself in it. I needed to take a lot of breaks.

Because it's at the heart of my story, I'm going to provide information to help foster an understanding of how people process emotional trauma, what it looks like, how it manifests, and how society sometimes deals with it. It's a quick tour of trauma, as I understand it, presented in a way that is hopefully more accessible and less intimidating than some other resources.

It is important to recognize that the discovery process can be difficult, and information like this might be hard for some people to read. This book is filled with terms and narratives that can be challenging, but as a courtesy, I will provide a bit of warning before sections that include graphic descriptions of sexual violence. When you see this—

—know that potentially triggering content is just around the corner, and I hope you will take care of yourself while you read. Don't force yourself to metabolize something quickly that requires time and tending. Take your time if you need to.

~ A Quick Tour of Trauma ~

trauma

noun

: a disordered psychic or behavioral state resulting from severe mental or emotional stress or physical injury.[2]

The world is filled with people walking around with unresolved past trauma, which affects their decisions in the present day. It looks different on everyone, the sources of it vary, and the degrees to which a person is affected depend on multiple factors. Gaining an understanding of trauma, in general, can give us clarity around our own life experiences, providing personal awareness. It can help us understand what's going on with others too.

To provide a little bit of context, here are a few foundational elements to understand the basics of trauma: fear responses such as fight, flight, freeze and appease, being triggered, the ways the body dysregulates, and how the mind dissociates when someone has a trauma response.

Trauma is experienced differently by everyone. Two people can experience the same event or conditions and walk away from it with completely different effects, which can manifest physically, mentally and emotionally. How someone deals with a traumatic event differs because of age, stability in their home, previous life experience, state of mental health before the event, how they process information, and what kind of emotional support system they have.

There are three types of trauma: acute—a single event, chronic—repeated and/or prolonged trauma such as domestic

---

2   Merriam-Webster

violence, and complex—exposure to various and multiple traumatic events over time.

Because of these multiple variations, it's unfair to judge one person's experience against another. Lumping trauma and how individuals deal with it into one pile can lead to downgrading and dismissing our own experience or unfairly judging others. Context matters when it comes to how a person navigates their own healing process. It's best to accept that there are complexities to everyone's internal landscape that we are likely not privy to and not to compare.

Immediate responses to trauma differ as well. "Fight, flight or freeze" are common reactions to scary or dangerous situations. "Appease" is a new category that refers to the way some people will accommodate or go along with the actions of being harmed in order to minimize further violence. All of them are normal modes of survival, and we can experience them in varying degrees at different times.

Trauma memories are stored in the brain differently than regular memories, deep in the right side near the primal part of the brain called the amygdala. Normally, a memory can be accessed by both sides of the brain, so there's a complete experience of it. A memory comes forward, we may have difficult emotions around it, but we can logically see it as something in the past.

When a trauma memory is triggered,[3] because of the way it's stored and the nature of the memory, the right side of the brain—where our emotions live—fires up, but the left—where logic, linear thinking and reasoning live—doesn't. Because of this, logic goes out the window, and the memory is experienced in a very different way. It can feel like it's happening in real time, like we've been swept into the memory experientially. The body doesn't differentiate between memory and real time. We can feel as if we're in danger in the present moment, even if we're not.

---

3   Triggered- adjective: (of a mechanism) activated by a trigger. "a triggered alarm": (of a response) caused by a particular action, process or situation. "a triggered memory of his childhood" Oxford Languages

Our bodies can also go through a dramatic change when experiencing trauma or when trauma memories are triggered. It can cause a disruption in normal emotional and physical functions. It's common to experience dissociation,[4] becoming numb and detached, or having a panic attack, and/or dysregulation,[5] which can manifest physically in many ways: blood pressure rising, irregular breathing like hyperventilating—we may even feel separated from our bodies.

Post-traumatic stress disorder[6] (PTSD) can result from a single traumatic event or compound and complex trauma situations, resulting in symptoms that can surface immediately or even years later. Symptoms can last for weeks to months or months to years. Symptoms can include but are not limited to panic attacks, dissociation, memory problems, difficulty experiencing positive emotions, a feeling of emotional numbness and self-destructive behavior.

Because of the way trauma memories are stored and the way the body will try to take care of itself by dissociating and dysregulating, it's important to understand that it's nearly impossible for someone with severe PTSD to just "get over it." Believe me, I wish it were that easy. PTSD appears in the *Diagnostic and Statistical Manual of Mental Disorders* for a reason. But here's the good news—it is treatable.

When I'm triggered by something that stimulates a memory of past trauma, I emotionally go back in time to the genesis of whatever traumatic event caused damage. I begin to function more primally.

---

4   Dissociation- noun: the separation of whole segments of the personality or of discrete mental processes from the mainstream of consciousness or of behavior. Merriam-Webster

5   Dysregulation- noun: impairment of a physiological regulatory mechanism that allows one to manage emotional responses. Merriam-Webster

6   Post-traumatic stress disorder- noun: a condition of persistent mental and emotional stress occurring as a result of injury or severe psychological shock, typically involving disturbance of sleep and constant vivid recall of the experience, with dulled responses to others and to the outside world. Oxford Languages

My amygdala is hijacked, and logic goes out the window. I can't think straight or find the right words. I sometimes make childlike decisions. The triggering event can be a real-life one, like seeing the person who assaulted me walking down the street or just something that reminds me of a past event, such as hearing a name associated with that time period in my life. It doesn't matter, my body reacts, and I go into an altered state.

~ Sexual Violence ~

Trauma can result from overwhelming negative events such as experiencing or witnessing physical or sexual violence, domestic abuse, natural disasters, severe illness, injury, or death of loved ones. I'm focusing on sexual violence because that's the root of my complex trauma.

There is no "one size fits all" when it comes to the trauma effects of sexual violence, but victims have one thing in common—they have been fractured at the core as human beings. In our society, we're taught early that our genitals define us, more so than our culture or the color of our skin. That message creates an image of how we see ourselves and how we experience our existence on the planet. When a person is violated sexually, it's not only a physical violation, but an emotional wound in the belly of our experience as a human being. The depth of this wound will vary, and the consequences will be different from person to person.

Sexual violence is a broad term. Here are the forms of sexual violence as defined by The National Sexual Violence Resource Center:

- Rape or sexual assault.

- Child sexual assault and incest.

- Intimate partner sexual assault.

- Unwanted sexual contact/touching.

- Sexual harassment.

- Sexual exploitation.

- Showing one's genitals or naked body to other(s) without consent.

- Masturbating in public.

- Watching someone in a private act without their knowledge or permission.

I would add electronic or internet offenses such as revenge pornography, sending or receiving sexual images electronically, solicitation for sex from minors, and producing or possessing child pornography, now referred to more accurately as "child sexual abuse images." Simply calling it pornography doesn't really address the criminality of forcing or coercing a child to participate in producing the images or the impact on the victim.

Criminal sexual assault is also a broad term that might be confusing. There are several degrees of assault and levels of punishment, and each US state has its own laws. What most people don't know is that criminal sexual assault isn't limited to rape or attempted rape by force or coercion. You don't need to have been penetrated to have been assaulted. Sexual assault includes:

- Coercing a victim to touch you intimately or touching a victim's intimate areas under or over clothing.

- Non-consensual sexual touching.

- Exposure of genitalia or masturbation in the presence of a minor sixteen years or younger.

The age of consent in the United States varies from state to state but ranges between sixteen to eighteen. In Minnesota, the age of consent is sixteen, but in 1984, a provision was added that if the abuser is in a position of authority over the victim—a teacher, coach or clergy, for example—the age of consent changes to eighteen. In this book, when I use the word "children" in a broad way, I'm talking about ages eighteen and under.

In eight out of ten rapes, the victim knows the perpetrator, usually a family member, friend, fellow student, neighbor, clergy, teacher or coach. Parents often teach young children to stay away from strangers but ignore signs of abuse being perpetrated by people they know and trust. Women aren't the only ones who get raped, and they can also be rapists—statistics show that most sex offenders are men, but between 1 and 9 percent of them are women. Children and adolescents can also exhibit predatory sexual behavior.

Statistics of sexual violence are staggering; one in four girls and one in six boys will experience sexual violence before the age of sixteen. The numbers are more horrific for minorities: 60 percent of black girls are sexually assaulted, and indigenous women are three and a half times more likely to be assaulted than any other group. Eighty-six percent of trans women are assaulted *per year*. People with disabilities are seven times more likely to be violated. Sexual violence is a worldwide pandemic of harm that no one wants to see. Think about it this way: more than four-hundred-fifty million people have contracted COVID-19 so far, which is tragic, but there are literally billions of people walking around on this planet who are victims of sexual violence.

Culturally, a lot more energy is spent on ensuring that children, women and other vulnerable targets know how to protect themselves from assault and rape rather than teaching the offenders not to offend. This, of course, puts the burden on victims and not perpetrators. We need to teach boys and men how to control their impulses, not just make sure that girls aren't wearing provocative clothing. I have a friend who was raped while wearing sweatpants, a sweatshirt and no makeup. Appearance had nothing to do with it.

The nature of those who perpetrate sexual abuse against children is complex; there are pathological distinctions. Pedophiles are sexual predators attracted to pre-pubescent children, and hebephiles are those attracted to pubescent children. There are also people who assault children not because they're compelled to violate children specifically but because children are easy targets. Sometimes sexual violence is a continuation of a cycle of abuse. The abuser may not be abusive by nature but was the victim of abuse and perpetuated the cycle by violating others. For simplicity, I will use the terms pedophiles, predators and perpetrators in this book, steering clear of more complicated distinctions I'm not qualified to make.

Most of the perpetrators identified at CTC were in residence there in the early 1980s when I was a child actor and student. The artistic director, John Clark Donahue, was a predator who built a shield of protection for himself that extended to those around him who also took advantage of children. The more they got away with it, the bolder they became, growing in numbers. It's not hyperbole to claim that CTC under Donahue was a safe haven for sexual predators.

~ Grooming ~

You may have heard the term "grooming" bandied about and may not know exactly what it means in this context. It describes what sexual predators do to prepare their victims so they can be easily manipulated and controlled. Kids are the easiest to groom for sexual abuse, but adults can be groomed as well. Not only to be more easily abused themselves but to unwittingly assist in the abuse of a child in their care.

When speaking with a friend about the history of CTC, she asked me how these criminals knew what to do. She couldn't fathom how a person could inherently know these grooming techniques.

"They talk to each other, look out for each other," I said. "They share information, they even share victims."

My guess is that much of it comes naturally to the mind of someone geared for deception. And if they don't have an in-person perpetrator network to tap into for tips, there is a well-orchestrated global network of people who abuse kids and share their techniques. You can find anything you want on the darker side of the internet, including how to groom a child and coerce them into sex. The situation at CTC would have been far worse if they'd had the internet as a resource.

These people aren't evil-looking villains who twirl their mustaches—though some mug shots I've seen have caused me to say out loud, "Um, yeah, you're a creeper, you even *look* like a child molester." That's not always the case. They can be con artists who look great on the surface, who surround themselves with people who will vouch for them, charming them into a place of believing the good intentions they profess to be guided by. It's a long game. They can give plenty of evidence to appear trustworthy, while at the same time they search for easy targets, children who are vulnerable to deception.

Dr. Michael Welner provided excellent examples of the techniques offenders use to coerce and control their victims. He described the six stages of sexual grooming on Oprah.com in 2010:

Stage 1: Targeting the victim. The offender targets a victim by sizing up the child's vulnerability—emotional neediness, isolation and lower self-confidence. Children with less parental oversight are more desirable prey.

Stage 2: Gaining the victim's trust. The sex offender gains trust by watching and gathering information about the child, getting to know his needs and how to fill them. In this regard, sex offenders mix effortlessly with responsible caretakers because they generate warm and calibrated attention. Only more awkward and overly personal attention, or gooey intrusiveness, provokes the suspicion of parents. Otherwise, a more suave [sic] sex offender is better disciplined for how to push and poke without revealing themselves. Think of the grooming sex offender on the prowl as akin to a spy—and just as stealth [sic].

Stage 3: Filling a need. Once the sex offender begins to fill the child's needs, that adult may assume noticeably more importance in the child's life and may become idealized. Gifts, extra attention, affection may distinguish one adult in particular and should raise concern and greater vigilance to be accountable for that adult.

Stage 4: Isolating the child. The grooming sex offender uses the developing special relationship with the child to create situations in which they are alone together. This isolation further reinforces a special connection. Babysitting, tutoring, coaching and special trips all enable this isolation. A special relationship can be even more reinforced when an offender cultivates a sense in the child that he is loved or appreciated in a way that others, not even parents, provide. Parents may unwittingly feed into this through their own appreciation for the unique relationship.

Stage 5: Sexualizing the relationship. At a stage of sufficient emotional dependence and trust, the offender progressively sexualizes the relationship. Desensitization occurs through talking, pictures, even creating situations (like going swimming) in which both offender and victim are naked. At that point, the adult exploits a child's natural curiosity, using feelings of stimulation to advance the sexuality of the relationship. When teaching a child, the grooming sex offender has the opportunity to shape the child's sexual preferences and can manipulate what a child finds exciting and extend the relationship in this way. The child comes to see himself as a more sexual being and to define the relationship with the offender in more sexual and special terms.

Stage 6: Maintaining control. Once the sex abuse is occurring, offenders commonly use secrecy and blame to maintain the child's continued participation and silence— particularly because the sexual activity may cause the child to withdraw from the relationship. Children in these entangled relationships—and at this point, they are entangled— confront threats to blame them, to end the relationship and to end the emotional and material needs they associate with the relationship, whether it be the dirt bikes the child gets to ride, the coaching one receives, special outings or other gifts. The child may feel that the loss of the relationship and the consequences of exposing it will humiliate and render them even more unwanted.

I find this description of grooming thoroughly disturbing because I recognize in it what happened to me and countless others at CTC. Donahue used our "otherness" as artists to isolate us from the outside world, telling us that no one "out there" understood us the way he did. He veiled his deceit in altruism and good intentions, making us believe he had our best interest at heart and wanted us to soar in our artistry. But, at the same time, he was sizing up which kids he could coerce into his web.

What child doesn't want to be considered special? This form of conditioning is very effective in earning trust and making a child believe they're a willing participant in the abuse. I can attest directly to this. Company actor and teacher Jason McLean made me believe I was special. He took advantage of my age and inexperience, persuading me that I was falling in love with him. Because I was groomed to think that way, I believed I was at least partly responsible for what he did to me. This was an effective silencing tool, enough to keep me quiet.

One of my friends, a victim of Donahue, described to me how as a nine-year-old, he would be lifted up by Donohue and set on his lap during gatherings of students. Casually, Donohue would work his hand to my friend's tiny bottom and massage his sphincter with his finger. This vile act normalized sexual sensations in a public setting, making my friend believe this behavior was okay. It also led him to the false conclusion that he wanted more from Donohue, who later took the abuse to another level. Another former female student described being set on the laps of men with erections and told to stay there regardless of their visible discomfort. These are all acts of grooming.

Our bodies are designed to find pleasure in the act of sexual stimulation. It's part of the grand design to perpetuate the species. When we're touched in the area of our genitals, our body reacts, and we have little control over it. Predators know this. A rape victim might actually orgasm, not because they find pleasure in the violent act but because their body is responding to the stimulation. This reality has kept many victims of sexual violence from reporting the incidents. They believed it wasn't a rape at all or that they wanted the violence because they had an orgasm. They feel shame and responsibility. But the physical phenomenon of sexual stimulation doesn't cancel the violence. It doesn't negate the fact that a sexual assault occurred; it only confirms that the victim is human.

Some of the perpetrators at CTC used long-term grooming techniques, waiting until the targeted victim reached the age of consent before making their move. The sexualizing of boys by gay men was more covert than the men abusing girls. I believe this was partly because sodomy was illegal then (the Supreme Court didn't decriminalize it until 2003). If grooming techniques of boys by gay men were noticed, they were excused because liberal thinkers in the arts didn't want to demonize gay men. They chalked such conduct up to "discovery of sexuality" and left it at that. I think that's one of the key reasons Donahue got away with much of his abuse, particularly with the older boys—people ignored it, or worse, thought of it as a service to the boys. Donahue was very careful not to be seen with the younger ones, knowing it wasn't only illegal but socially abhorrent.

Conversely, men taking advantage of young girls is so popular in our culture that there's an abundance of songs containing public service announcements for how to practice it right in the lyrics. They warn men not to get too close until "it's time" (translation: she's sixteen.) Every time I hear the lyric "Girl, you'll be a woman soon. Soon, you'll need a man," I feel like I'll lose my lunch. Sexually victimizing girls has been normalized in society. Consequently, people weren't thinking twice about the girls being assaulted at CTC; it went with the territory of being a girl.

Parents teach their children to stay away from creepy strangers: "Don't get in a car with someone you don't know." But not all predators and pedophiles drive around alone in grungy old cars looking for kids to abduct. Some are so good at what they do they're able to groom the parents of the victim too. They normalize predatory behaviors to put the parents at ease. Donahue groomed an entire city to allow him to carry out his wicked agenda. Bill Cosby groomed a country. Michael Jackson groomed the planet. These predators were black belts at attunement and deception.

Award-winning Pennsylvania State University football coach Jerry Sandusky is an excellent example of the craftiness and charm of many expert sexual predators. He was highly respected in the community and had founded a nonprofit organization that served at-risk youth. This gave him unlimited access to a group of young children who were already vulnerable—easy pickin's. He victimized over forty of them, and those are just the ones who reported. Sandusky didn't get away with more than thirty years of abusing boys without the people around him pretending they didn't see or suspect anything and some outright lying about it.

Olympic gymnastics team physician Dr. Larry Nassar couldn't have sexually assaulted more than three hundred girls and women in the program without people looking the other way or disregarding the reports. Even the FBI allowed him continued access to athletes when they knew he was abusing them. Victims were ignored and blamed to protect the perpetrator and the organization he worked for.

I understand that people have reasons for being silent—maybe their livelihoods would be threatened. But it takes a village to allow this level of abuse.

~ Silence Around Sexual Violence ~

Sexual violence is the most underreported crime. Often, assaults are downgraded by the victims as a coping mechanism. We not only tend to silence ourselves when we're assaulted, but we can be silenced by others as well. Sometimes an assault is downgraded by the person receiving the report. *Yes, but what were you wearing?* One former student from CTC describes how she had told a female stage manager that a male staff member had forced her to have sex. The stage manager told her, "Every girl's first time is a rape," and left it at that. The stage manager did nothing, said nothing more and didn't report the perpetrator.

A variety of elements can cause victims to live with shame and fear instead of exposing their abusers. Society often blames the victim, and the judicial system is biased in favor of the perpetrator. Most of the time, even adults who understand what happened to them don't come forward, so it shouldn't be surprising that kids report their assaults even less frequently. Because a child's brain is undeveloped, they're sometimes unaware that a crime has even been committed against them.

When perpetrators of sexual violence are caught, they often engage in a victim-blaming response that psychologist Jennifer Freyd has dubbed DARVO—Deny, Attack, and Reverse Victim and Offender. We've seen this behavior in people like R. Kelly, Donald Trump and Harvey Weinstein. Perpetrators deny allegations, attack their victims for "spreading lies," then turn attention away from themselves by claiming they did nothing wrong—it was their victim who caused harm, not them. This can turn the victim into the offender and the perpetrator into the victim. This kind of gaslighting can cause a victim to believe they were actually a willing participant or perhaps even responsible for the abuse.

It's not uncommon for kids to have fragmented memories or completely forget about the sexual abuse they suffered and then remember it later in life. That coping mechanism can happen for a variety of reasons. When the perpetrator is someone the child knows, especially if it's a family member, it can be safer to ignore or forget about it than to recognize the horrors of it. Silence can be safer than admission if the child fears exposing the abuse will also cause them to lose a provider of food and shelter. Many victims care about their abuser and may be attempting to appease, protect or accommodate them through their silence. If the abuser is outside the home but in a position of authority, the child may choose to ignore abuse for fear of losing something important to them such as an education or extracurricular activities.

I was ten the first time I was sexually abused. I didn't mention it in a therapeutic setting until I was twenty-eight. Statistically, waiting eighteen years is considered a short time. I didn't start serious work about my childhood sexual abuse until I was well into my thirties. It can take decades for a victim to fully understand and come to terms with the reality of what happened to them. They can live a lifetime of trauma symptoms not realizing the root cause was sexual abuse. By the time they put the pieces together, all statutes for reporting have expired.

It's important for people to believe victims when they reveal abuse. Yes, people do falsely report abuse or abusers, but statistically, that is rare. Around 5 percent of reports are considered false by the authorities. Even then, a report may be classified as false because there is insufficient evidence to back up the claim, not because the victim is lying.

Sexual violence is bad enough, but the re-wounding inflicted upon victims who are not believed when they report it can be worse than the assault itself, causing anxiety, depression, and even self-harm or suicide. I always assume someone is telling the truth, partly because of my personal experience and training but also because I don't believe people say they've been harmed unless some form of harm was experienced.

Abuse isn't always intentional—for example, non-verbal messages about permission can get mixed or misinterpreted—but if the impact of an action wounds the receiver, regardless of the intent, that's what matters to me. I deal with feelings honoring the human being and creating space for healing. Why should we withhold support for someone in pain? The verbal or emotional validation of a victim does *not* cause an accused perpetrator to be fired or arrested. Due process and due diligence by authorities do. We should always err on the side of believing the victim.

~ Changing the Culture ~

Through sharing my story, listening to other survivors, and educating myself, I started to see the larger connections of Rape Culture—it isn't just about victim-blaming and sexual harassment. It's about unbalanced gender roles, the normalization of sexual dominance and submission, tolerance of unacceptable behavior, ignorance of the realities of how women walk through the world in a state of fear that men are never subjected to, and how no one wants to look at the harsh reality of the prevalence of child sexual abuse. It's about reinforcing harmful societal norms that are baked into our culture, into our family dynamics, which we don't question because "that's the way we've always been."

I don't want you to walk away from this book despondent or without understanding that there are actions we can take to make things better. So, I'm sharing some content after the epilogue at the end of this book that talks about dismantling Rape Culture. It's a bonus chapter from my companion book to this memoir called *Daring to Heal: Growing Beyond Trauma Through Awareness, Acceptance, and Action,* which focuses on the universal effects of trauma as a natural response to traumatic events, and how we can transform our core belief system to shift society away from Rape Culture towards a culture of accountability and consent.

I'm providing this content to help you understand that Rape Culture is the social attitude that allowed for the silencing of children at CTC and part of the reason the sexual predators were so successful. It's why the community looked away from what was obviously going on and why the legal process was so painful for me.

Because children in the arts are especially vulnerable and personal boundaries are blurred by antiquated adages like "you must suffer for your art," it's of the utmost importance that those around them create safe spaces for our young artists to grow and learn. Understanding how Rape Culture works and how to dismantle it will help prevent what happened at CTC from happening again.

~ An Important Definition ~

In preparation for the damages interview for my civil case, which is part of the discovery process for litigation, I read the journals I'd kept as a teenager during my time at CTC. I often laughed at the immaturity on display in my sophomoric writing. Then I came across an entry that shocked me. It referred to what happened to me in 1977 when I was ten years old. In my journal, I had called that experience a "rape."

For years, when speaking of that incident with the few people who knew about it, I always referred to it as being "assaulted" or "molested." Both of those terms are true, but they lack the impact of the word "rape." Somewhere along the line, I had stopped using the word "rape," downplaying the event in my mind and changing the intensity of it to something more...well, more acceptable. Rape is an ugly, violent word in both sound and meaning.

I slept restlessly after reading my journal. The word kept tumbling around in my head. When I got up the next morning to get ready for the appointment with my lawyer, the first thing I did was check the dictionary on my phone. Had I been raped? At fifteen, I had described it as such. Was that what had happened?

Here's what I read on Dictionary.com:

rape

: unlawful sexual intercourse or any other sexual penetration of the vagina, anus, or mouth of another person, with or without force, by a sex organ, other body part, or foreign object, without the consent of the victim.

I slowly walked into the bathroom, turned on the shower, got undressed and stepped into the hot stream of water. Deep inside, I felt a pressure building, and I began to cry—softly at first, and then sobbing uncontrollably. From a place of overwhelming anguish—I bawled. Part of me cracked open, and I allowed myself to access some kind of a primal well. My tears and spit mixed with the steaming water swirling down the drain. As I stood there, the silent poison of shame began to seep out of me, and I started to feel emotions I hadn't allowed myself to feel, like desolation and rage. After decades of downgrading that terrible invasion, I finally began to accept the full reality of what had happened to me.

Chapter Two
Altered

My mother, a spinster as far as her peers were concerned, married my father one month before her twenty-third birthday. She was voted "friendliest" in her senior high school yearbook. Most of her high school friends were married and had at least one baby by that point, but my mother wasn't in a rush. She was waiting for the right guy to show up. My handsome and charming father was younger, only twenty, with a singing voice to die for. He swept her off her feet by crooning to her in a local bar.

My older brothers were born within thirteen months of each other. I was the "oops baby," not planned but loved completely—and the only girl. I was born in Minneapolis in July 1967, exactly two years before Neil Armstrong took that "giant leap for mankind."

While my mother was friendly, she was more stoic than Dad, definitely the enforcer in the family. My father was affable and gregarious. Everyone loved him. He was often more like a fourth child for Mom than her co-parenting partner. He had a huge personality, loved to have fun and would make impulsive decisions that affected the whole family. Mom would make them work. She was capable and organized.

My memories of Minnesota as a small child are filled with ample mosquito bites in the summers and huge snow drifts in the winters. I was always big for my age—being a nine-pound baby can do that. I remember how devastated I was when Dad said he couldn't put me on his shoulders anymore. I think I was four or five.

~ Decisions I Made ~

Children make decisions about themselves and their world based on personal experiences and what they see and hear. These conclusions are based on a limited ability to comprehend the meaning of things. I have several early childhood memories that certainly contributed to my opinions of the world and my own existence in it.

When I was about four or five, I had severe pain in my hip joint. When I complained, Dad thought I was just being dramatic. In his defense, I was the third child, and by that point, most parents were pretty tired of their kids being sick or hurt. Also, I'm an actor, so being dramatic was probably part of my nature back then. At the time, I was hurt by his dismissal of my pain, which was real. I could barely walk.

It turns out I had a viral condition called toxic synovitis and was put into a wheelchair. I graduated to crutches within a month and spent almost a year hobbling around on them. This inflammatory illness isn't treated the same way today. In fact, it's rather common and usually disappears without treatment within a couple of months. But in the early 1970s, my condition was a bit of a mystery. The medical logic of the day was to immobilize the painful joint. They stopped putting kids in wheelchairs for this virus a long time ago.

I had to go in for blood tests a couple of times a week for a few months—I had a real aversion to needles after that. Being treated as a "cripple" made me feel like I was broken.[7] I remember my brothers taking me out of my wheelchair so they could race around the house in it. I sat on the couch watching them, wanting them to stop but

---

7   The term "cripple" is no longer considered a socially acceptable way to describe someone, but I use it here because it's how I saw myself at the time.

doing nothing about it. They were having so much fun. But for me, they essentially had my legs, and having been told not to walk for fear of damaging myself, I was powerless to stop them. This is a formative memory in which I felt out of control and sacrificed my wants and needs for the enjoyment of others. This led to a few decisions about my life and the world:

- I'm broken.

- I don't matter.

- The enjoyment of others is more important than my own.

At this same time, I also suffered from chronic bladder infections, so frequently the doctors scanned my bladder to see if there was something wrong. My dominant memory of this procedure was having a man insert a tube into my urethra. I didn't really understand what was happening, and it was the first time I felt paralyzed into inaction having a man touching my genitals. The decision I made:

- I don't have much say in what happens to my body.

Me at age four. Photo: Stearns Family

My stoic mother seldom shared her feelings—especially the dark ones. One day, when I was around seven and was walking upstairs to my bedroom, I heard someone crying in my brother's room. This was odd—it was unusual for anyone to cry in our house unless they had a bloody knee or a bee sting. And I could tell it wasn't my brother crying. The sobs were too high-pitched.

As I rounded the corner, I saw the hunched silhouette of my mother framed by the light coming in from the window. She was sitting on the end of my brother's bed, slightly turned away from the door, her shoulders shaking. I was stunned. I'd never seen her cry before. I watched her for a few seconds but began to feel uncomfortable like I was seeing something I shouldn't, so I spoke.

"Mom?" I said quietly.

She was startled because she hadn't heard me coming. I saw her pushing her fingers into the corners of her eyes as if she were trying to push the tears back in. Then she turned to me with a big smile as if nothing were wrong. Her smile said one thing, but her eyes said another. She stood up, said she had something she needed to do and hurriedly disappeared down the stairs leaving a trail of wordless emotions behind. I never learned why she was crying, but I did make a decision about how to behave in the world:

- Don't show people how you're really feeling.

My fourth-grade science teacher was one of my favorites. I loved his class and thought science was cool. The subject for class one day was nuclear war—the atomic bomb was an excellent topic for eight-year-old kids. This was back in the days when we did tornado safety drills by climbing under our desks and then crouching down with our heads on our knees and clasped hands on the backs of our necks to protect us from flying debris. I doubt this protocol ever saved anyone from physical harm, but we practiced it, and it gave us a sliver of hope that if a tornado came, we might be able to avoid certain death.

Our science teacher made it clear, though, that crouching under our desks wasn't going to save us. "Nothing can save you from the A-bomb," he said. His description of what would happen is burned into my memory. "When the sky goes orange, that's it. It's over." He was describing the inescapable fireball that would overtake the city if the bomb went off.

Not long after this lesson, I was lying in bed waiting for my mom to come in and say goodnight. I'm not sure what kind of weather phenomenon was occurring, but the lights of the city were bouncing off the clouds and creating an orange hue. My eyes grew big, and I looked for the fireball, convinced that it was the end of the world because the sky was orange, just like my teacher said it would be.

My mother finally came to tuck me in. I had often watched her put on a good face, and I didn't want to tell her what was coming, that the world was about to end. So, I pretended like everything was okay. She kissed me goodnight, and I stared out the window at the marmalade-colored sky until I fell asleep, certain I'd never wake up again.

Of course, in the morning, I woke up, and the world was still there. I knew that my choice to spare my mother from my fear of impending doom was justified. That's when I made another decision:

- Don't talk about things that scare you because you might be wrong. You might upset people for no reason, so keep it to yourself.

This series of personal decisions set me up for a lifetime of relating to trauma in a very unhealthy way. There's really no one to blame; it's just what happened. Could things have turned out differently if I'd made some different decisions? Probably. But I see no point in second-guessing, blaming someone or wishing things had played out differently. My past is my past, and the only constructive thing I can do is to learn from it.

When my bedroom was redecorated, Mom and Dad let me pick out the wallpaper and carpeting for my room. My father brought home huge wallpaper sample books, and I leafed through them until I found the perfect look—pink, green and yellow butterflies. My carpet choice was pink. I had desperately wanted a canopy bed, and to my delight, my parents let me have one. Mom found a bed covering set that matched so well with the wallpaper it seemed as if they were made to go together. I remember lying on my bed, looking up at the butterflies on the sheer canopy and thinking I had it all. What more could I ever want?

Our house had a basement large enough for a pool table, ping-pong table and a TV with an Atari console. Any new electronic gadgets were quickly acquired by my father, who loved to be the favorite dad in the neighborhood. There were always kids at our house. When VCRs came out, he got two of them, one for my parents' bedroom and one for the basement. Not only were we the best house for games, but we were also the place where the best parties happened.

In their teenage years, both of my brothers smoked pot as well as cigarettes. They'd drink out of my parents' liquor cabinet and replace what they drank with water. My brothers turned a crawl space above the garage into a pot-smoking den and devised a rope and plank ladder to climb up to it. At first, they wouldn't let me go up—I was the irritating little sister—but eventually, they did. I smoked pot for the first time up there when I was nine or ten. I didn't like it but said I did—no way was I going to look like a dork. When my parents discovered the den, they shut it down and confiscated the stash. This didn't stop my brothers from their delinquent behavior, though. They just went down the alley to smoke.

My brothers were very popular—the party house was good for their reputation. I knew most of their friends who came over. Since my brothers were only thirteen months apart, most of their friends were friends to both, so I got to know them all pretty well. There was one pot-smoking friend I didn't know who started hanging out with them. He wasn't from the neighborhood. His name was Jeff Rusthoven—Rusty for short. He was fifteen, tall and thin, and creepy.

~ Rusty ~

♥ ♥ ♥

It happened one day as I was alone in my bedroom. My brothers and their friends were down in the basement, probably playing Pong on the Atari, eating sour cream and onion potato chips and drinking copious amounts of Mountain Dew. I didn't know Rusty was in the house until he just appeared in my bedroom. I'd met him a few times, but I had no idea how dangerous he was.

As I was playing with my stuffed animals on my pretty pink bedroom carpet, he sat down behind me, his long legs stretching out beside my own. It made me uncomfortable, but I wasn't one to say anything. He began to tickle me playfully on my sides. I was extremely ticklish—when my father tickled me, it was a game to see how hard he could make me laugh. Rusty's touch was different—measured, slow, intentional—but I liked the feeling. It gave me butterflies in my stomach.

He worked his hand under my clothes and tickled the area just above my underpants. I was ten years old, and no one had ever done something like this to me. Then he slipped his hand under my panties and down to where I wiped myself when I went to the bathroom. I didn't understand what was happening. But this is a very sensitive area of the body, and it felt good, so I didn't resist. His hand slid down further and found the opening of my vagina.

In a flash, he was no longer being playful but had become dark and sinister, an animal pouncing on his prey. Suddenly, his other arm was around my waist, violently pulling me close to him, so my back was against his body. As he forced his hand inside the mysterious space between my legs, a sharp pain shot through my body and I cried out. He slapped his hand over my mouth to silence me, and I froze. Then he jammed his other hand deep inside me with quick, forceful, repetitive movements, in and out repeatedly. I was incapable of stopping him. My stuffed animals and the colorful butterflies were the only witnesses.

I don't have a clear memory of getting away. The next thing I remember is being in the bathroom. As I was seated on the toilet cleaning myself, I felt the sinking weight of panic in my belly when I pulled my hand away and saw the stark contrast of bright red blood on the white toilet paper. I'd heard that when a girl bleeds between her legs, she was then a woman, so I assumed I was a woman now. I didn't get my actual period for two more years.

The day after Rusty raped me, he came by the house again. I was there alone and saw him through an open window. He grabbed me by the wrist and tried to yank me through the window, threatening to hurt me again if I told anyone what he'd done. I was horrified, but thankfully my "fight" response kicked in. I wrenched myself free and slammed the window shut. Then I went around the house, closing and locking all the doors and windows.

I was scared and ashamed. For five years, I didn't tell anyone what he had done to me. The decision I had made earlier—that I don't have much say in what happens to my body—was reinforced by this experience.

I stopped being able to fall asleep without an auditory distraction like a radio or a fan. Silence had become unbearable. And I always had to have a light on; usually, the closet light with the door cracked to ward off monsters. When I was twelve, my parents gave me a small TV for Christmas, and I'd fall asleep with it switched on. When the daily programming was done, the screen would go to static. Even the sound of that was better than silence.

Not long after my assault, I began to masturbate almost daily. I didn't understand why, but it became an absolute compulsion. I tried to recreate the fluttery feeling I had in my stomach as Rusty was "tickling" me. Touching myself made me feel good and took away my dark thoughts for a while, but it increased my shame. I felt like there was something wrong with me because I couldn't stop.

Then I discovered a bunch of Playboy magazines under my father's side of the bed. The cover photos were shiny and provocative. Inside was a whole new world for my tweener brain. Sometimes there were men in the pictures with the naked ladies. The men didn't really interest me, but the women—holy cow. I'd take the magazines from under the bed during the day when my dad was at work and carefully replace them just as I'd found them before he got home.

Around the time I discovered the magazines, I had a few physically intimate encounters with a friend's sister. These felt comfortable and safe, and somehow not embarrassing or filled with shame. I wanted more of that, but it didn't continue. I had crushes on a few boys, but I craved their attention, not their bodies. I wanted their hands on me, not in me.

My compulsive behavior continued into my adulthood. I often preferred that to having sex. Later, when I was in my thirties, I finally confessed this to a therapist. This was more than twenty years after Rusty raped me. I was so ashamed and afraid she'd tell me I was a freak, damaged beyond repair and in need of serious help. What she explained, however, was that masturbation was a coping mechanism. I was trying to comfort myself, and because the assault was of my genitalia, that's where I focused my act of comforting. Because the crime had happened at such a young age, part of me was frozen at the age of ten. My ability to process that event was also frozen. Though my body had grown and, in other ways, I had matured, I was still reacting to this event with the limited capacity of a ten-year-old. Her affirmation made me cry; I finally began to understand what I'd been doing. After that therapy session, the compulsive behavior stopped.

When I decided to go public with my experience at the Children's Theatre Company, I began working with a different therapist. While working with her, I decided to search the internet for Rusty. What had happened to him? Did he have a criminal record? In my heart, I knew I wasn't the only person he'd raped. I believed I wasn't the first or the last of his victims.

More than thirty years had passed, but I found his mug shot immediately. His face was older, but the eyes were the same. My stomach turned, and I felt like I was going to vomit. Those eyes, those hands—I'll never forget them. He had gone to prison for an assault on the eight-year-old daughter of his girlfriend back in the nineties. The criminal report showed that his crime was less egregious than what he'd done to me, and yet he had spent eleven years in prison for it. Knowing this helped me fully accept the level of his assault on me. The way I had coped with my emotional and psychological wounds made sense now.

At the time of my internet search, Rusty was doing another short stint in prison for lying about his sex offender status on an apartment application. I was relieved to know he'd been caught and was in the registry, but the search, which I did at work, caused me to have a severe reaction. My body was remembering that assault just as much as my mind, but it didn't recognize I wasn't in any present danger. I was shaking at my core and felt pain in my vagina, even though it had been decades since the event. The pain took several hours to dissipate. If my doctor had examined me at that moment, she wouldn't have seen a wound, but my body felt injury as if it had just happened.

This is the nature of triggers. I could feel so clearly the ghostly presence of Rusty's body pressed to my back that I jumped, yet no one was there. It freaked me out. For ten minutes, I sobbed uncontrollably in the arms of a co-worker.

Through my shaking and tears, I told her, "It's like I'm having a PTSD episode or something."

She replied, "It's not *like* you're having one—you *are* having one."

Even now, as I write about this episode, my body is tense, it's hard to swallow, my breath catches in my throat, my heart is racing and my pelvic area hurts. These events I'm describing are not happening at this moment, but my body remembers them. I have no control over that. I'm choosing to engage with these memories so I can accurately write this book, but these kinds of bodily responses can happen at any time. They can be triggered by a memory, a sound, an image, or a name. When triggered, a neural pathway fires up, which sets off a chain reaction, and then my body takes over. I'm no longer in the driver's seat.

Me at age ten. Photo: Stearns Family

*For trauma survivors, simply reading this account
can be extremely triggering. If you find yourself
dysregulating or dissociating, going for a walk can help
immensely. It engages both sides of the body and brain,
which can reboot your system. Also, alternately tapping
lightly on both sides of your body with your hands
can sometimes be enough to get both sides of the brain
firing and mitigate the effects. Even shifting your eyes
from side to side can help.*

~ Junior High ~

I had a very perceptive school counselor. Halfway through my seventh-grade year, he recognized that something wasn't quite right with me. He asked if anyone at my home was a heavy drinker. My dad was a three-martini business lunch kind of guy, so I said yes—and I was very concerned about the amount of weed my brothers were smoking. My counselor suggested something I'd never heard of—a Twelve Step program for kids affected by someone else's drinking or drug use.

My grandfather died of alcoholism, and I was concerned about how much my dad drank, but I didn't see a correlation between my increasing sadness and my father's drinking. It was more likely that the cause of my depression was the hidden, slowly festering effects of sexual violence. I decided to try out the Twelve Step meetings because they were totally anonymous and held at different times during the school day, so I wouldn't miss any one class too often.

At the first meeting, I was astonished to see kids I knew. It was like a private club, and no one knew we were gathering. An adult supervised, but the kids shared openly around him. I didn't say much in that first meeting, but I learned something I didn't know before—I wasn't alone. Other kids were struggling with difficult things too. They talked about abusive parents, alcoholic family members and their own depression. It was the first time I'd ever heard people talking openly about things that were so upsetting. Over time, I shared some of my concerns about my dad and brothers but never could speak about being sexually assaulted.

The popular preppy girls at school hated me until they learned I knew how to braid hair. Then I was their best friend—well, at least in homeroom, when they would ask me to braid their hair. The rest of the day, they had no time for me.

My best friend, Lisa, was tall like me and had blonde hair. Some of our friends called us Salt and Pepper, not to be confused with the hip-hop team Salt-N-Pepa. It would be years before they became a thing, and there was nothing hip-hoppy about me. I was a complete dork. Lisa smoked cigarettes and would take her parents' car out at night after they went to bed. She was a rebel. No one messed with Lisa.

I was always nervous when we'd do things that were against the rules because I wasn't only a dork, I was a rule-follower. But there was something about Lisa that made me want to hang out with her—maybe because she was real with me and didn't play games, like pretending to be my friend to get something from me. She was free, spoke her mind and did what she wanted. I wished I could be more like her. I didn't feel free—I felt burdened.

Lisa gave me one of her mom's cigarettes, a Pall Mall long, and it made me feel cool, tough. I thought Lisa looked like a badass when she smoked, and I wanted to look tough too. If I was tough, maybe no one would mess with me either. Before long, smoking became a habit I'd carry into adulthood.

I felt like an outsider in public school. I loved to go to the theater, and I started doing the school plays, but really got the performing bug when I saw a play at the Children's Theatre Company in 1979 called *Good Morning Mr. Tillie*. I remember it vividly. I was sitting in the front row, house right. The students in the audience were being squirrelly and loud. I had seen professional tours of Broadway shows, so I knew how to sit properly in an audience. These kids weren't behaving themselves, and I was pissed.

I remember watching the child actors on stage working with adults in a professional show. I was sitting far enough to the side to see a smidgeon of movement backstage, and as I looked up into the fly-loft above the stage, I saw the lighting instruments. I was in awe. I wanted to be up there with them—the kids, not the lights—not sitting with the idiots in the audience throwing candy wrappers at each other. That performance lit a fire in me.

In eighth grade, I got the lead in the fall play, a musical. I'd done a lot of dance recitals as a little girl and several summer theater workshops, but this was the first time I really got to act. Before then, I always thought I wanted to be a singer, but I discovered that acting came naturally. I felt most like myself when pretending to be someone else.

Musicals were a wonderful combination of the things I was good at and loved. I started to dream of being a musical theater actor on Broadway. I spent many hours singing into my hairbrush and accepting awards in my bathroom mirror.

In December of 1980, my mother set up an audition for me at the prestigious Children's Theatre Company and School (CTC). If accepted, I'd be able to leave my public school every day at lunch and take theater classes in the afternoons until five o'clock. I was incredibly nervous but determined. My audition number was 69—I still have the paper slip that was pinned to my shirt.

We were in the dance studio on the fourth floor of the theater for the movement section of the audition when I met John Clark Donahue for the first time. He occupied a chair as if it were a throne, and his presence commanded attention. He made me nervous, but I wanted to impress him. Current students in the school's gray-and-black uniforms packed the doorways, leaning in to see the possible new kids. I was as nervous about auditioning in front of them as I was Donahue.

On December 15, 1980, I received a thick envelope in the mail from CTC. My heart started to race—a rejection letter would've been in a thin envelope. I'd been accepted into the Theater School and would start in January, joining the class of students who'd already done the fall semester. The envelope included lists of things I needed to know and items I needed to get, like ballet slippers. I was out of my mind with excitement and pride. I was going to be one of those theater kids.

I was thirteen and had no idea what I was walking into.

Because of my belief stemming from early childhood that I had no control over who touched me and that I had already been sexually assaulted once, I was primed for receiving more abuse if put into the right conditions. Statistically, once children have been sexually assaulted, they're more likely to have it happen again. I was no exception.

Polaroid audition photo of me at age thirteen from December 1980.

Chapter Three
Learning to Stop Trusting My Gut

The professional theater scene in Minnesota extends into the early 1900s. The Twin Cities of Minneapolis and St. Paul were not considered a theater hub until 1963, when famed English theater director Sir Tyrone Guthrie decided to establish a new theater company in Minneapolis. This effectively put The Guthrie Theater on the national map as the first regional theater company in the United States. At the same time Guthrie was making his historic move to the Midwest, the Children's Theatre Company (CTC) was putting down roots of its own.

~ Roots ~

From the beginning, profound levels of deception and willful ignorance were present at CTC and in the theater community at large. As I outline the development of CTC, I feel like I'm watching someone walk toward danger in a scary movie. I want to yell, *Don't go in there!* Nevertheless, this progression is important to understand for context:

- John Clark Donahue graduated from the University of Minnesota in 1961 at the age of twenty-three with a degree in theater.[8]

---

8   From p. 133 of the doctorate thesis of Martin John Costello entitled *Hating the Sin, Loving the Sinner: The Minneapolis Children's Theatre Company Adolescent*

- Donahue was arrested in October 1961 for child sexual abuse of a student where he taught at Carl Sandberg Jr. High, suspected involvement in child trafficking and production of child sexual abuse images.[9] He received a one-year suspended sentence and spent ninety days in the Hennepin County Workhouse.

- Donahue's college friend, Beth Linnerson, who knew of his criminal history, hired him in 1962 to work at her theater company for children called The Moppet Players. Linnerson later said she believed the kids would be safe from Donahue because she could "keep an eye on what was happening."[10]

- Donahue left The Moppet Players, bringing several of his colleagues with him, and started The Children's Theatre Company in 1965. The company moved into a performance space at the Minneapolis Institute of Arts.[11]

- When Linnerson had the opportunity to tell the newly formed CTC Board of Directors about Donahue's criminal history, she chose to remain silent.[12]

- Donahue was considered a brilliant director but difficult to work for. He often used shame and humiliation to control his performers, adult and child alike.[13]

Sexual Abuse Prosecutions, submitted to the faculty of the Graduate Program for his PhD in philosophy at The University of Minnesota, published 1987, henceforth known as *Costello Thesis*.

9   State of MN v. John Clark Donahue, 1961, case No. MN0271100

10 Deborah Caulfield, *The Scandal at the Children's Theatre*, LA Times Calendar, July 22, 1984, p. 4

11 CTC promotional materials, trial exhibit #53 from Laura Adams [Stearns] v. Children's Theatre Company and Jason McLean case No. 27-CV-15-20713, henceforth known as *Stearns v. CTC case No. 27-CV-15-20713*, and Costello Thesis, p. 137

12 Deborah Caulfield, *The Scandal at the Children's Theatre*, LA Times Calendar, July 22, 1984, p. 4, and Costello Thesis, p. 135

13 Kay Miller, "A Story of Denial: John Clark Donahue and the Children's Theatre—Parts 1, 2 and 3," for *Minneapolis StarTribune*, May 19, 20, 21, 1991

- At least five former male students report having been sexually assaulted by Donahue between 1965 and 1969.[14]

- In 1969, with endorsement from the Minnesota State Arts Board and the National Endowment for the Arts, Donahue established an official theater training program for high school students that was connected to the theater. It was part of the Minneapolis Public School System's Urban Arts Program. Students were given academic credit in their public schools for classes they attended at CTC.[15]

- Had Donahue ever again applied for accreditation for teaching in public schools, his criminal past would have been exposed, disqualifying him from acquiring a license to teach.[16]

- The Rockefeller Foundation gave CTC grants in 1972 and 1973 totaling $750 thousand dollars, putting the theater into a category with The Lincoln and Kennedy Centers for the Performing Arts.[17]

- World-famous Japanese master architect Kenzo Tange, who designed such famous buildings as the Tokyo Olympic Arena, was commissioned to design the new theater.[18]

- In addition to being both artistic and executive director of CTC, Donahue was an associate director of the Minneapolis Society of Fine Arts (MSFA) and had solid connections with the most affluent people in the Twin Cities.[19]

---

14 Protected victim statements and depositions with Jeff Anderson and Associates
15 Stearns v. CTC No. 27-CV-15-20713, trial exhibit #53, CTC promotional materials, and Costello Thesis, p. 137
16 Costello Thesis, p. 139
17 Stearns v. CTC No. 27-CV-15-20713, trial exhibit #53, CTC promotional materials, and Costello Thesis, p. 140
18 Stearns v. CTC No. 27-CV-15-20713, trial exhibit #53, CTC promotional materials
19 Costello Thesis, p. 143

- Donahue was becoming a darling of the community and CTC a gem of the city. In 1973, Donahue was named the American Theater Association Arts Administrator of the Year and won the Jennie Helden Award for Excellence in Professional Children's Theatre.[20]

- The Mandatory Reporting Law was passed in 1975, which requires anyone in a position of power, such as teachers, to report suspicion of child abuse to the authorities, stating that anyone who is a mandated reporter, "who has knowledge of or a reasonable cause to believe a child is being physically or sexually assaulted shall report." It goes on to say, "Any person required by this act to report suspected physical or sexual abuse, who willfully fails to do so, is guilty of a misdemeanor."[21]

- In approximately 1972, two students who were sixteen and seventeen told a friend's parent, Jacqui Smith, they were "having sex relations" with Donahue. They asked her not to tell anyone about it. Because the mandated reporting laws had not been established yet, Smith honored their request and did not report to the authorities at that time.[22]

- Despite rumors of his abuse of male students, referred to as the "worst kept secret in Minneapolis" by one public school teacher, Donahue's popularity and reverence within the community grew because people were enamored with Donahue's vision of theater and the level of artistry being produced at CTC. His abuse of students was ignored.[23]

---

20 Stearns v. CTC No. 27-CV-15-20713, trial exhibit #53, CTC promotional materials
21 Mandated Reporting Law, Minnesota Statute § 626.556 (1975)
22 Furst and McEnroe, "Donahue Was Topic of Rumors for Many Years," *Minneapolis Tribune*, April 29, 1984, p. 10A
23 Kay Miller, "A Story of Denial, John Clark Donahue and the Children's Theatre—Part 1," *Minneapolis StarTribune*, May 19, 1991

- In 1977–78, Jacqui Smith, now on the CTC Board, reported to Deborah Anderson, the director of sexual assault services for Hennepin County, information about students she knew had been abused by Donahue.[24] Anderson, noting Donahue's connections to influential and wealthy people, recalled Smith's information as "the biggest bomb" that could hit Minneapolis if an investigation found any truth in the allegations.[25]

- In the late 1970s, a former secretary reported to the Minneapolis Police Department (MPD) that she was aware of sexual abuse happening at CTC but was too afraid of the people at the theater to do more than just inform the police of the situation. Due to a lack of cooperation and willingness of anyone to talk, the investigation stalled. It wasn't picked up again until 1981, when the Bureau of Criminal Apprehension (BCA) took over the investigation.[26]

- At least nine male students report having been assaulted in the 1970s by Donahue.[27]

- Donahue established working relationships with such famous children's book illustrators and authors as Tomie dePaola and Dr. Seuss.[28] In fact, at that time, the only theater in the world that was granted rights to produce a play based on Dr. Seuss' work was CTC.

- By 1980 the teaching and artistic staff at CTC was almost entirely made up of people who believed Donahue was a

---

24 Stearns v. CTC No. 27-CV-15-20713, Testimony of Deborah Anderson, trial transcript, p. 1640
25 Grand Jury transcript, testimony of Deborah Anderson, vol. 3, p. 1
26 Stearns v. CTC No. 27-CV-15-20713, testimony of investigator Michael Campion, trial transcript, pp. 23–24
27 Protected victim statements and depositions with Jeff Anderson and Associates
28 Stearns v. CTC No. 27-CV-15-20713, trial exhibit #53, CTC promotional materials, and Costello Thesis, p. 145

genius and could do no wrong and his former students—
people who had grown up with no boundaries between
adults and children, and for whom the sexualization of
children was normalized.[29]

- In the early 1980s, CTC had been highly acclaimed
internationally and considered a premier theater for children
in the United States with a budget of $2.7 million and an
annual audience of more than a quarter-million people.[30]

- Donahue had created a safe haven for himself as a sexual
predator, which extended to the people around him. As
many as fifteen adult staff members have now been identified
by victims as perpetrators of child sexual abuse in the early
1980s.[31]

- In 1982, a former student gave a statement to the BCA that
he had been sexually involved with Donahue from the age
of fifteen. Because the statute of limitations was only three
years at the time, too much time had passed, and Donahue
could not be charged.[32]

- The BCA informed the CTC Board of Directors that
Donahue was being investigated in 1982 and told the board
not to interfere with the investigation.[33]

- In 1983, Donahue received the John F. Sherman Award for
Significant and Sustained Service to American Theater.[34]

---

29 Costello Thesis pp. 118–123, Protected victim statements and depositions with
Jeff Anderson and Associates, and multiple eyewitness accounts
30 Stearns v. CTC No. 27-CV-15-20713, trial exhibit #53, CTC promotional
materials, and Costello Thesis, p. 124
31 Protected victim statements and depositions with Jeff Anderson and Associates
32 Costello Thesis, p. 153
33 Stearns v. CTC No. 27-CV-15-20713, testimony of investigator Michael
Campion, trial transcript, pp. 23–24
34 CTC application for "Ongoing Ensembles Narrative Proposal," submitted to
the National Endowment for the Arts and MN State Arts Board, March 28,
1984

- Terri Hanson, South High School music teacher and director of the Urban Arts Summer Theater program, was arrested in April 1983 for molesting a male student and producing child abuse images. As part of a plea agreement, he gave information to the BCA about Donahue's involvement in the production of child pornography and the sex trafficking of children.[35]

- The National Center for Missing and Exploited Children was established in 1984.[36]

- Charming and charismatic, Donahue was lauded and loved in the community. A local restaurant offered a lunch named after him called the "John Donahue"— quiche du jour served with fresh fruit.[37]

- Donahue was arrested on April 18, 1984. He pled guilty to seven counts of first- and second-degree criminal sexual conduct, which was later reduced to three counts.[38]

- A grand jury was convened in the fall of 1984. Several staff members were investigated, and some were charged with criminal sexual conduct or failure to report suspected abuse. Due to a lack of evidence and cooperation from staff and students, only one other person was sentenced. Later, those charges were dismissed.[39]

- The former head of the Family Violence Division at the MPD, Rollo Mudge, recalled, "Of all the cases that came across my desk, that was the one that bugged me the most."[40]

35 Dave Anderson, "Ex-teacher Sentenced on Moral Charges," *Minneapolis StarTribune*, May 12, 1983, p. 1b, and Costello Thesis, p. 152
36 https://www.missingkids.org/footer/about/history
37 Deborah Caulfield, "The Scandal at the Children's Theatre," *LA Times Calendar*, July 22, 1984, p. 4
38 Costello Thesis, p. 165
39 Costello Thesis, p. 189
40 Furst and McEnroe, "Donahue Was Topic of Rumors for Many Years,"

At John Clark Donahue's 1984 sentencing, Judge Charles A. Porter, Jr. stated: "You created a fantasy world of Children's Theatre...and then you took that fantasy world and perverted it. You discriminated against female students. You tied the selection of roles in your plays to the relationships that the various performers had with you. And you took advantage of the very special relationship of respect and trust that your students had with you for the basest of your personal reasons."[41]

The true scope of what was happening—how many perpetrators were abusing children and just how many children were impacted—wouldn't be known for decades. The actual numbers will likely never be known. There was a powerful structure for abuse in place at CTC. These things didn't just happen. The trappings for large-scale abuse were constructed, and the community helped uphold this structure of abuse.

The details provided here are just a sample but sufficient to provide context. If you desire more content, an extended cited history with commentary is provided in the appendix at the back of this book.

I've had many conversations with former students about their experiences at CTC, ranging from glorious to horrifying. Some students never had anything bad happen to them and are astonished by what's now being revealed. It was a dream factory for some. A living nightmare for others. More often, it was a bit of both.

~ Theater School ~

When I began classes at CTC in January 1981 at the age of thirteen, I started my days by taking the school bus to my public school for morning classes. Because of the artistic nature of what I was learning at CTC, I didn't have to take classes like English. My public school

Minneapolis Tribune, April 29, 1984, p. 10A

41 State of Minnesota v. John Clark Donahue, November 7, 1984, transcript of sentencing hearing, pp. 7–8

classes consisted of math and sciences. At the lunch break, I'd leave school for CTC and an afternoon of theater classes.

I remember feeling supremely odd that first day as I left school alone to get on a city bus. I had never skipped school, so it felt like I was getting away with something. I'd never taken the city bus alone, so I was nervous I'd miss my stop. Fortunately, my dad would be picking me up after work.

I was both excited and nervous for theater classes to start, but I feared I wouldn't fit in, wouldn't be up to snuff. These kids were the best of the best and had already been in classes together for months. Would I meet their standards? Would they accept me?

In public school, I often felt different from my peers. I looked older and processed information in a way that seemed foreign to them. In junior high, I was "the theater geek." When I got to CTC, a group of young people immediately brought me into the fold. They were like me—weird, in a wonderful way. They didn't follow a trodden path. I had found my family. We were like the island of misfit toys; our uniqueness bound us to each other.

Friendships form quickly in a theater environment. One of my new friends, Rana, showed me how to open a pomegranate. I'd never even seen one before, and the taste of the little jewels that came out of it were bitter and sweet at the same time, completely new to my palate.

There were about fifty kids in the theater school when I started. I was blown away by the level of talent and work ethic. Our instructors told us we were special, and we worked our asses off. Being different set us apart and sadly also made us vulnerable to the people who were preying upon children. Our "specialness" could be used to isolate us.

We studied all forms of performance; there was no specializing as depicted in the movie *Fame*. We were separated into "years." As a First Year, some of my classmates were younger than me, some older. We were matched with those at our same level in the training process, not by age. We mostly studied classes with the kids in our same year, but occasionally classes would be combined. Our studies consisted of things like singing, spoken voice, multiple disciplines of dance, gymnastics, improvisation, acting and oral interpretation.

We were also required to learn about backstage production. Every student had to work on one of the professional main stage productions every year. We could work with the stage crew, stage management, props, wardrobe, and sound and lighting. There were also kids who worked in the box office, costumes, production management, theater administration, education, and as assistant teachers. We were exposed to everything and every department of the theater. We were learning things that most kids weren't even aware existed and were given responsibilities that went far beyond what children were typically expected to do.

Donahue's philosophy was that if you remove the boundaries between adults and children and treat them the same, the children will rise to the occasion because it gives them a different kind of ownership of their experience. He believed that if you expect great things of them, they'll produce great things. Using kids in positions normally occupied by paid adults was cost-effective for the theater but bordered on child labor. We used to joke about that, but there was a nugget of truth at the core. Because no one was telling us that we shouldn't be doing something, we did everything; we were there at all hours, given responsibilities that in other professional theaters would be done by employees. Because we were hand-picked and honored to be there, we delivered and were grateful for the opportunity. The chance to learn our craft at that level and at such a young age was unprecedented, but it came at a high cost. If we didn't do something perfectly, we were ridiculed for our mistakes. There was no room for imperfection.

CTC was a multi-million-dollar institution regarded as a national treasure. The school was prestigious and attracted a lot of attention nationally. We were working with world-renowned designers like Tanya Moiseiwitsch. Famous people would tour the building regularly.

Imagine being in the darkened womb-like atmosphere of a small theater space. Theatrical lights illuminate the center of the room where you sit with your classmates. The edges of the room are dark. And then a door opens, and an enormous figure appears in the doorway, surrounded by a halo of light from the hallway. The edges of his body are glowing, but you can't see his face. The door closes, and the man is now standing in the dark. Slowly, he steps into the light, and you see that it's James Earl Jones. *Holy shit, that's Darth Vader.* He was in a Guthrie Theater production at the time, and Donahue had invited him for a tour of CTC.

In the Green Room of the theater's basement hung a wall-size black and white photograph, a cast photo from a film version of *He Who Gets Slapped* that Donahue and company made back in the mid-seventies. There were about thirty people in it. Just about everyone who was a CTC staff member when I was a student was in that photograph. I wished I'd been in it. I wanted so badly to be part of the history—no, the legacy of CTC. I was in awe of the people whose faces were memorialized on that wall. I didn't want to see or hear anything that would contradict the love I felt for these people, the mentors who guided me in my artistry.

~ Rumors ~

From the get-go, the sexualization of children was normalized for me at CTC. I quickly became aware of rumors about Donahue and boys in the school. There was a joke going around that I now find disgusting but seemed normal back then. You would stand up and bend over, showing your ass to someone, and then say, "What's this?" The response was, "An audition at Children's Theatre." Hearing sex jokes about auditions was just part of the package. Everyone would laugh, but with a knowing undertone.

The "casting couch" is a term used in the theater and film world. It basically means that directors will cast you in shows or movies in exchange for sexual favors. The idea of a casting couch didn't set off alarms in me partly because our society, in general, accepted it as normal. *That's the way it is in the Biz.* Jokes and rumors about Donahue being sexual with students was just no big deal. I didn't know until many years later how prevalent sexual abuse was at CTC. Children crave attention and accolades, and Donahue used his power to groom and manipulate children for sexual favors.

Donahue orchestrated many elements of his predatory behavior. He would go into the boy's locker room and shower with them after Boys Class—a muscle-strengthening class created just for them. Pouring sweat and exhausted, the male students would go into the locker room where Donahue was already present. He would comment on their bodies, even jackoff in the shower. I now know that a student reported this behavior to a school administrator, but nothing was done about it.

It was common for students to warn new boys about Donahue; they were on their own after that. One of my male friends talked about the fresh young faces that would arrive every year. He said everyone could tell by the way the fresh faces changed over time who Donahue had gotten to.

In general, Donahue was aloof when he walked the halls of the theater. He'd show favoritism by engaging with a boy and ignoring the people around him. When this happened, rumors would start flying. Some of the boys in the school were gay, but certainly not all of them. I later heard that one way Donahue would ensnare a victim was to tell him he knew the boy was gay and wanted to help him "find himself" by embracing his homosexuality. It's doubly heartbreaking because this behavior is exactly what homophobes think being gay is all about—being a sexual predator.

A gay man supporting a young gay man to find his way can be a beautiful thing. It's a difficult transition for many, and gays often feel ostracized, bullied, unfriended and even disowned by their families because of their sexuality. I believe there were some men at CTC who had good intentions, but there were also predators who used the situation to their advantage.

For girls, the abuse at CTC was much more socially acceptable. I don't really remember rumors about girls—it was more like facts or common knowledge. Sadly, the idea of girls being victimized doesn't sound the same alarms as it does with boys. Men preying upon girls is so normalized in our society that it barely gets noticed. When I was new at school, no one warned me, "Watch out for Jason McLean."

Rumors of Donahue's sexual predilection for young boys were not confined to the CTC building. I've heard many stories about parents deciding to keep their male children from going to school at CTC because of Donahue's reputation. The flip side of that was also true. Some parents of prospective female students heard that if you had a female child, it would be fine to send them to CTC because it was the boys who were preyed upon. How wrong they were.

The rumors even went over the borders of our state. People in New York City were aware of them. It was an open secret.

~ The Conservatory School ~

During my first year of theater school, it was announced they were going to start a full-day school in the fall of 1981. The curriculum would include state-accredited academic classes. I was jazzed about the possibility of this because it meant I wouldn't have to go to public school anymore.

The design of classes would revolve around the shows being produced. For instance, when CTC produced an adaptation of Astrid Lindgren's *Pippi Longstocking*, our studies would include things like Swedish culture and food. I was excited about this teaching concept, and my parents were on board, so I signed up. There were still kids in the theater school who went to public school in the morning, but many of us opted to join The Conservatory School.

The first year included about twenty-five students. It was like a one-room schoolhouse with grades nine through twelve all moshed together learning the same curriculum. We were allowed to design individual classes. If we wanted to learn something, we merely had to present the idea to our academic teachers, who would help us make it happen.

When I was cast in *Alice in Wonderland*, I had to wear wigs. It was the first time I saw what a handmade wig looked like from the inside, and I was enthralled. At fifteen, I went into the wig shop and asked the wig master Victor, who was also a former student, if he would teach me how to make them. He was delighted to pass on his knowledge of this rare craft and get a little help in return. I started going to the wig shop whenever I had free time, and eventually, we made it an official class. I was basically his apprentice.

Those times with Victor are some of my favorite memories at CTC. They were filled with laughter and music and made use of my love for working with my hands and skills like braiding hair. The exposure set the foundation for my becoming the wig master at the prestigious Guthrie Theater later in life.

Because of the flexible curriculum, I got to know the company playwright, Tom Olson, another former student who'd adapted many plays for CTC. He became a mentor and guided me in my writing endeavors. I'd meet with him in his office down in the basement near the dressing rooms a couple of times a week, and we'd talk for hours about playwriting, often scrutinizing things I'd written. It was another opportunity to have a one-on-one mentorship with someone I respected greatly. There were seemingly no limits to my discovery process. If I wanted to learn something, I just made it a class.

The Conservatory School made it easier to do shows. Public schools don't love it when you miss classes, and there were performances for school groups Tuesdays through Fridays. Students performing in shows or fulfilling their crew requirements would miss a lot of school, but this new branch of the theater school solved that problem. Between the time I started working on shows in the 1981–82 season and the time I graduated in the spring of 1985, I was involved in sixteen of the twenty-five main stage productions that were produced, plus a few blackbox studio theater shows. This was in addition to attending full-time school. I basically lived at the theater, and the Conservatory School made it so much easier.

Sadly, the conservatory also isolated us from the outside world, and the predators at CTC took advantage of our lack of interaction with peers and adults in public education. Of course, I felt even more special, which was appealing as a kid. Many parents were pleased to know their child was part of an elite group. My parents loved to brag that I was at CTC. They were proud of me, and I was proud to be there.

~ The Man at the Center ~

John Clark Donahue's professional behavior was well known in the industry at large, even outside of Minneapolis. He was a charismatic figure, considered brilliant but difficult. If you had what it took to work with him, that was a badge of honor in some circles.

Donahue had removed the boundaries between adults and children in the name of creating more authentic art. He was loved for this because he believed in what we were capable of, and that, in turn, made us believe in ourselves. Many of his former students credit him for their successes, using phrases like "he saved my life" and "I wouldn't be the artist I am today without him." He was revered and admired because of how he was able to get the kids under his tutelage to blossom.

As a storyteller at heart, I was drawn to the level of quality storytelling I discovered at CTC. Donahue was approaching the art of storytelling from a vantage point beyond anything I'd experienced.

His energy was a demanding force, and he was masterful at using it to get what he wanted from people, including actors and donors. He could turn his charm on and off at will.

Like many kids, I was scared of Donahue as a First Year. He sauntered through the building with an air of ownership. When I started, I was mostly invisible to him, just another kid in the crowd. He didn't even bother learning our names. I knew what it was like for him to look through me.

But then, when he first saw me, I mean really looked at me, it was like a current of energy came off him and went right into me. His eyes came alive—it was palpable. It was the beginning of the fall term for the newly established Conservatory School. I'd just played Nancy in *Oliver* with the Urban Arts Summer Theater program directed by Terri Hanson. I had entered the elevator with another student when Donahue got on. Normally, he wouldn't say anything to me in a situation like this. He would just stand silently in that metal box, the energy of him bouncing off the walls. This time, he looked right at me and called me by name. He told me he'd heard I had done a great job as "Nancy" and congratulated me. Clearly, Terri had told him about my performance.

I beamed and said, "Thanks."

I was on Donahue's radar, and that made me desire his approval even more.

Donahue could be encouraging, but he could also be mean. When he was angry at someone, he'd ridicule them and tell them to "blow up." He said this to anyone who really annoyed him or pissed him off. His eyes would shift and become empty, withholding the life-force of approval, and then he'd look right through you. The effect was depleting—like being deprived of oxygen. When I experienced that part of him, all I wanted was to get back to the place where his eyes would connect to me, and I would become visible again and not irrelevant. I wanted to please him more than anything because when I did, I felt like I mattered.

I didn't have classes with him the first year I was there. Students didn't get that privilege until later. In my second year, I took his improvisation class. He would encourage us to dig down into the darker parts of ourselves to expose our fears and anger. He'd nod in approval or say "yeeeeees," like a long sigh of agreement for whatever we were exposing, a verbal citation for our commitment to stretch ourselves and take risks.

In one class, I dug so far down into my emotions I had a hard time bringing myself back. Donahue invited me to come to his office to talk about it, like a caring father or a close friend. His office was on the third floor of the theater. A wall of windows spanned the room and overlooked the stage. A door at the end of the windows led to the balcony seating. The windows had curtains that could be drawn. From the stage, you could clearly see the office windows in the balcony, and the curtains were usually drawn. When we were performing, we knew that if the office lights were out and the curtains were open, Donahue was most likely in there watching the show—and us. From the vantage point of the performer, you couldn't see people in the office, but they could see you.

That day, overwhelmed with emotions from class, I sat on his couch and cried. He listened intently. I didn't share specifics with him about being sexually assaulted, but I think I gave him enough information to know there was some deep trauma in my life. I had exposed my vulnerabilities, and he had filed them away in his mind.

By the time I'd arrived at CTC, Donahue was in his heyday. His abuse of boys was ignored by the people close to him. Rumors were rampant but weren't investigated. Donahue was considered too important, which I believe emboldened him. Men have told me horrible stories of being assaulted by Donahue as boys, some of them describing other adults being present while they were being abused, but they would ignore what was happening, or they would walk into the room, observe what was happening, then quickly exit, closing the door behind them. Donahue was enabled time and time again by the adults around him. They did nothing to stop him.

Polaroid cameras were used for things like audition photographs. Within minutes you could watch an image slowly develop right before your eyes. Donahue would use his Polaroid camera to take pictures of male students' genitalia. He kept a stack of these photographs, like a deck of cards. No faces, just the groins. One of these men told me that Donahue had taken several pictures of him over the years, eventually showing him how his own penis had developed over time.

~ The Shaving of the Head ~

Our uniform was very plain: a light grey T-shirt or sweatshirt bearing the CTC logo—a bird on a branch—silk-screened on the back and black karate pants. For dance classes, we wore black leg warmers if you wanted them and black ballet shoes; girls wore black leotards and grey tights, and boys wore T-shirts with dance belts and tights. Any combination of these items was acceptable, and we were required to wear these things during theater school classes. We'd get in trouble if we wore something else. The uniform dress required us to shed the things that connected us to the outside world when we entered the learning spaces.

Donahue would present what he called "The Shaving of the Head" speech in the studio theater on the fourth floor at the beginning of the school year and again after the winter break. It was always very theatrical. The doors would open, and the stage lighting would create a moody and mysterious atmosphere. The students would quietly enter and sit on the floor, slowly filling the room. Sometimes there would be a grand chair in the middle of the room (probably from prop storage). Donahue would be in it, perfectly lit and regally perched. Sometimes he'd wait until we were all seated and then make an entrance, grandly walking through the assemblage as we sat there with upturned faces, waiting with anticipation to hear his wise words. Depending on his mood, though, he sometimes would sit on the floor as if he were one of us. The event was treated like a ritual that required respect.

The speech was ceremonial in nature and offered reverentially. We listened intently as he poured his philosophy into us. He was his best self during these speeches, smiling and looking directly into our eyes, asking us for our thoughts on the elements, nodding in approval. He was our friend. He would be barefoot and in the same uniform as us, a demonstration of his own requirement of devotion to the work. Much of the eight elements of his speech were rooted in Buddhism:

- The Temple—the space where we learned and created our art, the theater.

- The Shaving of the Head—a mark of devotion, the giving over of self by wearing the uniform, and showing full commitment to the work.

- The Silent Focus— the shutting off of distractions, leaving the outside world "out there," appreciating the beauty of silence.

- The Master—speaking of himself and the other teachers. He said, "The Master is wise enough, if he is a Master at all, to know that the Master is the student, and that learning is a beautiful communion between some of us who have walked a while and a way. And so, I invite you to walk along with them, but also recognize that you have much to give."

- The Journey—our process, our learning, our growth. Our successes and failures.

- The Sanctuary Light—the light that burns inside of us, our potential. "Your fuel, your flame, your eye, your inner eye, the part of you that is divine."

- The Tools—our classes, our bodies, our voices, things we would use to reveal the light inside us.

- White Blindness and Freedom—the state of ecstasy, euphoria one feels when everything clicks, when what you have been striving for is achieved. "You are made greater by the greatness of your work."

It felt very sacred, and the fact that much of the philosophy he taught was based on centuries of Eastern philosophy, it sounded really good. He told us how special we were, took away the boundaries that separated students from teachers and gave us the sense that our work was sacred, our journey unique. He told us *he* understood us, highlighted our uniqueness and the potential that was burning inside us aching to be recognized. We were a family, he said, and we needed to be there for each other because the outside world wasn't there for us.

He made me want to leap in the air, to test my boundaries, find my limits. *If I do all those things, people will see my greatness and I'll feel ecstasy? Hell yeah, count me in.* I gobbled up his rhetoric like water found in a desert.

I still made efforts to show my individuality, however. I cut the neck off my T-shirts and sweatshirts, a la *Flashdance*, and wore a different color leg warmer when I could get away with it. After all, I was a teenager trying to figure out my place in the world. But I bought Donahue's wares and tried to do what he asked because I wanted his approval.

~ Working on Shows ~

Donahue had a reputation of being difficult to work for. Stories of his temper and indifference to those who didn't live up to expectations are legendary. An actress friend of mine who didn't grow up in Minnesota and wasn't aware of his abusive history recently told me she worked for Donahue in the 1990s. She considered him one of the best directors she'd ever known, but also said he was the kind of person who would "eat you alive in the shadows." He was notorious for humiliating people.

One of his favorite insults was to call someone "Betty" or "Mary" whether they were male or female. This derogatory use of women's names and the general disregard he had for women made it clear that females were on the low rung of the ladder. Being a girl was onerous in that misogynistic environment. Historically, the objectification, silencing and abuse of women in the world has been minimized; that's just the way it is. It was simply magnified at CTC.

The first main stage show I worked on was called *The Cookie Jar*, written and directed by Donahue. I worked stage crew and props, helped run the dry ice machine and baked the prop cookies in the little kitchen by the Green Room. At the end of each performance, the cast would throw wrapped pieces of cake into the audience—a highlight of the show for children in attendance. I helped wrap the cake in waxed paper. Being on the stage crew was fun. In addition to the professional acting company, the show had lots of kids on and off stage. This was when I realized that backstage production work was just as important as what happens onstage.

On this show, I first saw a glimmer of the power Donahue held and how mean he could be. During one of the technical rehearsals, I was backstage watching and waiting for the next thing I had to do. Donahue was out in the house, sitting in the dark, barking out directions on what we called the "God Mic." He was grumbling about a technical difficulty. Ranting and belligerent behavior, I would discover, was common for him.

Director of Production Frank McGovern came on stage and stood not far from where I was sitting. He began arguing with Donahue about the nature of the problem. They just kept going back and forth, Donahue on his God Mic and Frank defiantly spitting out his own vitriol. I'd never ever seen anyone question Donahue before, let alone argue with him. People could get pissy with him, tempers could flare, but I never saw anyone directly confront Donahue the way Frank did.

Tech rehearsals often went late into the night. No one considered that maybe the kids should go home. We were expected to stay just like everyone else. Starting a run-through at 11:00 pm was not unheard of. It was just the way things were. I remember one time sitting outside the theater alone after a late rehearsal. The building was locked and I was afraid that I might be attacked while waiting for a ride home at one o'clock in the morning. My brothers could drive, and they would often pick me up. My parents never questioned if I was supervised at rehearsals or while waiting to be picked up—they assumed I was being taken care of because it was such a professional environment. But the truth was, we mostly weren't supervised.

During my first opening night party I followed a fellow student crew member into the scene shop and they went and grabbed a beer. I was flabbergasted.

"Is that allowed?" I asked.

"Yeah, just grab one," he said.

"Holy crap," I said. "This is fucking awesome."

Supervision of students was spotty at best, and it felt like our well-being wasn't at the top of anyone's priority list.

In August 1982, *Smithsonian Magazine* featured the Children's Theatre Company as its cover story. Donahue had taken this tiny little troupe of theater artists and created a treasured gem in the local and national theater scene. The featured production for the story was *Alice in Wonderland*, the first show in which I performed at CTC, and the picture on the cover of *Smithsonian* featured the man who would later rape me, Jason McLean. An actor in the show told me McLean had bragged before the photo shoot about how he'd painted his prosthetic nose to look like a penis.

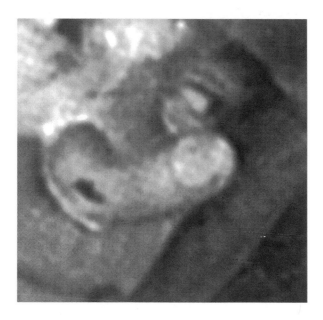

Closeup of McLean on the *Smithsonian* cover

Alice in Wonderland was filmed with The Television Theater Company for cable television release and is now available on YouTube. The *Smithsonian* version of his nose is not in the video.

Pippi Longstocking was produced in the fall 1982. By that time, I was constantly involved in main stage productions, so I was at the theater a lot. I wasn't one of the kids who got cast in leading roles—I was way too tall and looked like one of the grownups—so I was pretty much an ensemble player or worked backstage crews.

At the cast party for *Pippi*, Jason McLean began paying attention to me. A lot of teenage girls fawned over him, and I was flattered that a company actor was flirting with me. He was tall, thin and muscular with sandy brown hair and an impish smile—charming to my fifteen-year-old eye. I'd worked on a few shows with him, but this night he was being particularly flirtatious.

One of my friends, Melissa, had told me she had been sleeping with McLean for a while. It seemed weird that he'd be flirting with me if he was "with" her. I say "with" because that's how we talked about such things. We didn't say "dating;" we said "with" or "they're together."

For the production of *Pippi Longstocking*, the character of Pippi was double cast—meaning two performers would alternate playing the part. Both of the girls playing Pippi were in my same year. Double-casting children in plays is common today but was unheard of for CTC back then. The pressure of being the lead in a show at CTC was intense, but the part of Pippi was also physically demanding, requiring the young actress to do a lot of gymnastics. CTC productions were performed six days a week for several weeks in a row. We regularly performed two shows a day. I believe they had two girls playing the part because the risk of injury was so high.

I was on the stage crew and operated the puppet that was Pippi's horse. It was a complex design, tricky to manipulate and extremely heavy. I had to be strapped into it. After a few weeks, I started getting severe back pain—the beginning of a lifetime of back issues for me. At the top of the show, I was positioned within the set of Pippi's house, where I'd wait to maneuver the puppet through the window after Pippi made her grand entrance. When Pippi entered she would do a series of acrobatics, flips and handsprings.

One day, my friend Annie and I were in position to start the show. Annie would be performing as Pippi, but right before her entrance she had a breakdown. She was exhausted, and I heard her crying and whispering, "I can't. I can't." It seemed clear that she would be unable to make her entrance. It was just the two of us in the set piece, and I tried to assure her she'd be okay, but I was strapped into the horse puppet and couldn't move to console my friend.

The stage manager was whisper-yelling at Annie from their post offstage, telling her to get up and make her entrance. Another friend of hers crept over from behind a curtain and gently talked her into getting up and starting the show. She pulled it together and performed brilliantly, as she always did.

I felt horrible for her and thought it was stupid to make her perform when there was another actor who could do it in a heartbeat. The people in charge completely disregarded Annie's mental state.

That year, the 1982–83 season, the theater planned to do a new Christmas show based on the Charles Dickens novel *The Pickwick Papers*. Normally, the theater produced plays that were part of the CTC cannon, like *Cinderella* and *The Little Match Girl*, so a new Christmas show was exciting. *Mr. Pickwick's Christmas* would be an adaptation by resident playwright Thomas Olson and there would be a large cast. I decided to audition.

At the callbacks, all the key players were there—the full acting company, apprentices, some of the best child actors, and because it was going to be a large cast, a few local Twin Cities actors as well. Most of the acting company were also my teachers, so I felt a lot of pressure to do well. There was going to be singing in the show, and I was a singer, so I thought it was my best shot at being cast.

We were taught a new song and we each had to sing a line solo. I got more and more nervous the closer my turn came. Finally, when it was my time, my mouth went dry and I squeaked out some noise that sounded awful. I wanted to sink into the floor. I thought my biggest asset was my singing, so I figured I had blown my chance.

When the cast list went up, I reviewed the selected ensemble names and mine wasn't there—I hadn't made the cut. Then someone tapped me on the shoulder. "Congratulations," she said. Confused, I looked again. I was cast in the show, but not in the ensemble. I was under the list of characters. I'd been given a speaking part. Not only that, but I was cast as a supporting lead—the love interest of one of the main characters. And the actor playing my love interest was Jason McLean. I was giddy. I felt like I had finally arrived.

I would be cast regularly in shows and eventually became part of the "inner circle" comprised mainly of the acting company, certain teachers, people in leadership roles and select students. Those in the inner circle were regularly welcomed to hang out at Donahue's house and attend parties and gatherings.

The Christmas show marked the beginning of McLean's grooming of me in earnest. What began as flirting suddenly intensified. Once rehearsals started, we were required to spend a lot of time together. He had his hands on me all the time, hugging me, kissing my neck. I thought it was awesome to have this influential man paying such attention to me. I was infatuated with him.

In the play, my character fell for his character, at one point kissing him under the mistletoe. This meant I had to kiss McLean eight shows a week for five weeks. I felt like an adult and believed I was special to him.

During a tech rehearsal when I was in the wardrobe room and sitting with a few friends waiting for a music rehearsal to start, a nineteen-year-old acting apprentice came in. I knew him pretty well because he was "with" a friend of mine who was only fourteen at the time. This actor was in a strange mental state. He rushed toward me, got in my face and said, "Hit me." I was dumbfounded. The remark was so out of the blue. "Hit me," he said again more intensely.

"I'm not going to hit you," I said. "What's wrong with you?"

With no warning, he hit me in the face—hard. "Hit me back," he demanded.

The adult supervisor just sat there slack-jawed.

The other person in the room, another apprentice, told me, "Go ahead, hit him."

So, I did. I slapped him. He shook it off.

"Hit me again," he roared.

I refused and he stormed out of the room but came back a minute later with my friend, the girl he was "with." She had teary eyes and was holding her wrist, clearly in horrible pain. He had done something to sprain her wrist.

Somehow word of the incident reached those who were prepping for the rehearsal. I figured our stage manager, Mary Winchell, would come down to find out what was going on. But Donahue himself came to get the story directly from me. He didn't ask if I was okay, just wanted to know what had happened. I told him everything, then he went back upstairs. I figured the apprentice was in big trouble because he'd just assaulted two students.

Within minutes, the full company of actors was called to the stage. I assumed there would be some acknowledgement of the incident from Donahue or Winchell, but nothing was said. We were just told to get ready to sing. The assailant was across the stage from me still agitated but singing along with everyone else. It was as if nothing had happened.

Tech for this show was extremely stressful. Tom Olson had been rewriting the show up to the last minute, trying to keep up with Donahue's demands. We were getting new pages of script daily until we opened. Donahue was impatient and imperious. No one wanted to get caught in his wrath.

During one rehearsal, after a scene shift, the lights came up to reveal that a chair had been left on stage. Someone had forgotten to remove it or maybe choreography of the shift didn't allow time for the chair to be taken away. Donahue got on his God Mic and asked who was supposed to get the chair.

The culprit was one of the conservatory students, a sixteen-year-old girl in a class above me. Donahue made her stand there in the middle of the stage next to the chair while he publicly berated her until she started crying. She was shaking from trying to hold in the sobs and he just kept on humiliating her and making fun of her tears until he dismissed her, telling her to "blow up." No one even tried to stop this cruel behavior. I think we were all just so damn happy it wasn't us up there on the stage.

During another performance of the same production, I was waiting for my entrance near the edge of an open orchestra pit. One of my friends, a student from my class, made his entrance right before me. As he twirled around inside a giant rump roast costume, which was part of a dream sequence, he fell into the pit. The show kept going. Though I didn't know if my friend was dead or alive, I had to go out there and dance. Thankfully, it turned out okay, the costume had broken his fall and he wasn't injured.

After several shows, I had gotten to know Frank, the general manager who had confronted Donahue in the first show I worked on. Frank was a former student himself, part of Donahue's living legacy. Frank had a quick temper, so most people were afraid of him, including me; but he recognized my talents on the production side. Eventually, I got on his good side and became one of a small group of students who were allowed to hang out in his office between classes. I was given a key that gave me access to most of the building. Having that key and being one of the few students Frank liked was yet another thing that brought me into the inner circle, a marker that I had a different status.

In the spring of 1983, I was cast as the Jailer's Daughter in *The Wind and the Willows*. I was fifteen and didn't even have to audition; the director just asked me if I wanted to be in the show. I wore a corseted costume that made my chest billow up, exaggerating my cleavage. The designer of the show wanted to amplify this visual element even more, so I was taught how to add makeup highlights and lowlights in the right places to make me look more buxom.

During this time, Gilbert and Sullivan's *Trial by Jury* was being presented in the studio theater. Even though I was already cast in a main stage show, I auditioned for it and was cast in the chorus. The shows were not scheduled at the same time (there were also other people in both shows), but often I'd have to perform in both shows on the same day.

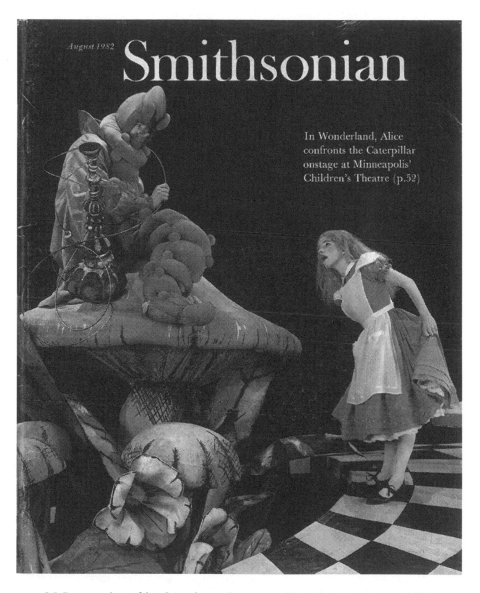

August 1982 **Smithsonian**

In Wonderland, Alice
confronts the Caterpillar
onstage at Minneapolis'
Children's Theatre (p.52)

McLean and my friend Annie on the cover of *Smithsonian*, August 1982

My character in the studio show was completely opposite of what I was doing on the main stage. I was in the chorus, but the director wanted me to be a beggar woman sitting in the audience next to the jury box. I was supposed to act like I was a fan of the musical, just there to watch, but I knew all the songs so I'd sing along with them. It was great fun. I ate peanuts and offered them to audience members, wore a raggedy costume, blacked out my teeth and smeared dirt on my feet and legs. I was disgusting to look at and loved every second of it.

By this point, my family had moved to a western suburb of Minneapolis, so it was harder to come and get me. Being in two shows at the same time was exhausting, and I'd often just stay in town, sleeping at friends' houses or in the out-of-town student housing, or sometimes in the dressing room at the theater on a couch. Between shows and school, I was at the theater pretty much all the time.

~ The Snake Nest ~

One night in late May 1983, after doing an afternoon *Wind in the Willows* and then immediately performing in *Trial by Jury* at night, I rushed out of the theater to attend a gathering at Donahue's house. I was now attending many parties there for opening nights, Christmas and birthdays, but I was also welcome at more casual gatherings. I don't recall what the occasion was, but the guests were mostly adults. McLean was making out with a woman on the front room couch, a former student who was now in her twenties.

I was jealous. McLean had spent about eight months grooming me to believe I was special to him, but we were not really "together" like I had seen him be with others.

I helped myself to some wine—it was completely normal in this crowd for a student to drink alcohol—then stood in the dining room, sipped my wine and took in the scene. Donahue's home had a beautiful bohemian aesthetic. It was filled with plush antique furniture, artful paintings, antique rugs on hardwood floors, velvety rich reds and dark wood. Clusters of people chatted and sipped wine together.

McLean, no longer on the couch, came toward me with an impish smile on his face. After some small talk, he leaned in and whispered, "Will you come home with me tonight?"

I was happy he asked and said I would. It's normal for teenage girls to have a crush on older influencers, to want to be viewed as mature. I thought I was head over heels, but I was in over my head.

When I said "yes," I expected we would make out as he'd just been doing with the woman on the couch. I wasn't thinking about having sex, and while I did wonder if that was what he was suggesting, we didn't mention it. I'd never had sexual intercourse with anyone before. The incident when I was ten wasn't an intimate encounter, it was an attack. I'd never even had a serious boyfriend, though I'd made out with a few. The comfort I'd found with my friend's sister had rocked my world, but I'd never been fully naked in a bed with another person.

I don't remember much more about being at Donahue's, except that I was drunk when McLean and I left together. I had to hold his arm as we walked to his house. I was completely vulnerable at that moment. He knew it and took advantage of the situation. As the adult, he should have been looking out for me. Instead, he used it as an opportunity to add another girl to his list of conquests.

I'm not certain if I was so drunk that I don't remember much after leaving Donahue's or if I've blocked those memories. I have no recollection of entering McLean's house or removing my clothes, but I'm sure I undressed myself because later on I saw my clothing folded neatly and sitting on the back of the couch next to the bed. Thinking about it now, that gesture of folding my clothes feels like confirmation of my state of mind. This wasn't a moment of passion. I didn't throw off my clothes in a trail on the way to the bed. I was scared and felt powerless, not knowing what else to do and trying to create a sense of normalcy in a moment that felt out of control.

My next clear memory is being naked in the bed with my legs tightly crossed and ankles locked, my arms wrapped around my upper body to hide my nakedness. I said, "No," but he kept trying to pry my legs apart. Eventually, he succeeded, forcing his body between my legs as I struggled. And then I felt him enter me.

Human beings have a natural fear response. Some fight, some flee. I froze, just as I'd done when Rusty had attacked me. That feeling of being powerless in the moment manifested in a visceral way, and I was unable to move or stop him. I was frozen. I could smell the musky scent of his armpits above my face mixing with the smell of my own fear.

He used no condom. The assault was impersonal and cold—his eyes were closed. I could have been anyone beneath him. He didn't listen when I told him to stop, he forced his way into me and fucked me as I lay there unable to move. When finished, he got off me without a word, rolled over beneath his framed picture of a naked Nastassja Kinski wrapped in a snake, and fell asleep.

I laid there for hours, terrified to move for fear that he would wake up and do it again. I wanted to get up and run away, but I couldn't move. Finally, after a couple hours of this paralysis, the first birds started chirping outside. I knew the sun would be up soon and my body began to relax. I was able to doze off.

To this day, I have sleep problems. Often, it isn't until I can hear the morning birds start to sing that I'm able to fall asleep. There is safety in sunlight.

When McLean began to stir, I woke up confused. Where was I? Then I realized I was in McLean's bed and the sun was up. I was able to quietly get out of bed, grab my clothes and get into the bathroom without waking him. All I wanted to do was get in the shower and wash off the smell of him.

I turned on the water but couldn't find a clean washcloth, so I got into the shower and started to wash with my hands. The sensible protocol of waiting to shower after being raped was not taught to young women in those days. Not that I was going to report this incident. I was aware of how women and girls were treated after accusing men of such things—they were called sluts and told it was their fault. The cops wouldn't believe them and their reputations would be destroyed. I wasn't going to inflict that on myself.

I scrubbed as hard as I could, lathering up the soap and running my hands over my body to remove any residue of him. And then I realized I still had dirt on my legs from the previous evening's performance, which felt like a hundred years ago. I looked at my chest and saw the makeup highlights and shading contours. It was absurd to find these remnants of a typical day at the theater on my body, which had just been violated.

Only a few months earlier, I had confessed to Stacey, my best friend in school, what Rusty had done to me. It had been five years and I had finally felt safe enough with someone to talk about it. It was an important conversation; I'd written about it in my journal. I needed someone to know about what happened. Telling Stacey helped some, but I still felt broken. In McLean I was looking for something that would help me feel normal, not more shattered. But now I felt worse.

I scrubbed hard to get all the dirt off my legs and watched the water at my feet change from murky to clear. What I really wanted to wash away I wasn't able to shed. A new level of shame had engulfed me. It would be with me for decades.

After dressing, I came out and found McLean cooking breakfast as if the world were normal. My world was completely altered, I was cracking open, and he was frying bacon. He looked at me with a smile.

I glared back at him.

"What's wrong with *you*?" he said, as if I were ruining his morning.

"You know what's wrong," I said and stormed out.

I walked as fast as I could toward the theater. I was reeling inside as I ferociously chanted, "This is so fucked up—this is so fucked up—this is so fucked up." I'd just been raped, and I knew that if I let myself fully feel what had just happened I'd spin out of control—and I had a show to do that morning. There was no time for feelings.

My chant changed to, "I can't deal with this right now. I'm not going to deal with this right now. I can't take it." I put my emotions into a mental box and locked it so I wouldn't have to feel anything. I shoved those emotions so deeply into that box that I'm still unpacking them.

The terrifying experience with McLean hardened a destructive belief that I wasn't able to break free of until recently—my body was not my own.

Production photograph of me from *Mr. Pickwick's Christmas*.
McLean used to be in the picture with me, but I ripped him out and burned the half he was in. Photo Credit unknown

After McLean raped me, I told no one. How could I have been so stupid to believe this person cared for me? I was ashamed and afraid that if my parents found out they'd remove me from the school. I didn't want to go back to public school—CTC was my home. And I didn't want to bring grief to my parents, fearing they would blame themselves.

For a short time afterward, I struggled to make sense of the incident. After all, I had gone willingly to McLean's house, and I had drunk too much wine—no one had forced me. When my foggy mind cleared, I saw the experience for what it was—rape. Finally, I started to allow myself to feel something, and what emerged was pure hatred for the man. And I didn't hide it.

Because I knew McLean had committed a crime, I decided to record on a legal pad the events of that night. When I was finished, I tore off the pages, folded them neatly, sealed them into a white envelope and tucked it deeply into a box of keepsakes where it stayed for more than twenty years.

I had to continue working with McLean for the next two years. He was never assigned to me as an acting instructor, thank God. I didn't tell anyone what had happened, but I didn't hide my disdain for him. When I saw him setting his sights on a girl, I warned her to steer clear. But it was too late, he'd already started his grooming process and they didn't want to listen to me.

After I turned sixteen, I lived for a time in an apartment with two other women who were apprentices. My parents didn't want me driving back and forth late at night from Minneapolis to the western suburbs, and they were no longer picking me up since I had my own car. By then, I was at the theater pretty much all day every day. If I didn't have performances, I had classes. Being closer to school made sense.

In the 1983–84 season, I heard rumors that Donahue was being investigated by the police, but nothing changed because of it. Then my mother told me I'd had some phone calls from the Bureau of Criminal Apprehension (BCA). They wanted to talk to me.

~ The Arrest ~

In spring 1984, my parents were planning a vacation in the Florida Keys and wanted me to join them. They said I could invite a friend at their expense, so I asked my friend Annie, the girl who had played Pippi. It was tough, but we worked our schedules around the trip.

We stayed in a condo that belonged to a friend of my parents. Annie and I decided to watch some television and started flipping through cable channels. As we switched to a relatively new national news channel called CNN, we stopped. The screen was showing a photograph of John Clark Donahue. Then a video clip played of Donahue being led out of the CTC building with Mary Winchell at his side, one of the women I had most respected at CTC.

It was bizarre, seeing these people I knew and loved on a TV screen. Not long before this event, an acting apprentice had told me something Donahue had said. "Ya know, John only really respects two women around here," he'd said. "Mary Winchell and you." I was astonished that Donahue would put me in the same category as Mary. But now, there they were—Donahue and Mary floating past my eyes on national cable news. The news reporter said that Donahue had been arrested for molesting boys at the school.

It was bewildering to have this important event happening two thousand miles away. Our vacation took on a different tone. We still had fun, but both of us wanted to be back in Minnesota with our CTC friends and teachers.

We came back to an altered reality. News networks had descended on the staff and theater students for comments. Reporters were ruthless in their pursuit of the story. The arrest stirred anti-gay backlash in the press, which resulted in an unfortunate outcome. Donahue's arrest prompted editor-publisher Tim Campbell of *The GLC Voice* to write a feature article supporting Donahue and advocating for the views of the Man-Boy Love Association (MAN-BLA).[42]

John Clark Donahue in a photograph from our 1983 Conservatory School yearbook. I'm sorry if this picture is triggering to people he abused. Please take care of yourself.

Everyone at the theater was shell-shocked. People wanted to know who the victims were—or rather, the squealers. Unfortunately, the kids who cooperated with the BCA were easy to identify. Their names didn't appear anywhere, but back then the authorities didn't use Doe numbers to provide anonymity of witnesses—they used the person's initials. It didn't take a genius to figure out who they were. I'm also sorry to say they were treated as if they'd betrayed the CTC family.

---

42 Deborah Caulfield, "The Scandal at the Children's Theatre," *LA Times Calendar*, July 22, 1984, p. 4

We learned that the BCA had been investigating Donahue for more than two years and finally had accumulated enough evidence to arrest him. Kids were saying things like, "I can't believe he would do that to John, he totally wanted to be with him," and "they've ruined everything."

Three boys had told the BCA what Donahue had done to them, but it was a phone call to the BCA from T. J. O'Donnell that prompted the arrest. Donahue had been abusing T. J. Despite all the grooming, when O'Donnell watched another young boy run screaming out of Donahue's bedroom, he realized something had to be done.

Ironically, T. J. told me he never intended for Donahue to be arrested. He just wanted Donahue to stop abusing children. At the time, he had no idea it would be the end of Donahue's reign. In reality, T. J. liberated many abused children, but that heroic act would not be appreciated for many years—and still isn't by many. All of Donahue's victims were vilified and ousted.

In this environment of finger pointing, I wasn't about to reveal my own rape. When my parents asked if I'd been abused, I said "no."

The BCA pressed me asking, "Are you *sure* nothing happened?" They told me McLean was being investigated and they had reason to believe he'd done something to me. But there was no way in hell I was going to climb into that circus ring. "No, nothing happened to me," I said.

McLean's reputation with young girls was not a secret. A former student recalled a conversation she'd had with a female staff member. When the former student said she thought one of the dancers in a show—a young woman around twenty—would be a good match for McLean, the staffer's response was that the dancer was "too old for him."

Apparently, one of the students had told the BCA she knew about McLean having sex with some of the female students; the informant was a classmate from my same year. She had named me as someone who may have been assaulted.[43] I'm not naming her, but

---

43 Stearns v. CTC No. 27-CV-15-20713, trial exhibit #1040B, BCA Investigation
    Report dated February 27, 1984

I want her to know that I'm grateful that she cared enough to try and help.

It's infuriating that children were bold enough to expose Donahue and McLean for their abuses but not a single adult was willing to step up and tell the truth.

Because of multiple rumors and reports to the BCA, McLean was asked to take a "voluntary leave of absence" and his understudy took over his role in the current production. The BCA began investigating him in earnest. McLean was terrified that he was going to end up in prison. He forced my friend Jina, one of my classmates and another of his victims, to reach out to me and the other girls he'd assaulted to arrange a meeting away from the theater. Jina by then was deeply in McLean's clutches, having been assaulted and trafficked by him, so she did what she was told. I didn't want to meet with him alone for fear he'd be violent, so I asked Melissa to go with me, knowing she'd also been with him. We met in a park.

When he arrived, I could see that he was agitated. He asked if I had talked to the BCA and if I planned to tell them anything. He made it sound like I would get in trouble for being with him.

I thought about how I'd gone to his house willingly, so I felt some responsibility for the incident. I didn't want to go through the kind of treatment other victims were getting, and I didn't want my parents to remove me from the school. I told him I wasn't going to say anything. Then he said, "That was consensual, right?"

Consent, of course, is irrelevant because I was fifteen when he raped me. Legally I couldn't give consent. This interaction was an extension of his abuse, manipulating me to believe that I was partly responsible and coercing me to protect him. But I didn't see it that way back then.

"Right," I said, starting to believe it was. McLean suggested that if anyone asked me why I'd been so mad at him I should say it had something to do with a show.

I nodded, and that was that. In the end, the investigation against him was dropped due to lack of evidence. He'd convinced us all to keep our mouths shut.

~ My Senior Year ~

Students, including me, referred to the investigation as a witch hunt. Our grooming to accept the sexualization of children was so strong we didn't see the investigators or therapists as wanting to save us. We saw them as trying to tear us apart. We sought comfort and understanding in each other, not in outsiders. And we knew that if we said anything about abuse to the counselors, they would be required to report it and our parents would probably remove us from the school, which would have been horrible.

The community didn't want CTC to fail. Ticket sales fell only slightly after Donahue's arrest, and the Minnesota State Arts Board gave CTC $96,000 as a "vote of confidence."[44] The prestige that theaters like CTC and the Guthrie brought to Minneapolis was a valuable commodity.

Between the effects of two childhood sexual assaults, the grief of losing my mentor (I still saw Donahue that way), lying to the authorities and my parents, going to school even though it felt like it was crumbling around me, and having to continually stuff my feelings when working with McLean, I was building up a solid case of complex trauma. I coped by finding even more to do. My perfectionism went into high gear. I kept myself moving so fast I didn't have time to think about anything but what was right in front of me. I stopped categorizing myself as a victim of a crime and began to think of it as just the way things were at CTC, like a family dynamic—we work hard, we make beautiful art, and adults fuck kids.

---

44 Mike Kaszuba, "Children's Theatre Receives $96,000 from Arts Board," *Minneapolis StarTribune*, November 30, 1984, p. 1B

Director of Education Wayne Jennings talked to the student body about "good touch and bad touch" that had us all rolling our eyes. As someone who'd been raped by a teacher, I found his description of bad touch laughable and his suggestions about good touch absurd. Those of us in my class had been together for years, literally breaking down the physical barriers with each other through trust exercises, sweating together in classes and shows and giving each other backrubs when our bodies were worn out. There was an intimacy there that new rules couldn't change.

In September of 1984 a grand jury was convened to investigate what was happening at CTC. Jennings and Scott Creeger, science teacher for the Conservatory School, were indicted for failure to report suspected sexual abuse of CTC students, which was required by the Mandatory Reporting and Maltreatment of Minors Act. These cases were the first ever indictments to challenge the State of Minnesota's Mandated Reporting Act. The charges were dismissed in November by the same judge who sentenced Donahue. Their lawyers successfully argued that the reporting act was too vague. Instead of challenging the judge's dismissal of the case, the prosecutors decided to focus on getting the Minnesota State Legislature to improve the wording in the mandated reporting law, in part by removing the word "suspected" and providing clear definitions of "knowledge" and "reason to believe." Their efforts were successful, and the loopholes were removed in the next legislative session.

In my research, I discovered that in 1980, Jennings was part of the statewide consortium that developed and wrote the training materials for teachers regarding the Mandated Reporting Act, and he trained teachers around the state of Minnesota. Jennings knew the law inside and out and designed the training, so I find it beyond belief that he didn't see what was going on around him at CTC. And how convenient for his defense lawyer that he was so well versed in it.

I agreed to be the student liaison to the CTC Board of Directors, which was wrestling with whether the school should stay open. Teacher and company actress Wendy Lehr was the theater staff liaison. I loved her—she was my idol and mentor. I wanted to *be* her. She didn't drive, so I volunteered to pick her up and bring her downtown to the board meetings. Time alone with Wendy was a bonus.

I felt detached during those board meetings. It was my first time getting an up-close view of the corporate world and it felt foreign. I believed the school should stay open and argued for that position. I was well spoken, so these adults listened to my arguments and thought I was helpful. In the end they decided to keep the school open.

Jason McLean in a photograph from our 1985 Conservatory School
yearbook after being re-instated as a teacher and company actor. I
decided to include a photo of him so people know what he looks
like and can warn others about him. Again, my apologies if this
photo is triggering to his victims.

I'm still learning to accept the contradiction of being a survivor of rape by a teacher and arguing for the continuation of an institution in which adults were sexually assaulting children. I know I was only a child, conditioned to believe it was okay, but this inconsistency is still hard for me to reconcile because I know now that abuses continued up until the school closed and beyond. But after I graduated, the school lasted only one more year, closing in the spring of 1986. I remember feeling like "why did I go through all that work to keep the school open if they're just going to shut it down a year later?" I think they thought it was more trouble than it was worth.

The events of the previous year hadn't discouraged McLean from his pursuit of teenage girls. In fact, getting away with his criminal behavior emboldened him—he became more violent, beating some of his victims.

My senior class was comprised of twenty-five people, and many of us were still close to Donahue. We continued to see him as our mentor despite what he'd done. Because of our conditioning to accept the clearly unacceptable, and the degree to which he was revered in the larger community, we were not appalled by his actions. I hate to admit this, but in some circumstances, we blamed the victims. Yes, me, a victim, blamed other victims.

I feel terrible about this because I understand how much pain these child victims were in. They didn't deserve to be vilified. The brave young people who were willing to speak the truth were called traitors, and they were cast out of our family by students and adults alike. I was still so swayed into believing Donahue was my guru— that it was he who had made me who I am—that I wrote to him in prison. I even visited him there. My desire to please him was intact. I remained stuck in a place where I could sanitize and package the wound tightly, like a neatly stacked pile of clothes sitting next to a violated body.

In spring 1985, Don Fogelberg, Conservatory School teacher and director of production, was fired when his wife discovered he was in a "sexual relationship" with a sixteen-year-old out-of-state student who was living with him and his family. He wasn't reported, just fired. There were no legal ramifications for his offense even though the statute for the age of consent changed in 1984 from sixteen to eighteen years of age when the offender is in a position of authority, such as a teacher.

A friend told me that in summer 1984, Fogelberg was part of a team promoting the Conservatory School to out-of-town students. He had assured her as a prospective student and her parents it was now safe for kids at CTC because all the "bad apples" were gone. Incidentally, Fogelberg's boss was Wayne Jennings, the guy who wrote the training manual for mandated reporters and was indicted for not reporting abuse of students.

I was cast as the ingénue in the spring production of *Penrod* directed by Jon Cranney, interim artistic director and a man who, in my opinion, showed outright distain for the younger members of the cast. After graduation, I wanted to stay at CTC perhaps joining the acting company and teaching classes to be part of the legacy—no matter how tainted or ugly it was.

Cranney was going to direct a production of *Little Women* after graduation in the fall, and I auditioned for the part of Jo. Cranney had called me in repeatedly to read with several of the child actors auditioning for the younger sisters, and I was certain he planned to cast me because he wasn't bringing anyone else in to read for Jo. I was livid when he called to tell me he wasn't putting me in the show because I was "too tall" for the part, then casting an adult company actress instead. To me, he'd taken advantage of my time; I felt used.

In that same call, he also told me he had decided not to allow me to go into the apprentice program. I was devastated. He said I should go out into the world and get different theater experiences.

He was right, of course. It's one of the only things for which I can find gratitude when it comes to Cranney.

Me in my CTC sweatshirt, rebelliously wearing it backwards with the sleeves cut, and a shot I took of Jina at a class outing. We were sixteen.

Me in the chorus of *Cinderella* December 1985, the fall after I
graduated. I don't remember the name of the person who took the photo.

Graduation was hard. There was a huge hole for us in the
proceedings, because Donahue wasn't allowed to be there to watch
us graduate. He was prohibited for life from setting foot on the CTC
property or ever working around children again. I recently listened
to an audio recording of a song I performed during the graduation
ceremony and was surprised and disturbed to hear myself dedicating
the song to Donahue. I remember being angry that no one was
saying his name during any of the speeches, and I didn't like the way
he was being erased so I had dared to say his name out loud.

We had the ceremony in the theater, and the graduates rode
up to stage level from the orchestra pit, rising out of the floor in
our white graduation gowns and wreaths of flowers on our heads.
We'd decided to be barefoot—we spent much of our time in theater
school wearing no shoes, so it was fitting, and it was in line with
Donahue's philosophy of shedding the trappings of normal society,
and vulnerability. To close the ceremony our class sang a composition
written by my classmate Rob Shapiro and me. I conducted the
singers, and when we finished, I spun around and threw my hands
in the air, celebrating the end of a tumultuous final year at CTC.

This photograph appeared in the Minneapolis newspaper announcing our graduation in 1985. The caption reads, "Laura Stearns, senior class president, led graduates of the Children's Theatre Company and School in song during Thursday's ceremony." Annie is almost directly behind me, and Jina is the third person from the right. Photo: Steve Schluter

~ Bad Apples and Victim Blaming ~

Donahue had been watched off and on by the Minneapolis Police Department since 1961, and The Bureau of Criminal Apprehension (BCA) took over the investigation in 1981. In 1982, the BCA informed the Children's Theatre Company (CTC) Board of Directors that they were investigating Donahue and told the board members not to interfere with the investigation. The board chose to interpret this instruction to mean they should do absolutely nothing different or change any of their policies.

The BCA denies any such instruction, saying they merely didn't want the board to do an investigation of their own. Instead of implementing measures that would make the environment safer for the kids, like ending rehearsals at a reasonable time or implementing the "rule of three," making sure kids were not left alone with adults, Executive Director Sarah Lawless chose to tell Donahue himself that he was being investigated. Of course, he denied he was doing anything wrong.[45] [46]

The BCA was instrumental in taking down Donahue. It would not have happened without its tenacity, but the tactics used to interview students were harmful and re-wounding to already traumatized children. Some abuse victims were treated as if they were hostile witnesses.

The man put in charge of the investigation was detective Mike Campion, a narcotics investigator who wasn't trained to deal with the complexities of a community of wounded child abuse victims. He and his team treated some students more like drug dealers than abuse victims, making them feel they were somehow guilty. One student who was interviewed told me an investigator threatened to tell his parents he was gay if he didn't cooperate.

After Donahue's arrest, the BCA investigated several other CTC staff members. A grand jury convened in the fall of 1984 to consider multiple rumors. Twenty-six students were subpoenaed. Some students now report they were ostracized from the theater if they talked. Others have said they were threatened or coerced by perpetrators and some of the students and staff to keep their mouths shut.

Donahue pled guilty to seven counts of criminal sexual conduct and entered into a plea bargain, bringing it down to three. Though the sentencing guidelines could have put him in federal prison for up to twenty years, Judge Charles A. Porter Jr. was lenient, ordering

---

45 Stearns v. CTC No. 27-CV-15-20713, testimony of Winthrop Rockwell, trial transcript, p. 1516
46 And how does telling Donahue he was being investigated not count as interference? It's mind boggling.

a bafflingly light sentence of one year in the workhouse. Donahue served less than a year before entering a work-release program.[47]

This scandal didn't ruin Donahue. And affluent CTC board member Mrs. Stanley Brooks Gregory paid all of his legal fees.

Though Donahue was forbidden to set foot on the premises of CTC for the rest of his life, or ever work with children again, when he got out, he was welcomed back into the theater community with open arms. People still considered him a genius. He was even given an impromptu standing ovation in 2009 at the McKnight Foundation awards banquet. Up until his death in 2019 I continued to hear comments about Donahue like, "Hasn't the guy suffered enough?"

In the fall of 1984, McLean was reinstated in the acting company. None of his victims would talk, so that investigation stalled. A male classmate who knew about McLean's abuse of girls recently told me that McLean threatened to kill him if he said anything to the BCA.

The grand jury indicted Steven Adamczak, one of the perpetrators. He was able to convince most of the girls who had reported him that if convicted he'd be raped by other prisoners. To save him from that fate, the girls recanted on the stand, saying they weren't abused.[48] He was acquitted, and the judge shook his finger at the girls telling them they were horrible children for lying about being assaulted.[49] The sexual abuse, the coercion to recant, the victim blaming and the unfair treatment by the judge profoundly affected the victims for their entire lives. It's tragedy upon tragedy.

Outreach Director Tony Steblay was one of the people who

---

47 Peter Vaughan, "Donahue to Direct Play at Mixed Blood," *Minneapolis StarTribune*, November 8, 1985, p. 2C
48 Protected victim statements and depositions with Jeff Anderson and Associates
49 Protected victim statements and depositions with Jeff Anderson and Associates, Costello Thesis, p. 181–183, State v. Adamczak file No. 86056-1, 86057-1, 85341-1

fell through the cracks. I've spoken to victims who described his predatory and abusive behavior to me. Donahue and Steblay had known each other since the early 1970s, and Donahue hired him as the director of outreach in 1981. Steblay had been fired a few years earlier from his teaching job at Hopkins High School for behavior described as "sexually molesting adolescent girls in his theater program" in Costello's doctoral thesis.[50]

In his 1987 doctorate thesis called *Hating the Sin, Loving the Sinner: The Minneapolis Children's Theatre Company Adolescent Sexual Abuse Prosecutions*, as well as in interviews, lawyer John Martin Costello categorized the CTC prosecution as a complete failure.[51] Understatement. He also mentions that the district court file for Donahue's arrest report in 1961 was "mysteriously" missing from the court records when he attempted to find them for his research.

Costello repeatedly refers to children who were victims of sexual violence as "victim-participants," and refers to the sexual assaults of one of Donahue's victims, who was twelve years old when the abuse started, as their "sexual relationship." It's not a relationship, it's rape. He also has the audacity to say that Donahue's victims used *him* to advance their own career, and categorizes the abuse as "trysts." There's even one section in reference to Adamczak where Costello actually calls him the girl's "lover." The dismissiveness of these labels are nauseating but typical of the downgrading of trauma sexual violence victims endure. This level of victim blaming is appalling. It's no wonder children didn't feel safe coming forward.

Also, Costello was the attorney who represented Conservatory School science teacher Scott Creeger, who was supervised by Wayne Jennings and indicted alongside him by the grand jury in September of 1984. Costello aided in helping these mandated reporters get away with the egregious offense of failing to report the abuse of

50 Costello Thesis, p. 141
51 Kay Miller, "Lawyer Costello's Book indicts Court's Handling of Sex Abuse Cases," *Minneapolis StarTribune*, May 20, 1991, p. 3E

children on their watch. Of all the things Costello could have put his brain power toward, he chose to praise Jennings in his thesis and wax philosophical about the evils of a pedophile.

Because of the lack of cooperation from students, parents and staff, the ignorance of the authorities and the silencing of victims, few people were held accountable for their crimes. The following is the list of people investigated and/or identified in 1984–85 as perpetrators, both charged and not charged, who were abusing students at CTC.[52]

- John Clark Donahue: Artistic director—Multiple victims identified, pled guilty to seven counts of criminal sexual conduct in 1984 and was sentenced to one year in the workhouse on three counts. Eventually, Donahue admitted publicly to sixteen victims. Authorities would later discover the true number was higher.

- William Herron: Dance instructor—One victim identified, criminally charged, then acquitted.

- Sean McNellis: Company actor—One victim identified, criminally charged, received a suspended sentence. Charges eventually dropped.

- Steven Adamczak: Sound technician, instructor—Multiple victims identified, criminally charged, then acquitted at trial.

- Steve Busher: Staff member—One victim identified. Never re-hired, never charged.

- Tony Steblay: Outreach director—Placed on leave while being investigated in 1984, never re-hired. Never charged.

- Jason McLean: Company actor/teacher—Multiple victims identified, put on leave and investigated by the BCA, no

52 Costello Thesis, p. 189

criminal charges filed. Re-hired at CTC in the fall of 1984.

- Don Fogelberg: Teacher/director of production education—
  One victim identified, fired in 1985 after his "relationship"
  with a sixteen-year-old student living at his home was
  discovered. Never charged.[53]

- Dennis Lambert: A teacher in the public school system and
  not on staff at CTC—Informed the BCA that Donahue
  was abusing a student starting when the child was twelve
  years old. It was revealed that Lambert was also abusing this
  boy. In his statement he referred to this child as "extremely
  seductive."[54]

~ Cult of Personality ~

Some former adult guest artists have told me they knew something
wrong was happening at CTC but couldn't put their finger on it. And
who could blame them, really—those of us who lived it didn't fully
get it. The BCA came up short when they did their investigation.
Counselors and therapists had no clue how to help us after Donahue
was arrested because they didn't understand that they were dealing
with a cult of personality.[55] They were trying to address individual
harms, not complex community trauma.

In recent years, I've spoken with people who weren't students at
CTC but had taken a class or been a child actor in the early 1980s.
They understood that something very wrong was happening around
them, and they didn't return to CTC. They had something I didn't
have—a working internal warning system that would ward them

53 Karren Mills, "Theater Staff Member Fired After Admitting Sex With Female
    Student," *Associated Press*, March 1, 1985
54 Costello Thesis, p. 160
55 Cult-of-Personality: A situation where a leader (often a dictator) has been
    falsely idolized and made into a national or group icon and is revered as a result.
    Yourdictionary.com

away from dangerous people who wanted to take advantage of them.

I've learned so much about what was happening at CTC behind the scenes. It's changed the experience for me. This is not to say that elements of what I learned weren't valuable. But I realized that much of the "positive" experiences I carried away from CTC have a residue of deceit smeared all over them. I'm letting go of things that no longer suit me, such as putting people on pedestals who don't deserve it. I'm reclaiming things I gave away, such as trusting my intuition and speaking my truth. I'm recognizing things I didn't see before. I've realized there was a fundamental piece of me that stopped working in that environment, like a compass that no longer pointed north. I lost something I wasn't old enough to understand was mine—self-agency.

This is the nature of abuse to children—why we were so vulnerable at CTC. We were so young. All of us thought we knew everything. Some of us were guided by broken compasses.

When I heard Donahue's *Shaving of the Head* speech as a child, it was affirming, made me feel I'd finally found the place where I belonged—my true family. Reading the words now, as an adult with kids of my own, I have an altered perspective. I see it as a grooming technique. Knowing it was created by a pedophile—capable of spouting sacred concepts he'd confiscated from sages to make himself look holy while at the same time stimulating the prostate of a child—makes me want to punch a hole in the wall.

Donahue used the language of scholars and centuries-old wisdom as lures, concealing his true intent to manipulate children under an altruistic façade. We were misunderstood adolescents on the fringes, and he used our kinship as a shield to mask his darker purpose. He utilized a philosophy of otherness to indoctrinate and validate us as people and as artists to make us feel special and understood. He won us over with the gift of attention, praising our uniqueness. We walked blindly toward a promise of heightened artistry like children following a Pied Piper under a spell that still lingers for many former students. His accolades, rarely given, were like gemstones, proof of our artistry. With such tools, he held us hostage to his abusive ways. Some who pushed against him were told they weren't special enough, so they'd better stay in line or they'd have to leave and try to make it by themselves in a hostile world where no one understood them.

He surrounded himself with brilliant people and used them as cover. Their loyalty to him was their downfall, and they failed the children. Adults are meant to hold clear boundaries and put a child's safety first and foremost. Hundreds of us were damaged because they refused to see what was going on around them.

Donahue instilled his ideology in us, allowing us to be taken advantage of by him and the other predators in our midst. Those of us who fell prey were primed for abuse, conditioned to believe that we were willing participants in the harm done to us. We "drank the Kool-Aid" and were manipulated into believing we were traitors if we revealed what was happening to us.

We were children lacking life experiences and we—as well as our parents—trusted those around us to guide us in the right direction.

Staff and company members, our teachers and mentors, created a culture of complicity. Antiquated adages such as "the show must go on" and "you must suffer for your art" were like dogma. As a child, when the adults around you are accepting harmful behavior, you learn that it's something to emulate. They might not have been fully cognizant of the lessons they were teaching us, but we learned things.

Because of the widespread abuse and how so many people were affected, in 1984 Dr. Richard Seely, director of the Intensive Treatment Program for Sexual Aggressives, referred to the situation at CTC as a "classic institutional incest structure." Today, psychologists say we experienced a complex community trauma, which is often connected to things like war or genocide.

What makes our situation so wounding and difficult to identify is the way trauma is bound to the beautiful thing that brought us all together—art. The joy and pain associated with our experience is a terribly complex emotional landscape. For those of us who were injured, be it physically or psychologically, our internal battle lives in the existence of multiple truths. The joy of what we were doing as artists has mingled with injury. Tragedy piggybacks on gratitude and it's damn near impossible to separate them.

A cult of personality is certainly not a term I would have used back then. In fact, I've only fully embraced it in the last few years. But that is what it was. Not a religious cult, but rather one of ideology. Ours revolved around the pursuit of art steeped in a bohemian aesthetic. Donahue was the leader; everything revolved around him. Donahue programmed us to please him. We dared not question him. Those who did felt his wrath.

As I gain more understanding of how I was affected as an individual, I also gain clarity about what we all went through together as a community. Most adults at CTC in the 1980s had grown up under the tutelage of Donahue, or were barely adults when they first started working with him, so their understanding of normal was skewed too. It's part of what makes the situation so convoluted.

The incestuous environment also makes it hard to distinguish perpetrator and victim because often an individual was both. Some identified perpetrators at CTC were victims of Donahue in their youth and went on to abuse others. Tragically, some students were sexually assaulting or beating other students. Some students who had experienced unrelenting pursuit by sexual predators, active abuse or had witnessed adults doing horrible things to other kids, ended up doing horrible things to each other out of frustration, anger, confusion and an inability to process what was happening because of their age.

Trauma memories live in the right side of the brain, the creative side, so our trauma memories associated with our experiences as kids are uniquely bound together with our artistic selves. It's very hard to decouple the harm from the joy, which is why I think it's difficult to see what's true. Humans in general have a hard time holding multiple truths at the same time. We lean toward black-and-white thinking because it's much easier to understand "x + y = z" than understand "x + y to the fifth power, unless Q happened before J, and in the dark instead of on a Tuesday, and if alcohol was involved its K, but otherwise, x + y = z."

Some victims are just beginning to understand they were abused or had abused others. Their ability to process their abuse has evolved as they've aged. Others can't let go of their admiration of Donahue, so they can't admit his failings and ulterior motives. Perhaps deniers fear that if they do, they must also let go of the hard-earned accolades he bestowed on them, diminishing their own intrinsic talents and gift.

The problem with Donahue's philosophy was that it removed all boundaries that were typically in place to keep children safe. I often wonder if he had believed his rhetoric and held our wellbeing with care as he professed, what would my life have looked like after CTC? If perpetrators had not been provided a safe place to choose their victims, and abuse wasn't so rampant, if we'd been given the freedom to explore our artistry in a boundless way, given the opportunities to experience that level of professionalism *and* been provided clear and safe boundaries, what would we have been able to accomplish as artists?

If you're an alum of CTC now recognizing that your personal experience there was abusive, that you participated in harming others or that you just need someone to talk to about what happened, there's help. Please visit CTAWellness.org

~ Anatomy of a Culture of Complicity ~

complicity
noun
: *association or participation in or as if in a wrongful act*[56]

---

56 Merriam-Webster

The adults at CTC rallied around Donahue, and the theater community welcomed him back into their workplaces, refusing to see him for what he was.

In the book *Blind to Betrayal*, Jennifer Freyd, PhD, and Pamela Birrell, PhD, investigate the complexities of choosing *not* to see things happening around you that are dangerous to know. Staying blind to ugly truths can be safer than seeing them.

The 1960s and 1970s comprised a different era, part of the counterculture movement of peace and love. I think that was part of the explanation for Donahue's success as a pedophile, but it's more than that. Human beings are programmed to look outside themselves for validation. It starts at a very early age, even before we understand words. We see approval in the faces around us, and it helps us know if we're okay or if we're doing something wrong or dangerous.

The need for external validation is intrinsic. It's vital to our safety when we're little, yet we don't stop looking for it when we get older. We continue to search outside ourselves to find our value, trying to please our parents and family, looking to the church to give us answers, to educators or other experts to tell us how to think. It's ingrained in us to do so. I believe the core of what causes a culture of complicity is that we aren't encouraged to go within ourselves to find our own truth.

Because of this need for external validation, we're also paying close attention to the way other people appear to have value. Those in the public eye grab our attention, and when they receive public accolades, one of two things usually happen—we get jealous—"What's so special about them?"—or we admire them—"I love them, they're so good at [fill in the blank]."

When we lean toward admiration of public figures, a part of us gets attached to them, and we can find personal value vicariously through their success. For example, the success or failure of a sports team can make us feel wonderful or terrible, depending on how they perform. When our favorite actor wins an award, we feel good about ourselves for liking that performer. We picked a winner, and our admiration of them makes us feel more valuable.

When our "hero" abuses someone, acknowledging or accepting that brutal reality challenges us to examine our attachment to them. We may fear our own value will diminish because our hero failed. We might wonder how we failed to recognize our hero's faults. We might even discover we've been duped, which can be embarrassing. This kind of investigation is extremely difficult to do, so instead, we look away, call the speakers of truth liars, or deny their truth, so we don't have to look closely at our own attachment to the fallen hero.

It's common to ignore the ugliest parts of humanity. It's human nature to gawk at a car crash, yet when it comes to an intentional act of harm against our most vulnerable members of society, like our children, we can't bear to look. It makes us think of someone hurting our own loved ones, which can be unbearable to consider. So we look away. People who prey on children know this—they rely on it to keep them safe.

The perpetrator—possibly the nice neighbor who always volunteers, the teacher, the police officer, the coach, the priest or rabbi, the famous actor, the movie maker, or the international pop singer—uses their perceived value in society as a shield for their criminal actions. They know that social admiration and the built-in tendency of people to look away from the ugliest aspects of humanity will protect them from the consequences of their actions.

We don't want to believe that someone who was doing something wonderful for kids could have the capacity to harm them. And if we've financially supported a perpetrator, that raises the stakes because we've invested in the perpetrator with our admiration and our money. Admitting the hero has committed a crime would make us an accomplice of sorts. If the criminal is our employer, our livelihood may also be at risk. If they were a mentor, our own value as a person is in question. There's so much to lose. The more we have emotionally invested in the facade created by the perpetrator, the higher the stakes and the harder it is to see the truth. We say things like, "It wasn't that bad," or "those kids wanted it." We separate the perpetrator from the crime because it can be too hard to bear being so closely attached to something so ugly and painful. We convince ourselves we didn't see. We say nothing. We turn truth to lies and lies to truth. We do nothing.

The anatomy of complicity looks like this: the need for external validation trains us to look outside ourselves instead of inward for guidance, which leads us to admiration of those we perceive as valuable, which tethers us to them and amplifies our own sense of value. If the hero falls from grace, we look away because examination might reveal our own failings, which leads to denial, which leads to silence, which leads to complicity.

It can take decades to understand childhood abuse. Sometimes we recognize nuances we didn't see before when we hear the stories of others. If you were at the Children's Theatre Company and School during these years and would like someone to talk to about your experience, please visit CTAWellness.org. If you related to this account but didn't attend CTC, RAINN.org is an excellent resource to find support.

Chapter Four
Hidden Trauma

By the time I left the Children's Theatre Company (CTC), I was very good at pretending to be okay. After all, I'd spent two years having to work beside the man who had raped me. Because I wanted the gifts that went along with being at CTC, I had to tamp down and ignore the emotional pain to participate in my classes and performances. My coping skills and ability to compartmentalize became so well tuned that I could smile, sing and dance on the outside while my insides were on fire.

I'm an overachiever—partly because it's the way I'm wired, but largely because I've worked hard to distract myself from the mess in the shadows of my mind. If you live life like you're always on a speeding train, you can't focus on the smaller details—they're just a blur. I was moving so fast I didn't notice the torment, but I was failing in my ability to share myself authentically, even with people I considered safe.

~ No Matter Where You Go, There You Are ~

When I graduated from CTC in the spring of 1985, I walked away with a sense of who I was as an artist, grateful for what I'd learned and ready to move into a career as an actor. The path to continuing my education at CTC, however, had been shut down by Cranney, so I decided to find a job and work. For a couple of years I moved around from California to Montana doing theater and side jobs, working retail, being an office assistant, even trying out telemarketing. Everything I owned fit into my car.

I lived in LA for a while with my friend Molly, who was a CTC alum. We were in a house with a few Scientologists, and I got scooped into the church for a while. But Molly had a horrible experience with some of their more pushy people, and we both got out. The last thing we needed was another cultish environment. Although the people we lived with were very kind, I'm glad we escaped a more entangled connection with that church.

I was used to being part of an ensemble and not focusing on a personal image, so I didn't like LA much. The attitudes of people in the industry seemed insular and myopic. I found an agent, a necessary thing in LA, and was getting some good auditions—even callbacks for films and television—but I didn't like the studio executives I was meeting. When I left LA, I told people it was because I didn't like the "everyone for themselves" element and was looking for the community environment you find in theater.

This was true, though not the full truth. Actually, I feared success because that made more room for failure, and failure was unacceptable. My perfectionism was immobilizing me. When I got a second callback for a major motion picture, I called my agent and told her I was leaving LA. She was stunned. I'd only been there about six months and was starting to get noticed. She tried to talk me out of leaving, but I was adamant.

At the time, I was still in communication with Donahue, who'd finished his time in the workhouse and was now in Arizona. He encouraged me to audition for the theater company that had taken him in, so I flew down and stayed with him and his partner. I loved Arizona and could imagine myself happy there acting with Wendy

Lehr and the others who'd followed Donahue. When I wasn't cast in the season, though, I was crushed. Looking back, it's probably the best thing that could've happened to me.

During these years of bouncing around, I had two short relationships with men who raped me. The first man, I'll call him Steve, would be devastated by my defining our initial time together as a rape. I was eighteen, and we were fooling around, which led to more than I bargained for. He paid no attention to my protests. Because I was already primed by two previous rapes, and he didn't stop when I said "no," I went into freeze mode and lay there, waiting for him to finish, hoping it wouldn't last long. Afterward, I was numb emotionally and felt disconnected from my body—I have no recollection of leaving the building or of the next few days. There are photos of me during that period, but I have no memory of them being taken. It's one of my coping mechanIsms—I disappear.

After that, I continued to see Steve for a while and found him very respectful; but that first sexual experience with him wasn't good. It was not consensual. Sometimes this is what rape looks like—it's quiet. It exists for one person as a good time and the other person as a nightmare. But one person's good time doesn't make it right.

Let me be clear about this: "I'm enjoying making out with you" doesn't translate to "I want to fuck you." "No" doesn't mean "keep going, I'm just a little uncomfortable." "No" means no. Period.

I'll call the second man Matt. He was different. It happened in spring 1987 when I was nineteen. In a room, a group of us were lying around and chatting in the dark. Matt and I were making out, fondling each other. His energy went from playful to aggressive in a heartbeat, alarmingly like the assault when I was ten. Matt yanked me toward him, and I tried to struggle, but then his hand went over my mouth to stifle any sounds, exactly the way Rusty had done. My body's response was immediate and dramatic—I froze—again. Flashes of all my previous rapes whirled through my mind, and suddenly he was inside me. It wasn't a hand this time—Matt was aggressively fucking me, and I was unable to move. I was raped in a dark room full of people, and I couldn't make a sound. Rape can happen anywhere.

By the age of nineteen, I'd been raped four times, each one very different from the others and all by people I knew. No dark alleys were involved. Each event left lasting invisible wounds that shaped how I'd participate in my life moving forward and how I would view future intimate relationships.

Me in an ironic *MPLS St. Paul Magazine* print ad for North
Women's Center, July 1986.

Reading about these events might cause you to reevaluate your past. If you're questioning whether you had an experience that could be categorized as sexual violence, please take a break, nourish your body with something healthy, and find someone to talk to for support.

In the fall of 1987, I decided to attend college. I flew to Boston to audition for acting and directing programs. I discovered a love for directing when I wrote and directed a play for my senior project the last year I was at CTC. I was still in touch with one of my favorite teachers, Aleks, who had come from Boston to teach during my senior year and was not at CTC when the proverbial shit hit the fan. He'd never even met Donahue. To me, Aleks was a breath of fresh air.

Aleks's good friend Alan, who lived in Cambridge, offered to rent a room to me. Aleks was working at Israel Horowitz's theater, the Gloucester Stage Company. The theater was managed by the infamous Frank McGovern, the CTC general manager who had left before Donahue was arrested—I believe he knew what was coming and got out before everything fell apart. Frank told me if I moved to Massachusetts, I'd have a job.

I made plans to move there in January 1988, rent a room with Alan and his male partner Shelley for a ridiculously small amount of money, work in the field I love with people I respect, go to school to hone my craft and focus my attention on a bright future. A major discrepancy in this equation canceled out the prospect of "happily ever after." I was not well in my mind. I wasn't sleeping much, was depressed and flirted with the idea of anorexia as a good way to control my weight.

My audition for Boston University was exceptional—I nailed it. When I was done, one of the men on the audition panel said to me, "I can tell you right now, we want you in our program. But are you sure this is what you want? You just did a four-year conservatory—are you sure you want to go back to school?"

This really threw me. I was honored to be chosen on the spot, but this male authority figure questioned my desire to go to school, which made me question myself. I thought I had made up my mind, but now I had doubts. If I'd listened to my gut, I would have ignored what he said, but I still didn't trust my instincts. I still gave more weight to the opinion of someone I didn't even know because he was a male authority figure. When my acceptance letter came, I declined the offer, although I moved to Boston anyway.

My sleep issues were getting worse, so one of my first purchases in Massachusetts was a TV with a timer that could turn itself off. At bedtime, I'd try to determine if it would take one, two or three hours to fall asleep. It didn't occur to me that my difficulty falling asleep without this technique might have something to do with being sexually assaulted. Why would I know that? And don't most people have problems sleeping? I'd hear people complaining about it all the time. Why would my sleep problems be any more significant than the average bad night's sleep? I was "asleep" to the fact that my sleep issues had a cause.

When I arrived in January for work at Gloucester Stage, Frank informed me that he was leaving to take a job in Utah. I was blindsided. His offer of employment was one of the reasons I decided to move to Massachusetts. My secure job was now a "maybe" depending on whether the incoming managing director would hire me. I decided to stick around and apply for the resident assistant stage manager position, which I was already doing alongside Aleks, the resident stage manager. Although I was mad at Frank for giving a false impression that moving there would be a smooth transition, I said nothing to him. Frank was as volatile as ever, so I remained silent.

Frank was in a relationship with a lovely woman named Sally, who was a board member at the theater. I loved Sal immediately. She, Aleks and I formed a happy trio during the months before she followed Frank to Utah. Sal and I became the best of friends, and I'd visit her and Frank for long weekends over the next twenty-plus years. Frank continued to be part of my life into adulthood, but it's unlikely I would've stayed connected to him if it weren't for Sal.

I was hired full-time by the new manager as the resident assistant stage manager and lighting technician. This is where I met the man I would eventually marry. Lee was a ruggedly handsome actor who could turn heads when entering a room. Lee was a badass, and when I was with him in public, I always felt safe because I knew he would beat the shit out of anyone who would try to hurt me. But he was also tender and respectful, incredibly talented, and quite possibly the funniest person I've ever met. No one can make me laugh the way Lee does. He felt like a perfect match for me.

When he showed up in my life, I was a pretty, competent twenty-year-old woman on the outside. I'd also stopped referring to, or even thinking about, the four assaults as "rape." It was easier to say, "I had a boyfriend who was a jerk," or "some guy hurt me when I was ten" than admit the truth. I was functioning in some vital ways with the mental capacity of a ten-year-old. What I could do really well was pretend everything was fine and not talk about what was really going on.

~ Going Back ~

About a year after getting together in Boston, Lee and I decided to move to Minnesota. Relocating also meant moving in together. I was in completely new relationship territory.

When I arrived in Minneapolis in August 1989, I went back to the Children's Theatre Company to see if my skills in the wig shop would be handy. The new wig master, Ivy, was running the department singlehandedly and really needed the help. She hired me on the spot. Ivy taught me all the things I hadn't learned from Victor when I was a student. Wig maker became my main job.

I brought Lee on a tour of the building so he could see the place I had considered my home growing up. I told him stories about what it was like as a student, assuming he would understand because he had also worked at a theater for children when he was younger. Having never known a different kind of theater school, I had no other reference and assumed all of them were like mine.

When I was done telling him some personal history connected to this amazing theater, he said, "That's really fucked up. That's not normal, you know."

No, I didn't know. I was twenty-two before I got my first inkling that what we'd all experienced as kids was not typical. When it was happening, I knew the whole episode with McLean was wrong, but the rest of it—I just thought that's the way it was for theater students.

Lee's reaction was the beginning of a long, slow revelation of how deeply affected I was by my experience at CTC.

Being at the theater as an adult was different from when I was a student. Some of the old acting company were still there, but it felt different. Ivy wasn't part of that old culture, which I liked. We worked really hard, our two-person department doing the work of several people, and she and I became good friends. Looking back, it was the most fulfilling time I had there because I was able to do a job I loved and wasn't under the pressures I'd had as a kid.

The best part about being in Minneapolis was spending time in a building that felt like home—CTC. McLean was no longer in the acting company, so I didn't have to worry about bumping into him. I knew all the nooks and crannies of the building, and I felt safe—as if I were visiting an old friend.

Being near McLean's home was the worst part about being in that area of town. And because they were next to the highway entrance that took me home, I had to drive past his new restaurant and theater near Loring Park called The Loring Cafe and The Loring Playhouse all of the time. McLean had hired a ton of CTC alums to work for him at the restaurant. It was becoming a hot spot in town, but there was no way in hell I was going anywhere near that place. I didn't want to see him, and I didn't want to be seen.

I got a call from a former company member from CTC who was directing a show and wanted me to be in it. I was flattered, and wanted to do it until she told me it would be at The Loring Playhouse. I curtly said, "I can't work at Jason's theater. He's a criminal." She didn't respond, so I just thanked her for the offer and declined.

Lee and I got married in August of 1990. Sally and Frank had bought a farm in Minnesota, and Sally was a bridesmaid. The day of the wedding, Sally and Frank's dog gave birth to a litter of puppies. Frank was calling the farm constantly, checking in on the birth progress. We loved that the puppies were born on our wedding day, and we told them we'd like to have one. Two months later, we visited their sheep farm in northern Minnesota and picked out a puppy that would be our family dog for the next twelve years. Another puppy from the litter went to Donahue, a connection I was proud of at the time. Today, family pictures that include our beloved dog are forever linked for me to a painful past.

Donahue and company had returned to the Twin Cities theater scene after trying to set down roots elsewhere, and he was back in his house on Stevens Avenue near CTC. I was just as swept up in his masquerade as when I was a child and still wanted to please him despite the burgeoning doubts planted by Lee during his building tour. Though I was starting to recognize the levels of harm that had happened to my friends and me as children, I wasn't seeing Donahue as a criminal—yet. I was still very much under his spell—I hadn't "peed out the Kool-Aid," as a friend says—and I visited him occasionally on my breaks at work.

One time, when I brought the dog to work with me, I took him over to Donahue's house on my lunch break so the puppies could play together. Donahue wasn't allowed on the CTC premises because of the court orders, so this was the easiest way the dogs could see each other. Today, knowing that numerous kids were abused in Donohue's house, I want to scream at my younger self, "What the hell is wrong with you? Why would you go in there?" But I was doing exactly what I was programmed to do—trying to get Donahue's approval.

Donahue's long-time associate, Bain Boehlke, started his own theater company in Minneapolis called The Jungle Theater, and Donahue was hired for a variety of jobs. Boehlke eventually incorporated a weekend children's program of storytelling hosted by Wendy Lehr, who would read to the children. Donahue's sentencing had prohibited him from ever working at CTC again because of his criminal behavior. I find it unsettling that he was working at a theater with programming designed to serve young children. And Costell's thesis refers to him as never fulfilling his community service hours. Who was supposed to be supervising him?

In May 1991, the local paper ran an in-depth series written by Kay Miller about Donahue's arrest and what had happened at CTC. The statute of limitations regarding the scandal had expired, and I believe the paper felt safe to print an investigative piece. The series dug deep. Miller interviewed T. J. O'Donnell, who'd been the whistle blower in 1984, and several other former students and staff. The articles were shocking but helped me develop a better understanding of what I'd been through.

In the summer of 1992, I was pregnant with our first child. Lee's eight-year-old daughter from a previous marriage, Jill, came to live with us a couple of months before the baby was born. I quit my assistant job in the wig shop, and my son Tucker was born in November. He was a whopper—twelve pounds and two ounces of bouncing baby boy. And yes, it was a vaginal birth.

Tucker was—and is—a beautiful human being I'm proud to call my child, and I'd do it all again if I had to. When I was pregnant, I prayed for a boy. I didn't want to go through raising a girl, trying to keep her safe. I wanted boys so I could teach them how to be good men. I was thrilled when Tucker was born, even with the physical trauma that accompanied the process.

The birth of my ginormous baby did quite a number on my "undercarriage" as well as my back. Within a couple of months, I was nursing a baby who was growing at an astonishing rate. At two months old, he was already seventeen pounds. My back was becoming increasingly painful, and fiery jolts regularly shot down my leg. The damage to my back from hauling that horse puppet around was getting worse. An MRI showed two herniated disks. The doctor presented two options: surgery that would prevent me from picking up my baby for six months—not really an option—or extensive rehabilitation and occupational therapy to learn how to manage without surgery. I chose the latter.

After several months of rehab, I was able to deal with the pain, but the experience stirred something in me psychologically. A difficult childbirth had caused underlying back issues to surface, but it had also cracked something open in my psyche. Trauma energy lives between my waist and my thighs, and it caused something that had been locked up for years to start moving.

My old boss, Ivy, had moved on from the wig shop at CTC to become the new wig master at the world-renowned Guthrie Theater. I'd worked on a show there before marrying Lee and was excited to go back when Ivy hired me for some freelance wig building.

I was attending a performance at the Guthrie of the show I'd built wigs for when, during the intermission, as I navigated through the crowd toward the concession area, I saw McLean descending the staircase from the balcony. I had successfully avoided him for years, yet there he was in the flesh. I panicked and left the theater, skipping the second act.

I was surprised by the intensity of my physical reaction to him. I had always been angry at him, but as the years passed, my anger had morphed into fear. After that brief Guthrie sighting, I started having nightmares and extreme reactions to the smell of body odor, even my own. When out in public, I'd scan crowds for his face. Even a man with the same body type as McLean triggered panic.

In addition to my longstanding sleep problems, I started experiencing a form of night paralysis. Sometimes I would wake up filled with rage and wanting to scream, "Get your fucking hands off me." But instead, I'd lay there feeling paralyzed for hours—until I heard those first morning birds start to sing. I didn't share what was happening with Lee. I wasn't able to talk about it.

In my late twenties and pregnant with my second child, I tried therapy but didn't find it very helpful. My therapist was the sort who said very little, nodded a lot and jotted things down on a yellow legal pad. That was the first time I talked about Rusty or McLean with a professional—nearly two decades after the first rape.

Calvin was born in 1996 at nine pounds three ounces, significantly smaller than his big brother and full of vim and vigor. He stopped napping after two weeks but thankfully slept through the night. I had fewer back issues this time, but Calvin's inability to sleep during the day aggravated my horrible sleep patterns, and I had severe postpartum depression. I took Prozac for a while, which shut down my emotions even more and messed up my decision-making. I was a bit zombie-esque. Getting off Prozac restored my judgment, and the depression got better with time, but my sleep issues didn't go away.

We were living in the suburbs, and friends didn't live nearby, so I felt rather isolated. A lot of feelings about the past abuse were surfacing, and I wanted to separate myself from anyone from those years at CTC. I had no contact with any of my classmates—they were reminders of past harm.

Physical intimacy was becoming a major problem for me. I was haunted by images of past abuse. Lee showed a lot of understanding, but I felt like I was failing my partner. I decided to try one-on-one therapy again, this time with someone who specialized in childhood trauma.

~ New Understanding ~

My new therapist, Judith, was the one who helped me understand that my compulsive behavior was normal, loosening the grip of that shame. After that epiphany, however, I went from compulsively trying to comfort myself to being nearly devoid of sexuality. Something had switched off in me—I just didn't want to be touched. I figured that was just the way it was going to be now. To be a good partner, I would have to do whatever was necessary.

I told Judith about the incidents with Rusty and McLean— the foundation of my problems. When Judith referred to Rusty as a "perpetrator," I was thunderstruck. Before then, I had never thought of his behavior as a crime. "Perps" were characters in cop shows, not people I knew who came into my home or worked at my school. When I told her the story about McLean and how we'd been cast as love interests in *Pickwick*, she referred to the casting as "a set-up" and explained that I had been "fed to him by Donahue." I didn't want to believe that Donahue would do that to me. But then I thought about the way he conducted improv classes, regularly putting us into positions to reveal our vulnerabilities. I remembered the conversation we had and how I'd confessed to him that I was struggling. I began to see the possibility that he might have set me up, though I still didn't want to believe it.

I found my way back to Twelve Step work which, in tandem with therapy, started making sense of the jumble in my mind. Rusty was my main focus in therapy. I wasn't ready to tackle certain things or accept the larger reality of what had happened to me at CTC.

When my stepdaughter Jill was nine, I was quite sure she was gay. I could see her energy shift when she was around girls. Surprising neither Lee nor I, she came out to us at the age of eleven. At fifteen, she was struggling with school and finding her place in the LGBT[57] community (the rest of that acronym didn't exist yet). I wanted her to know she wasn't alone, that we all go through difficulties in our teenage years, and so I confessed to her that I had been sexually assaulted at her age.

---

57 LGBT: Lesbian, gay, bisexual and trangender

This intimate conversation gave me a different perspective on my rape and helped me see what fifteen actually looks like. I'd thought of myself as mature when I was that age, but I was a baby in a woman's body. I didn't know the first thing about being a woman. At fifteen, inside development doesn't match the outside, yet the world treats you as if it does. This was the first moment when I began to see the sexual violence at CTC through a different lens.

I was making some progress. The combination of therapy and the tools I was learning in my recovery program were the perfect duo for me. I started finding answers to questions that had baffled me my entire life.

Most people have stories from when they were little told to them by people who were there when it happened. For me, memories from early childhood live in flashes or through the recollections of others. I have three such stories that yielded healing once I investigated them further.

Story one: Throughout my life, I've had a visceral reaction when something unexpected comes at my face, like water splashing in a pool. My body's reaction is way out of proportion—I burst into tears, and I can't catch my breath. I had always been perplexed by this.

I have tiny scars on my face and ear from something that happened when I was about eighteen months old. According to the story, I was playing on the kitchen floor while my mother prepared dinner. Somehow, I got hold of a small glass bottle of tonic water and started shaking it wildly—a toddler with a fancy rattle. Then I dropped it, and the bottle shattered. The force of the bubbles from my shaking caused glass shards to go flying with great force in every direction, including my face. The story always emphasized how grateful my mom was that I wasn't hurt and that the shards had missed my eyes. But some glass did strike my face, though I didn't need stitches. I was hurt more than I was initially led to believe, both physically and psychologically. I don't remember the event, yet my body does. The injury pre-dates cognitive memory, but as Dr. Van Der Kolk says, "the body keeps the score." Now that I know this, I have the ability to process in real-time. Something can come at my face, and the visceral reaction will kick in, but I'm able to stay connected, and my body doesn't completely dysregulate. I can recognize what's happening, understand that I'm not in imminent danger, and stay in the present moment.

Story two: My dad and my uncle used to toss me through the air to each other. I have euphoric memories of flying through the air into my father's arm. These two burly men thought it was a good idea to practice my flying act in the kitchen. Back and forth I went, all giggles and glee until my knee smashed against the countertop just as I was landing in my father's arms. That was the last time I remember being tossed like that. Around this time, I started emotionally reacting to the smell of sautéed mushrooms. I didn't like the texture of mushrooms, but they had never made me sad before.

My investigation of childhood memories helped me recognize that mushrooms had been sautéing in a pan when I hit my knee. The smell was a connection to that physically painful experience. More than that, the smell of sautéed mushrooms was a reminder of my sadness at getting too big to be on my father's shoulders. Now I embrace that it's normal to be sad when you have to let go of something that brings you joy, and mushrooms weren't at fault.[58]

Story three: Wigs were a popular fashion accessory in the late 1960s when I was a little girl. Mom came home one day wearing a long blonde wig. Since she was a redhead, I didn't recognize her. I cried and ran away, and she followed me around, trying to pick me up. I wouldn't let her near me until she took the wig off. Whenever she wore the wig, I ran away in tears. I don't remember any of this, but there is an eight-millimeter film as proof.

---

58 Public Service Announcement: Kitchens are dangerous. Don't throw your babies around in them.

As an adult, I had a mysterious distrust of women, which I now see stemmed from an erroneous belief that my mother was an imposter. Perhaps my work with wigs was partly a quest for answers, an unconscious investigation into appearances, trust and authenticity. Once I understood these connections, I was able to open up to my female friends, and our relationships were enriched because of it.

As I opened each of these mental boxes, I found pieces of my puzzle and snapped them into place. Sorting out these things was giving me some peace of mind, and it seemed I was on the mend. But a lot of my trauma was buried deeply and not being addressed. If the smaller emotional baggage I unpacked revealed such profound awareness, imagine what the larger unopened ones were doing to me still hidden under the surface.

~ Starting to Wake Up ~

Not long after Calvin was born, I went back to work at CTC as wig master. Ivy had moved to the Guthrie, and her replacement at CTC was leaving. It may seem strange that I would return to CTC considering my therapeutic journey, but I still had affection for the *place* and wanted to stay connected to the artistic gifts I received there. The building didn't ask questions about my life, how I was doing or what I'd done since leaving school. It represented the good stuff—the memories of performing and the rewarding work I'd done with Victor. At this point in my therapeutic process, I was dealing with events, not diving into the broader complexities of the culture.

During this last period in which I would work at CTC, something happened that helped me recognize things I wasn't willing to acknowledge before. We were in technical rehearsals for *How the Grinch Stole Christmas*. The orchestra was in the pit playing music, and the actors were on stage dancing in full costume. I was watching from about ten rows up in the house. The Whos in the Dr. Seuss book are shaped like pears, so all the actors were in some kind of padding or pod to make them look like the characters in the book.

Cindy Lou Who was played by an eight- or nine-year-old actor. Her pod-styled costume was wide at the hip and small at her feet. She could only take tiny little steps because of the design, and she was dancing by the edge of the orchestra pit. Suddenly, she toppled in, and everything stopped. There was a collective holding of breath by everyone—except for me.

I flew through that space, my feet barely touching the tops of the seats. I found her unconscious and surrounded by shocked musicians. There were plenty of sharp things she could have hit, but she hit nothing and ended up being okay. I had flashbacks of that performance of *Mr. Pickwick's Christmas*, standing backstage waiting to go on and watching my friend fall into the same orchestra pit.

I was terribly upset the day after Cindy Lou Who fell, and I asked for a private meeting with Peter Brosius, the new artistic director. I told him about the *Pickwick* incident and what it was like at the theater when I was a child. I started to cry and then said, "Nobody was advocating for the children back then, and nobody is doing it now. Why the fuck isn't there a net over the orchestra pit? And why the fuck do you have a small child dancing inches away from a hole in the floor? Who is advocating for the children here?"

They got a net and changed the choreography. But watching that child fall did something to me. I didn't continue to work at CTC for much longer. The spell was broken, and I started to wake up.

~ To Be Seen, or Not to Be Seen ~

It's difficult to move around in the Twin Cities theater scene without bumping into someone who was either harmed, caused harm or was willfully blind to the abuse occurring at CTC during the Donahue era. In order for me to work in my chosen field, I had to ignore what was going on inside me; and if I couldn't overlook something, I had to opt-out.

In the late 1990s, I did one small show at The Minneapolis Women's Club next to Loring Park during the Minnesota Fringe Festival. After one performance, a couple of young women in the show were chattering away while changing out of their costumes.

"Oh my God, Jason McLean was at the show today," one of them said. "I'm so glad he got to see me in this show."

"My god, you're kidding me. That's so awesome that he was here," said the other one.

I was pretty sure I was going to throw up, so I went into the bathroom and splashed cold water on my face. Knowing that he'd been watching me without my knowledge made me physically ill. I didn't act in the Twin Cities again for many years. I limited myself to shows at my husband's dinner theater in the suburbs or small business theater projects that felt safe.

The only person I saw socially from my CTC days was Frank McGovern, and that was because of my friendship with Sal. I'd go to their farm for long weekends to get a break from my children and spend some time in the fresh air. Frank was his best self on the farm, yet he was still Frank. I knew he'd had a terrible childhood and suspected Donahue had done something to him as a teenager at CTC. I tried to get him to talk about it once, but he went silent.

Living in the suburbs kept me sheltered. I could disconnect from things happening in town. I knew that McLean had lost his restaurant space at some point. I didn't try to find out where he went. I was getting better at letting go, using my practices in recovery, self-help and a therapy session now and then. I lost track of McLean, and it felt good.

~ The Eye of the Hurricane ~

The early 2000s were relatively frictionless. My inner turmoil had declined from a boil to a simmer, which was livable. My aversion to being touched hadn't disappeared but had diminished. I was in and out of therapy. When something flared up, I'd call up someone in my support system. I didn't see a need to spend money on weekly therapy if I was doing well—or well enough.

In 2004, I reconnected with my old friend Annie, who'd been with me in Florida when Donahue was arrested. She was the only one with whom I chose to reestablish connections. It was now twenty years after the fact, and she was the first former CTC person I told about McLean raping me.

As Tucker and Calvin got older, they wanted to audition for shows at CTC. I used the excuse that we lived too far away from the theater. I didn't want them to be child actors. Performing at their school was okay, but I was fiercely protective of how they were treated. They didn't fully understand why I was so opposed to it at the time—but now they do.

I decided to attend community college in 2006, never having pursued an undergraduate degree. I studied studio arts, philosophy and a bunch of "ologies"—psychology, sociology, meteorology. I loved being back in school. For much of my adult life, I'd felt like an idiot because of the spotty academic education I got at CTC. I discovered that I wasn't stupid after all. I got my associate degree with a 4.0 grade point average and honors.

In 2007, I was deciding where I'd go to get my bachelor's degree and planning for a career in art therapy when I got a call from my old friend Ivy. She was still working at the Guthrie—the theater's location had moved a year before, from the sinking patch of land down by Loring Park to a beautiful location in downtown Minneapolis overlooking the Mississippi River. One of her assistants had given notice, and she wanted to know if I was interested in the job. I was hired as an assistant to the wig master.

Promotional shot for *Michele! A Musical Bachumanntary*
in 2010 at The Theater Garage in Minneapolis
Photo: Used with permission from producer James Detmar

In 2008, I came out of my self-imposed isolation to perform again in various theaters around town. It felt good to be doing what I loved, but I would always peek through the curtains from backstage to make sure McLean wasn't in the audience—I never saw him.

I was still experiencing some denial and wanted nothing to do with most of my old associates from CTC because they were a reminder of a time I wanted to forget. But I had a craving to connect with people who would understand the messed up, complex nuances of CTC. We had been a family—totally fucked up, dysfunctional, and incestuous, but a family. I tried to explain to therapists what it was like, but none of them really understood because they weren't trained in complex community trauma.

On the rare occasions that I'd talk with someone from that time, the part of me that craved a connection of true understanding would fire up. I longed to be around someone who knew every inch of the building as I did, and what it was like to be in Donahue's improvisation class when he was drunk or receive a simple look of knowing from someone who could make me feel seen in a way no one else could. I imagine this is how soldiers who've fought together feel when they get together.

Finally, in 2009 I actively considered reconnecting with CTC alums. A reunion had been planned for people from the Donahue era, and it was scheduled near the twenty-fifth anniversary of our graduating class. I learned that many people would be attending from out of town. So, after much deliberation and conversations with Annie, I resolved to go. This was a huge step for me. Seeing people I hadn't seen in decades felt strangely okay—in fact, there were people I wanted to see. Aware of my fear that McLean would attend, Annie reminded me that if he showed up, I could leave immediately.

The gathering was at a picnic setting near Minnehaha Falls in Minneapolis—there were about seventy people, former students and teachers, staff members, company actors. A dozen of us from the class of 1985 were there, most of them I hadn't seen since graduation day. A few of the old acting company and teachers were there, including Wendy Lehr. Frank came too, but without Sally.

The attendees were from a whole spectrum of CTC experiences; from people who hadn't been abused and loved every minute of being there, to those who were sexually assaulted and lived with deep wounds; from people who were bystanders and did nothing to stop abuse, to perpetrators themselves; people who would identify as both a survivor of abuse as well as abusing others. Of course, none of this was spoken. That would be a betrayal of the unwritten law of keeping secrets hidden. Thankfully, McLean didn't show up.

That weekend, I went to one social gathering attended by Donahue. I hadn't seen him in years. He was starting to look old and a little pathetic. It was disappointing that so many people were still vying for his attention. I hung out with the people I wanted to see, those who wanted nothing to do with Donahue. After that, I never went to another large reunion.

Occasionally, I would see Donahue in public. I went to a play at The Jungle Theater, and he was sitting on a couch in the lobby, holding court with an entourage, some of them literally sitting on the floor at his feet like we did when we were kids. I couldn't believe he still had so much power over them.

I also ran into him at the Guthrie a few years before I publicly came forward about McLean. By then, the veil had been lifted for me. I'd done enough processing to see him for the sexual predator he was. And yet, I found myself wanting to do something to get him to shine his light of approval on me. This made no sense. How could both feelings be true—that I despised this man and also desired his approval? I wanted to kick myself for having such a thought.

Neural pathways in the brain don't just go away. They're there for life and can fire up at any time. Sometimes you think you've dismantled a thought pattern only to find it reassembling when you're not paying attention. It's important to recognize and embrace the humanness in that. It's not a failure but rather an opportunity to recommit to what you now know is true.

One of the last times I saw Frank was when his relationship with Sal was ending. Things had gotten bad between them, and I went to visit and support her, knowing how intimidating Frank could be. Sweet Sally had always brought out the best in him—but that was over now. He had acquired Donahue's level of arrogance and aloofness, and it was disquieting.

A couple of years later, Wendy Lehr contacted me to design a wig for a production at The Jungle Theater, where Bain Boehlke was still the artistic director. This gig spawned a series of shows I designed for them over the next few years. I found Bain a challenging person to work with, but there was one thing he did that made me feel seen— he acknowledged my dual artistry. He respected the fact that I was both a talented actor and an offstage artist. He had also succeeded in juggling multiple endeavors in theater, and he recognized that in me. We were taught to wear multiple hats at CTC, and it wasn't common or appreciated by most theater folks—you either did one or the other. When I'd show up at general auditions around town, I'd get raised eyebrows from fellow actors who only knew me as a wig person. Bain knew I was more.

I had spent a few years in the "eye of the hurricane" emotionally. I'd quit smoking in 2000 and managed to stay that way through 9/11, the Great Recession and financial woes. My night issues were still there, but I managed. I thought I was doing pretty well, all things considered, so I was surprised when Lee shared the observation that sometimes, after being around my parents, I would "go away" for days. I had no idea what he was talking about.

Lee described what it was like to be around me after visits with them—my eyes were distant, I was distracted and became unavailable emotionally to him and the kids for several days. Honestly, I really didn't see that happening until he brought it up. Then I started to see it for myself. I wasn't in therapy anymore, so I discussed it with my close friend and spiritual advisor, Ellie, who knew me well. With her help, I was able to trace back to the source of my distance and sadness. I'm convinced it was due to my being raped when I was ten years old in my own bedroom and having never told my parents. I didn't want them to feel bad. I held it inside, and it kept me from being fully present to my love for them.

I had been doing emotional healing work for almost two decades when Lee helped me recognize this problem. That's how buried these issues can be. Now I understand that my behavior was typical of PTSD and triggered by being around my parents.

It can be disconcerting to know that even after so much effort and commitment to bettering ourselves, there are still things that can have us trapped. Here's the beauty of it, though. I was able to use my therapeutic tools to free myself from those destructive patterns. I finally found joy in being around my parents before they died. The sadness didn't fully go away, but I was no longer at its mercy.

~ Tugging on Threads ~

After I'd worked at the Guthrie for a couple of years, I was walking down a long hallway that had production photos from past shows on the wall. I'd walked that hallway countless times, but this time I read the little signs describing what show each picture was from and who was in it. I came across one picture I'd never really studied and saw a face that made me shiver. I checked the description to make sure I was right. Yes, it was Matt, the man who had assaulted me twenty years earlier in a dark room full of people. The second man to put his hand over my mouth to keep me from making noise while being raped.

I got dizzy and short of breath. I thought I was going to collapse. My knees turned to jelly. Then the strangest thing happened; I was so disoriented the walls appeared to move and elongate. I'd seen special effects in movies that were similar, like in *The Lord of the Rings* when Frodo feels the presence of the Wraith on the horse coming, and he tells everyone to "get off the road."

Hugging the wall, I felt my way to a doorway and found a chair on the other side. I sat there for about five minutes, crying and trying to catch my breath so I wouldn't pass out.

Once I calmed down, I went back to the shop and shared this with my co-workers, who had become good friends of mine. I was starting to let a few trusted people in on bits and pieces of my trauma story.

I had done a releasing ritual in 2005 regarding McLean with Ellie. I opened the sealed letter I had written to myself about the night he had raped me and read it out loud to her, my voice quivering and tears flowing gently down my cheeks. Then I burned it, along with the half of the production photo from *Pickwick* that McLean was in with me. I took the ashes and put them in a small raft I'd made of natural materials, like sticks and raffia grass, then sent it down the Mississippi. After doing that, when memories of McLean surfaced in me, I would call up the memory of that ritual, and in my mind, I would place him on that raft and watch him drift down the river just as I'd watched those ashes drift away. It helped.

After discussing the discovery of the photograph of Matt with Ellie, I decided to do a similar ritual regarding him. I hadn't seen him in over twenty years, and I'd never discussed the incident with a therapist. It was clear by the way my body reacted to the picture that the assault still held great power over me, so I did another burning.

I like the exercise of ritual—it establishes a new neural pathway that can give the trauma response in the brain a different place to go. When it comes to healing from trauma, I believe that when we're ready to address harm, the mind can send out a call for healing energy, attracting opportunities to see things and heal.

About six months later, another "opportunity for healing" popped up. I was at work going over a cast list for an upcoming production when I came across a name that made me freeze for a moment—it was Matt again. He'd been cast in the next show and would be coming to town in a few weeks. I went into a panic. One of the threads in my tapestry had been tugged, and it seemed like the universe was telling me it was time to do some deeper work. Thankfully, I'd had conversations with my co-workers, and they were able to help me come up with a plan of how I would take care of myself while he was there.

During that production, which lasted close to three months, I walked around in a constant state of being triggered, jumping at every sudden noise. This is not fun when you're raising noisy little kids. Having the support of Ellie and my friends certainly helped, but what I should have been doing was working with a skilled therapist. Unfortunately, the ones I'd previously worked with had either retired or passed away. Trying to establish mental health care is daunting; when you're in crisis, it's practically impossible. I had no mental capacity to find a therapist. All I could do was just get through it. I was relieved when the show closed and Matt departed.

~ Sightings ~

I moved from the position of assistant to the head of the wig and makeup department in 2014, the same year Calvin graduated from high school. On the day of his graduation ceremony, I was jolted back into my fear and shame. I was meeting some out-of-town family members who were in town for the occasion.

The high school didn't have a space large enough for the graduation event—Calvin's class had over seven hundred students in it—so the ceremony was being held on the University of Minnesota campus. My brother-in-law had made a reservation at a Chinese restaurant not far from the arena. A few of us were to meet there for lunch before walking to the arena through an area called Dinkytown. As I walked along, following Google map directions on my phone and counting the numbers on the buildings across the street, I came across a sign that gave me pause: Loring Pasta Bar. My first thought was that Loring Park was nowhere near here, why would someone use that name in Dinkytown? Then a dark feeling filled my body. Could this be—?

I looked at a person who was arranging outdoor seating for the lunch rush. It was McLean. The place where I was meeting my family was right next door to McLean's restaurant.

My stomach turned over, and I pivoted quickly and walked a few paces up the street, hoping he hadn't seen me. I had successfully avoided seeing him again for over fifteen years, and now I was catapulted back into my fear.

I calmly asked my sister-in-law, who was unaware of my past with McLean, to join me in the foyer of the Chinese restaurant. I started trembling fiercely and then spilled out the main details of the McLean story as I cried into her arm. With her support, I was able to pull myself together and join my friends and family. As I sat with them, I started to feel hopeful that McLean was too distracted to have noticed me.

After lunch, our group automatically embarked on the most direct route to the graduation ceremony. It took us right past the Pasta Bar. Just my luck—McLean was outside again amongst the tables full of people having lunch. He stood there with his arms crossed, staring right at me with a look on his face I can only describe as demonic. It was bone-chilling. He didn't say a word, just stared at me as I walked toward him. His eyes said, "I see you. I am powerful. You are nothing." It was so disturbing I had to look away. I tucked my head down, watching the sidewalk pass under my feet as I walked by him as fast as I could.

At the graduation ceremony, I told Lee about it, and he was enraged. Every time I mentioned McLean, he would get so angry he'd talk about going to his restaurant and beating the living shit out of him—or worse. I understood his rage, and as appealing as it sounded, I had forbidden him decades earlier from doing anything like that. Not because I didn't want McLean to feel the consequences of his actions—I absolutely did—but I was afraid Lee would be sent to jail for aggravated assault. I did my usual compartmentalizing and shoved down my emotions.

I saw McLean again a few weeks later in front of the Guthrie with some actors who had just finished a matinee. I hadn't seen him in all those years, and now I'd seen him twice. *Is this a coincidence, or is he stalking me?* I was feeling very exposed and scared.

The following day, I was scheduled for a mammogram. Typically, when I'm done with the test, I shuffle off to whatever's next in my daily planner. This is what women do—we just keep moving. But I was so emotionally and physically triggered by sightings of McLean that my trauma was very close to the surface. The exam felt like an assault, and afterward, I sat in the changing room for ten minutes crying and holding my breasts, apologizing to my body for putting it through that offensive ritual. I didn't have another one for seven years.

At work about two weeks later, I walked by the callboard for actors that was near the wig room, and something caught my eye—a very simple white card with three words printed on the cover—Loring Pasta Bar. I pushed the card open with one finger and read the note addressed to the cast of the show and signed by McLean. In it, he congratulated them on a fine performance and invited them to his restaurant for a free drink.

Anger shot through me, and I ripped the card off the board. It's one thing to see him in his own setting or in front of my workplace, but he wasn't allowed *in the building* in any way, shape or form.

I needed to get rid of the card. Throwing it in the garbage wasn't sufficient. That card could not stay in the building. I wondered, "Should I burn it?" Then I thought of the perfect place to put it. I hurried outside, walked over to the area where people walk their dogs, and tossed it in the garbage can with all the dog shit.

McLean appeared for a fourth time on my Facebook feed. I'd blocked his name long ago, yet this photograph showed up because it was on a friend's page. His name wasn't tagged, so his image wasn't blocked. This time I was sitting in my own house, and still, he invaded my space. It was getting ridiculous, but I felt that maybe the universe was trying to tell me something. I sent a message to the friend who had posted his picture, explaining that he had hurt me in the past and requested that she remove the image from her feed. She apologized and removed it immediately. I was starting to find my voice.

This image appeared in the *St. Paul Pioneer Press* for an article written in the spring of 2015 about my job as wig master at the Guthrie.
Photo: Lauren Mueller

The rapid succession of sightings had stirred up everything once dormant inside me. No imagery of rafts carrying him away could expel him from my mind. My sleep problems magnified—

insomnia, night rage, nightmares and paralysis. I was experiencing extreme anxiety, and my depression ramped up. I was haunted by the past I had tried to bury. And it wasn't just McLean that was haunting me now. It was all of them.

At this point, I didn't have a therapist, so I decided to share what was going on with my friend Shanan, who was becoming a close confidante. I needed to talk to someone about the things that were surfacing. I told her what had happened when I was a child, how McLean kept resurfacing and what it was doing to me psychologically. She held my hands and cried with me. It was so hard to tell her such ugly things but also so liberating. I could feel strength rising in me, the beginning of a new stage in my life—the era of truth.

~ The Facebook Thread ~

The Facebook conversation referenced in this section has become known within the Children's Theatre Company alumni community as "The Thread." It was a private conversation that happened in a closed virtual room accessible only to members of the group. I will not reveal any specifics of content in the telling of this story. If I mention someone's name or something they said, I do so with their permission.

On May 23, 2015, I first saw the Facebook post that would change everything. I was sitting at my kitchen table in my pajamas, scrolling through my page, when I saw a picture that looked familiar. It was a painting in a style that reminded me of my youth—of CTC.

Steven Rydberg was a brilliant artist. His artwork was on all CTC promos and posters back in the day. I knew this image wasn't done by him, but it was in his style. Rydberg's work is very recognizable—this was a cheap imitation.

I looked more closely. The picture showed a sad child perched on a stool in a spotlight on a stage. A theatrical curtain swag bordered one side, and from the other came an arm of a faceless person reaching out to the child. The hand, painted in a vile shade of green, was placed delicately on the child's shoulder.

The image was posted by someone on the CTC alumni page, of which I was a member. I clicked to see more. The picture was accompanied by an article written by Kay Miller about Donahue and what had happened at CTC. I remembered seeing the picture on the cover of the arts and entertainment section of the *Minneapolis Star Tribune* when I read the series back in 1991.

I looked at the picture again and started reading the comments people were sharing about the article. Memories of those painful years started to flood my mind. People were looking back on that time and sharing the difficulty of what we'd endured, careful not to say too much. To speak out and tell the truth was an unspoken violation of protocol. Down the long list of comments, people started saying things that went a little deeper, and I thought, *I guess we're talking some truth for a change.*

Then people started talking about their abuse—at first, in casual ways, then with more depth. The comments grew more intense. When I spotted a comment from my old friend Jina, who was also a victim of McLean's, I lost it emotionally. "I want to thank those of you who came forward back in the day," she wrote. "You saved my life." And that was it. I had an emotional meltdown and sobbed so hard I broke blood vessels in my face.

My son Calvin pulled into the driveway while I was crying. I didn't try to put on a good face—I'm not sure I could have. I just sat there bawling, knowing I'd have to tell him what was going on.

A few years earlier, I had confessed vaguely to Calvin that something had happened to me at CTC. He had had a basic understanding that kids had been sexually abused and that I had gone through a difficult time, but nothing more. Later, when I was helping Calvin practice parallel parking in an empty lot, the subject of CTC came up. I don't remember how or why, but when we were done, he put the car in park, turned to me and said, "Mom, were you one of the kids that was abused at CTC?"

There was my son asking me point blank if I was one of the sexual assault victims. I couldn't lie to him. My eyes filled with tears, and I said, "Yes," and began to cry. My beautiful fifteen-year-old man-child reached over, took me in his arms and said, "It's okay, Mom."

The parking lot faded away, and I could see him striding up the driveway. I knew there was no hiding it. He was going to see the depth of my pain. He walked in, saw my tears and immediately sat down at the table and asked what was wrong.

The full weight of guilt from my inability to tell the truth about what had happened overwhelmed me. The reality of how my silence had allowed others to be hurt was unbearable, and it was crushing me.

I told Calvin that for the first time, people were sharing the truth about what had happened to us, and I was feeling the force of it. And that's when this young man, no longer a gangly teenager yet barely old enough to understand the significance of his insight, spoke the words that brought me back from the abyss. He said, "Mom, you were a *child*. You did the best you could."

I don't know where that wisdom came from but thank God it did. Calvin made it possible for me to come back to reality, to recognize that I was powerless back then to do anything other than what I did—self-preservation.

I spent the next few days glued to the computer, watching the truth unfold. I told Lee that people were starting to share honestly about being abused.

He said, "It's time for you to say the truth, too, to your friends. This guy's been living rent-free in your head long enough."

I agreed and told him I would say something.

I was afraid to break my silence regarding what happened to me at CTC, but I went to my computer, composed a message to share on The Thread, read it over and sent it. At that moment, I knew it might not stay private to the group, but Lee was right. It was time.

The emotions stirred up by The Thread caused group members to seek each other. A few women still living in the Twin Cities decided to have an overnight retreat to share stories. It was incredible to be in each other's presence, to feel the walls of secrecy fall away and the barriers that kept us isolated disintegrate.

We ate together, laughed and cried. I told them what happened with McLean. One of my friends asked if I'd read the Minnesota Child Victims Act. I thought it was about kids abused by priests but learned it was created for situations like ours as well. Once I read it, I recognized it as a possible truth-telling platform.

Partly because of Lee's support, I was able to take that big first step to disclose what had happened all those years ago. His comment about McLean living "rent-free" in my mind stuck with me.

I had told Tucker what happened to me—it didn't feel right to have one child know and not the other. And I had already opened up to my friend Shanan, which had been incredibly healing. I decided to start telling people I worked with about McLean. Until then, whenever his name had come up, I'd get silent, change the subject or just walk away. The first co-worker I told was a Guthrie actress with whom I had frequently worked with when she was in my chair for a wig fitting. This "coming out" in a work setting was a pivotal moment for me, and it felt damn good. Scary, but good.

Something started changing in my brain, and my heart was beginning to open. I found myself freer to think, to feel, to speak about things I had never allowed myself to reveal.

I often say I hate technology, and it's true—computers frustrate me, cell phones are a pain, and I think people spend too much time looking at screens. Still, were it not for technology, which enabled The Thread to reach so many of us, I probably never would have come forward in a public way, and for that, I'm grateful. I hadn't attended any CTC reunion activities since 2009. Now that we were speaking the truth out loud, I wanted to look people in the eyes and have a common experience—one planted in truth, not lies and deception. The fiftieth anniversary of CTC was happening that summer. Anniversary events were scheduled over several days, culminating in a big celebration at Target Field in Minneapolis, where the Minnesota Twins baseball team plays, a venue big enough for a large crowd of alumni and supporters to congregate. A video retrospective showed highlights of CTC's first half-decade. Nothing was said about Donahue and the abuses suffered by the kids who were students there. The silence about this tragedy spoke volumes.

I didn't go to any of the scheduled events, only small side gatherings not connected directly to the anniversary celebration. By then, going anywhere near the building was too upsetting. I did attend a social gathering in which a former company member referred to Donahue's artistry and what it was like to meet him back in the 1960s. "He was like Mozart or Picasso," he said, "Just imagine—John asking you to do theater with him was like Picasso asking you to come over and play with his paint."

This actor's attitude was incredibly dismissive of the victims— Donahue's artistry doesn't cancel his crimes.

On Sunday, August 10, an exclusive story broke on Fox 9 News about the dark side of CTC's history that wasn't mentioned in the celebrations. In the segment, investigative reporter Tom Lyden revealed that he had been given access to our private conversation on Facebook and that former students who had been sexually assaulted at CTC back in the day were talking openly to each other about the abuse. He made references to the side gatherings we'd been having that weekend and quoted from some of the comments on The Thread, showing screenshots of comments from victims.

Someone in our private group had leaked this information to Lyden. Though he hadn't used names in the story, it was still a huge breach of trust—and devastating to the group. People who had finally felt safe to discuss their abuse scurried back into the shadows. I hope that those who were wounded by that story were able to find another safe place in which to unpack their trauma. Clearly, Facebook is not a safe space.

Annie, me and Rana at The Black Forrest Inn the weekend of the fiftieth-anniversary celebration. I forget who took the picture.

That next day, I gathered with a small group of women and watched the Fox 9 story online. Jina and Annie were there, and another old friend, Rana, who was in town for the reunion. We'd all reconnected through Facebook but hadn't spent much time together. One of the people interviewed for the news segment was attorney Jeff Anderson, a local powerhouse prosecutor from

St. Paul who specializes in childhood sexual abuse civil cases. I wasn't familiar with him, but Jina was. We decided we'd meet with Jeff Anderson and tell him about what McLean had done to us.

If this were a play, I'd place the intermission here. Take some time now to stretch your legs, to nurture yourself if you need to. We've only been in the shallows. Go fortify your spirit before we jump into the deep end of the trauma pool.

Chapter Five
Finding My Voice and Myself

Special Note: Seventeen former students filed suits under the Minnesota Child Victims Act against the Children's Theatre Company (CTC) and/or their perpetrators. We were a fraction of the people who could have filed. Each plaintiff had a different opinion of Jeff Anderson and his team, just as each had a personal trauma experience. We viewed the legal process and attorneys through our individualized lens. Some of us came through the process feeling liberated and filled with gratitude. Others believed they were mentally or emotionally worse at the end. In telling this part of my story, I speak from my own experience and don't want the other plaintiffs to think I'm trying to speak for them or dismiss how they experienced the process. Many plaintiffs filed under an anonymous "Doe" status and were assigned a number to protect their identities. In the 1980s, a plaintiff's initials were used and could easily be matched to a name; this method thankfully has been abandoned. I will not share names or identifiers of people who have chosen to maintain their anonymity. If I talk about someone by name, it's with their permission, or I'm referring to information the plaintiff has shared publicly. The following is my personal perspective and is not reflective of everyone's experience.

In May 2013, Minnesota became the sixth state in the United States to create a Child Victims Act, removing the statute of limitations for victims of childhood sexual assault and providing a legal platform for them to report abuse and seek damages in civil court. A three-year retroactive window was opened for people whose statutes had expired prior to the signing of the law. I'm grateful for the Minnesota Child Victims Act because it effectively remedied the senseless silencing of victims who needed more time to understand what had been done to them as children. It can take decades for victims to process and prepare to speak about their abuse. The Thread occurred while the window for filing retroactively was still open. That window closed in May 2016.

Before The Thread, I never thought I would litigate for damages in court, or attempt to hold accountable the person responsible for raping me or call out the institution that protected him. Sharing my experiences with a small circle of trusted and caring people was sufficient in my eyes; I had no intent to open myself up to wide exposure, revealing things I'd nicely tucked away in the deepest parts of my mind. I felt no need to publicly stir up trouble. But the scope of harm that revealed itself through The Thread was impossible to ignore.

Maybe, because I find it easier to feel anger on behalf of others, my own abuse wasn't enough to propel me into action, but when I saw how deeply our community had been wounded, I was inspired to expose the institution for its negligence. This meant I needed to publicly expose my own trauma experience and my perpetrator. Knowing that others would benefit from breaking my silence gave me strength. I was compelled to act.

~ Jeff Anderson and Associates ~

Jeff Anderson and Associates (JAA) are considered nationally to be the best attorneys in prosecuting civil cases for adults who were sexually assaulted as children. Jeff and his team have legal offices across the country, and as the laws change in different states, they help support survivors in breaking their silence while taking on predators such as priests and Boy Scout leaders as well as the institutions that protect them. JAA was an integral part of getting the Minnesota Child Victims Act passed in the legislature.

Jeff Anderson has been working on these kinds of cases since the early 1980s. He was a lawyer in St. Paul, Minnesota, when Donahue was arrested and followed the case with interest. He told me he knew then that justice hadn't been served and had always thought a reckoning for CTC should happen. He wasn't surprised when people started coming to him after the Child Victims Act became law.

Some people criticize Jeff for making money off the pain of survivors of sexual violence. I've thought about this a lot: "Isn't he just exploiting the survivors even more?" I understand why some people feel that way. The legal process is extremely painful for survivors of sexual violence, and money is made by lawyers in the survivor's pursuit of justice in civil court. The re-wounding of survivors occurs because of the nature of the legal process, and I don't want that to be hidden in the recitation of my story.

Victims who become plaintiffs must publicly expose the most painful and vulnerable parts of themselves in the legal arena, and it's a brutal system to navigate. That being true, I'd rather have Jeff make money while guiding survivors through the process of holding pedophiles and their institutions accountable than for Jeff to do none of those things.

The historical pattern of sexual predators escaping punishment for their crimes is changing because of people like Jeff. The rules are changing for this ugly game of exploiting kids for sex, and a message is being sent to people who perpetrate crimes against children—they are no longer safely hiding in the safe harbor of legal statutes. And victims are learning there's a place for them to reveal their abuse in a legal system that's beginning to understand the importance of truth-telling in the survivor's healing process.

So yes, I'm okay with JAA earning money by helping survivors because for every case that concludes with financial reparations, there are thousands that don't. And JAA is still there, holding space for survivors to tell their stories and be heard. To help survivors find resources, Jeff founded a non-profit called Zero Abuse Project in 2018, a national resource for victims of childhood sexual abuse past and present.

A lawyer's job is to navigate the law, and Jeff does it very well. I believe he and his team care about their clients. They're a good group of people trying to help victims of sexual violence find some form of justice. Jeff also tries to be a redeemer of sorts by helping people reclaim autonomy over their bodies and find emotional healing from childhood trauma. It's a mighty task, and he attempts to do it altruistically in part. The problem is—there's nothing altruistic about a legal system that continually retraumatizes victims of sexual violence. It's all well and good to have the intention of holding the welfare of a victim in high regard, but the system requires a victim's unflinching willingness to keep the tenderest parts of themselves exposed if they want to hold accountable those responsible for their abuse.

~ Bookends ~

I first met Jeff Anderson in August 2015. Jina and I had gone to his St. Paul office to discuss the abuse we had suffered at the hands of McLean at CTC. We met with him and his associate, Molly Burke, in the small conference room. The week before, I had watched his interview with Channel 9 reporter Tom Lyden about the anonymously revealed Facebook thread.

Meeting Jeff in person was scary—not because of him, but because telling the truth about what happened to us was taboo and grounds for dismissal from a family of artists I still had affections for. I was grateful for Jina's presence—I'd never spoken about my trauma to anyone but the people closest to me or therapists.

Jeff is well-practiced at being calm and validating to survivors. He lets his clients know he believes them. Part of his job is to help them find the power that was taken from them as children. If everyone in the legal field treated victims of sexual violence so kindly when they walk through the door, it would be a different world. I'm sure he finds it gratifying, having built a legacy of taking down sexual predators. Notably, he took great pleasure in naming the renovated building that houses his St. Paul office the *Guardian* Building.

The first meeting was loaded with emotions but easier than I'd expected. He told us we were not the first to approach him about abuse at CTC. He suspected more would come forward, and his firm was already aware of McLean. He told us that he believed us. Hearing someone in a position of authority say those words was particularly affirming.

We told Jeff we had no interest in putting CTC out of business. We wanted to bring light to the history of abuse, seek justice, and pave the way for others to do the same if they wanted to. We believe that the culture created by Donahue and upheld for decades by enablers and complicit staff allowed for the normalization of sexualizing children and encouraged people like McLean to abuse us at will without consequences. The well-being of children was sacrificed to save the institution, we explained. Justice and retribution needed to come from the organization because its success and very existence today was a direct result of abused children being silenced. But no, we didn't want to take down CTC.

Jeff made it clear our cases fell under liability insurance, that the theater had ample coverage and we wouldn't be ruining them financially by bringing the truth forward. He wouldn't be required to prove that CTC knew what Donahue and the other abusers had been doing, only that CTC *should have known*, and he was confident he could do that. Jeff said he'd take our cases, that I'd be the lead case and Jina would be the last.

Jina and I looked at each other.

She said, "We're bookends."

I agreed. "Bookends."

I was surprised that he wanted his lead case to be mine—Jina's abuse was far more egregious. Later, I came to understand that the straightforward nature of my case would probably make it easier for the public to understand. Also, I was known and respected in the theater community. And if we ended up in court, Jeff knew from this meeting that I'd perform well in front of a jury.

I signed an agreement to have Jeff represent me. I had the option to remain an anonymous Jane Doe with a number, but I felt pretty certain I would go public. However, I needed to talk to my family about it first. I told Lee I'd signed with Jeff and was seriously considering using my name. I wanted his advice.

He said, "I expect no less of you. It's who you are."

After talking to my kids and getting a similar response, I decided to attach my name to the complaint because it would have far more power and create a stronger platform for others to come forward. To take that step publicly, I needed to be prepared for a backlash—to be called a slut, a gold digger, a liar; to be shunned, lose my job, my friends, my reputation, maybe even be forced out of the theater community entirely. Having the support of my family and closest friends helped me stand in courage and not let fear stop me from doing what I knew was right.

Jeff said it would be a difficult path that could take years. This was an understatement. The litigation process was much worse than what he had described.

~ Stepping into the Unknown ~

My decision to file was made before the #MeToo movement went viral. I stepped into the unknown with support from the few people who knew about my abuse but without knowing how the community would respond. McLean was a big deal in Minneapolis—he owned The Loring Pasta Bar and The Varsity Theater, a popular music venue. I knew he still had power over me, as illustrated by our recent encounters.

I was scared but also inspired by the women who were taking on Bill Cosby, a huge story at the time. If they could take on an icon and living legend in the entertainment world, I could take on McLean. Those women were heroes to me.

I asked Jeff to whom and how much of my story should I share? Was I supposed to keep it to myself? He set no limits and encouraged me to share as much as I wanted with people of my choice. He emphasized that having a good support network would be crucial to my mental well-being throughout the litigation process.

I started building my circle of support, telling one friend at a time that I was filing a lawsuit. Slowly, my network widened. Before long, I had over a dozen women in support. Some of them were close friends, others were respected colleagues. A few were former students at CTC who understood what it had been like there.

My father's health was declining, so I worried about adding stress to my parent's lives. Nevertheless, I needed to tell them what I was doing. My adult relationship was different with each of them. Dad was a big teddy bear, always ready with a hug and easy to talk to. Mom wasn't a stern woman—she was sweet and kind—but less emotionally available than my father.

I drove to their home in rural Minnesota, talking to myself the entire way, trying to find the words. In their living room, I sat in a chair with my parents on either side of me. My father's face was warm and inviting; mom's was reserved. I didn't unfurl the whole narrative, just the part about CTC and McLean. In the end, I told them I was attaching my name to the lawsuit, which meant I'd be in the news.

My father told me he was proud of me. "Go get the bastard," he said, giving me a big hug. Mom didn't say much, though she hugged me and said, "Thank you for telling us."

~ The Press Conference ~

Jeff decided to file my case alongside another plaintiff, a male victim named Todd Hildebrandt, referred to as Doe 84 at the time of the press conference. Several months later, Todd chose to reveal his identity. Todd filed against the theater and Donahue. Both of us were included in the official complaint filed on December 1, 2015. Jeff explained that there was more strength in having our cases joined, showing there were both female and male victims and more than one perpetrator. He also wanted future litigants to know anonymity was possible. Publicly revealing along with an anonymous plaintiff showed there were options. Although our cases were being filed together, and our process of jumping through the legal hoops would run parallel to each other, he explained that all cases were still separate. This wasn't a class-action suit. We each had the autonomy to make our own decisions.

The morning of the press conference, Jeff asked if I wanted to meet Doe 84— he was interested in meeting me. I said, of course, and Jeff led me to a private area in the firm's offices. I'd never met Todd before—he had attended theater school in the 1970s. It didn't matter, though—we embraced immediately, feeling we knew the other because of the common experience we'd shared.

Todd told me about himself, his abuse by Donahue, and how his life had been affected by it. He said he would be in the conference room with me along with a slew of JAA staff members as I spoke to the press. He felt confident there wouldn't be anyone there who could identify him, and his anonymity would be maintained. I was grateful to know he'd be in the room with me.

During a show, I don't get nervous until just before I walk on stage. This was similar, but it wasn't a theatrical performance. This was my life. At the press conference, I was going to be speaking my own words about the life I'd lived. This was not a role scripted by a playwright—I would be *me*. My nerves swelled.

When I walked into the conference room, I could see Lee, a few friends and other former CTC students at the back. Shanan, Annie and my old friend Stacey were there for support. Todd was there off to the side, completely anonymous. Then I saw the wall of cameras.

I turned to one of the lawyers and said, "I think I'm going to need a glass of water."

During the press conference, I felt separated from my body and emotions. I remember what I was wearing but very little about what I said. I remember looking to Jeff to keep me on track. My clearest memory was looking down at the podium as I lifted my hand and saw the moist print of my sweaty palm on the wooden surface.

After answering some questions, I closed with an Audre Lourde quote that hung over my desk at work. "When I dare to be powerful, to use my strength in the service of my vision, then it becomes less and less important whether I am afraid." I got halfway into it, and my mind went blank. I was terrified I wouldn't be able to finish it. *Everyone's watching, come on brain*—then the final words came into focus. Hoping my lapse had been interpreted as a dramatic pause, I finished the quote, left the room, and walked into the little room where we had stowed my stuff, my friends' coats, and bags. I'm really good at holding it all together—until I'm not. Years of silence had just been broken—I did that. I had said out loud secrets that had been hidden for decades. It was terrifying and liberating at the same time. I broke down in a torrent of tears. Emotions gushed out of me. Lee came into the room, saw my emotional state and was worried that something was terribly wrong.

I told him no, everything was very right.

CTC quickly put out a statement explaining that they were sorry for what happened to me and all the children harmed back in the Donahue years. That was the first public validation of past harm by CTC in over three decades, though they made it very clear they were not responsible for what had happened. They carefully distanced themselves as an institution from the harm caused by "former employees." I was grateful, though, that they didn't deny the abuse. Even so, it was obvious they weren't going to take responsibility as an institution for the harm.

In the following days, JAA received over two hundred phone calls from people wanting to give information. These people expressed appreciation and support and were grateful the truth was finally being revealed.

I was both surprised and relieved by the community response. Artists my age from Minneapolis knew about what had happened at CTC, though they didn't really understand its scope until I had spoken out. Younger artists, however, had no clue and were astonished that such insidious things were allowed to be forgotten.

I heard many stories of abuse from people who wanted me to know they'd also suffered at CTC and other theaters around the country, not only as kids but as adults. Suddenly, strangers were saying to me, "I've never told anyone this, but..." I understood the emotional cost of holding secrets. Inspired by this confessional outpouring, I enrolled in rape crisis advocacy training so I'd be able to refer people to the best resources if they needed help.

When the truth is spoken out loud, it gives other people permission to do the same. All sexual violence is unacceptable, so being courageous enough to point it out is essential. If a perpetrator did something to one person, it's possible they did it to someone else too. Two isolated incidents can be a coincidence. Additional assaults turn a coincidence into a pattern.

There were people who were unhappy with me, and unkind comments were posted on newspaper websites, but I chose not to read them. Those misinformed people didn't know me, didn't know what had happened and how my life had been altered. The people who were at CTC—those who had been part of that world—mattered to me.

The reactions have varied from people who were adults during my time at CTC. A few people have said they suspected something nefarious was happening and wished they'd done something. Some will no longer look me in the eye. Others are cautious around me, unsure of how I will respond to their presence. Some profess their sorrow about what happened to the victims but assume no responsibility for their part.

~ McLean ~

After I decided to file my suit against McLean, I reached out to Melissa, one of his victims. We hadn't spoken in decades. Catching up on our lives, I told her about the lawsuit and she was very supportive. She explained that she had moved on and didn't want to pursue a civil suit for herself. She said she was proud of me for taking a stand, and I thanked her for supporting me and left it at that.

After my press conference, McLean vigorously denied wrongdoing, declaring that he was innocent and would clear his "good name." Almost immediately, Melissa phoned me. "I'm going to file," she said. "After hearing McLean's denial, I said, 'Oh, hell no.' and knew I needed to come forward too so you wouldn't be alone."

I wept with gratitude.

It wasn't surprising that McLean professed his innocence—he's a sociopath who has no remorse for the harm he inflicts on others. In his eyes, he's the victim and I was the one ruining his life. Once he was exposed and multiple women came forward, however, the community took notice. His restaurant and entertainment venue were picketed. Other businesses cut ties with him, and musicians canceled concerts—and this was before #MeToo. The pressure eventually ran him out of town.

JAA turned over evidence for pretrial discovery to the prominent defense attorneys McLean had retained, Jon Hopeman and Marnie Fearon. One of the most damaging bits of evidence was a cache of 230 papers provided to JAA by a confidential source. Apparently, McLean had kept things beneath the floorboards of his old house—trophies from his victims. Who keeps trophies like pictures and love letters from their teenage conquests under their floorboards?

Jina told me she knew about the hiding spot in the floor—it was in the room where he raped me. This was like a crime movie that writes itself. The papers yielded a lot of damaging evidence. Hopeman and Fearon withdrew as McLean's lawyers a few weeks after reviewing these papers. McLean claimed he fired them because they were too expensive and started representing himself.

In 2018, McLean cashed in his Minnesota assets for about $4.75 million dollars. He fled to Mexico and bought a lovely rental property in Cabo San Lucas, where he resides.

~ The Media ~

The first flurry of media coverage focused on McLean and Donahue, less about Children's Theatre Company as the institution that harbored them. I was interviewed several times by Rohan Preston of the *Minneapolis StarTribune* , a theater critic writing for the arts and entertainment section.

Jeff chose Preston rather than an investigative reporter because he knew the theater community well, but I believe giving Preston an exclusive line to this ongoing story was a mistake. I have nothing personal against Preston, but he had too many relationships in the theater community, which was lagging behind in its appreciation for the damage that had been done. I think Jeff should have chosen someone more neutral.

Preston interviewed several former students, including me, at one point, asking if we considered CTC to be a cult. My immediate response was, "I'm not comfortable calling it that, though there were definitely elements that resembled one." Even as a plaintiff, I felt like a traitor for even considering CTC to be a cult.

At that time, openly admitting that CTC was a cult was like admitting I was weak and mentally unstable. In my mind, anyone who would fall prey to a cult was an idiot. And that's the genius of a cult, isn't it? It's a built-in way people like Donahue can protect themselves because those who fall into it don't want to look that closely at it or admit they participated in something that was such a total mind-fuck, even if they were children at the time.

When Preston's big article came out three months after the press conference in February 2016, he mentioned the cult aspect, quoted several former students, and misquoted me. I was terribly disappointed that he failed to point out CTC's part in institutional harm and betrayal of the students. The newspaper's lawyers were very timid about criticizing the beloved CTC.

I get it—they weren't going to expose themselves to lawsuits. The effort to reveal the truth about institutional negligence was going to be much harder than just breaking the silence.

I believe Preston should not have been allowed exclusive access to cover the plaintiffs' cases against CTC while continuing to write about the glories of CTC itself. Over the years of litigation, whenever there was an article about the nasty business in CTC's past, Preston always followed it later with a cover story filled with praise. He played both sides, which made me feel dismissed and diminished.

Because I was a survivor of sexual violence in a constant battle to expose the truth, those glowing articles landed like a blow to my gut. They seemed obvious and predictable, scattering sunshine to distract from the darkness and keep the current CTC administrators in good light. Despite the supposed journalistic firewall between news gathering and advertising departments, it also seemed like a conflict of interest that CTC was a large advertiser, contributing to the financial well-being of the newspaper.

Reporters frequently interviewed Jeff as more cases against CTC were filed. Jina blasted Jeff at one point because he had described McLean as a "Svengali," implying that he had "seduced" his victims. She believed, and I agree, that it's inappropriate to perpetuate a narrative that romanticizes childhood sexual abuse. "He isn't a Svengali. He's a pedophile," she said. "He didn't seduce us. He groomed us. Would you say a priest seduced an eleven-year-old boy?"

Jeff is a clever wordsmith; he tries to find just the right way to say something so the press will grab it. But calling McLean a Svengali was completely dismissive of the criminality of his acts and our vulnerability as children. It didn't capture that McLean's duty—and that of every other adult around us—was to reinforce clear and protective boundaries around young kids and adolescents. Jeff had made it appear as if we were willing participants who were wooed rather than raped.

We complained to Jeff, and to his credit, he understood, apologized and immediately changed the way he talked about perpetrators.

In early 2018, I was contacted by Elizabeth Foy Larsen, a local journalist commissioned by *Minneapolis St. Paul Magazine* to write a piece about McLean. She requested an interview. I was willing to talk to anyone who wanted to tell the story. I met with her several times and also answered questions via email.

Foy Larsen's article *"The Exit Strategy"* came out in the May 2018 edition of *Minneapolis St. Paul Magazine*. Her excellent piece is expert investigative reporting and can be found online. In it, McLean was quoted as claiming he never did anything wrong, referring to his accusers as "libidos in training," blaming his victims and insisting that he was pursued by us, the plaintiffs. This is deny, attack, and reverse the victim and offender (DARVO) in action. Foy Larsen interviewed McLean exclusively through email as he was in Mexico by then.

When I read the article online, I saw a link to another page: "To read McLean's full response, click here." I ignored the link at first and kept reading, expecting to see a link to my written responses. There was none. Why was the magazine giving McLean's defense so much more exposure? Unknown to me, when McLean agreed to respond to Foy Larsen's questions, he made the publication of any part of his response conditional on the editors including access to his entire written response. The editors complied.

I had also given Foy Larsen written responses to several questions. Where was the link to my words, I wondered? I immediately called the editor and said that if the magazine allowed a rapist like McLean the privilege of having his full statement available, they should extend the same courtesy to his victims.

The editor apologized and said they'd add a link to my written responses as soon as possible, which they did. I was tired of the media treating survivors like an afterthought, and it felt good to confront them. There are some excellent reporters and journalists doing fine work, and Foy Larsen was very respectful, but there are also some who are causing damage to already wounded people.

One of the CTC alums who was angry with Tom Lyden for his reporting about The Thread on Facebook, rebuked the reporter via email for his lack of compassion or moral compass. Lyden's report had shown computer screenshots revealing things posted in private about abuse that group members had suffered as children.

Lyden's email response was curt: "We did not identify them. If they thought their comments were private, they were truly misled by the moderators." Nothing more. No apology for the pain he'd caused an already wounded community. No accountability.

On the flip side, reporter Marianne Combs took great care in her dealings with survivors. She went through training in trauma-informed practices before interviewing survivors.

Reporting news doesn't have to be heartless. Finding the line of reporting and doing no harm can be difficult, but this is their job.

~ Healing in Community ~

When I initially met with attorney Jeff Anderson, he suggested I get a therapist. I knew that was good advice. The first person I reached out to was Cordelia Anderson. Jeff had spoken highly of her, and I wanted to talk to someone who understood childhood trauma. She wasn't seeing patients anymore and was focusing on advocacy, consulting, education and public speaking about sex traffickers and those producing child sexual abuse images. She was truly a star in her field.

I was honored that she agreed to meet me. She told me right away that she had been one of the therapists who was brought in to help students at CTC after Donahue was arrested.

Cordelia suggested a clinic for therapy, but more importantly, she became a source of support, a mentor and a friend. We organized gatherings for sharing between CTC alums in Minneapolis that greatly informed later efforts to come together to heal in community.

Getting back into therapy was hard. I had struggled to tap into the deepest trauma with my former therapists. While I could acknowledge my sadness and the other effects of the abuses, I just couldn't see how emotionally shut down I was. I had discussed Rusty in-depth with former therapist Judith, but I was never able to get very far into the work around McLean or my time at CTC.

For several months, I worked weekly with a therapist at the new clinic. I was finally delving into the more complicated elements of my time at CTC, and McLean specifically, when she informed me she was leaving her practice. I'd been putting myself wholeheartedly into the work with her, finally unpacking some very dusty old emotional baggage, and now I was going to have to pick that all up and find someone else. I was hurt and, fairly or unfairly, felt abandoned. My faith in the therapeutic process took a hit.

After our final session, I decided against more therapy. I just couldn't go through all the foundational information again with someone else. It's exhausting, and it seemed like it would be less work to just manage on my own. My father was dying, and I was caring for him. I didn't need more stress trying to find a new therapist too. Several months later, however, it became clear that I was floundering in the frustrating, intrusive and impersonal legal process on top of my unaddressed childhood trauma. I had no professional help to guide me.

What kept me grounded was the group of CTC survivors I had bonded with. We had experienced community trauma in addition to individual abuses, and our bonds were strong. For about a year, a group of us gathered weekly in church basements and coffee shops. Our honest and vulnerable conversations allowed us to form a more complete picture of our pasts, to fill in the gaps. We found ourselves through listening to each other's stories, which gave us new perspectives on how to participate in our own lives. We were experiencing collateral growth. These women became my teachers and helped me begin to climb out of my trauma.

During community truth-telling, sometimes you hear things you don't want to hear. When a name comes up connected to a story of abuse that hits close to home, it can cause a cascade of realizations that shift your present reality. When I heard from a couple of women that Frank McGovern pursued them as soon as they turned sixteen,[59] I had to look at my adult friendship with him through an updated lens. It was heartbreaking to hear how much harm he had caused, knowing how our lives had continued to intersect because of

---

59 Protected victim statements and depositions with Jeff Anderson and Associates

my relationship with Sal. My family dog was not only connected to Donahue because he had my dog's littermate, but Frank had raised my dog's mother. It was a kinship I wanted to erase, but there are things that can't be undone.

Admitting that I still needed help, I found a new therapist through a friend's recommendation. She knew a lot about the history of CTC, so I didn't have to trudge through every detail. I dedicated a lot of energy to evicting the demons "living rent-free" in my head, moving the energy of harm through my body and tending to invisible wounds.

Once I had a solid relationship with a therapist again, I started doing EMDR, a trauma therapy technique that kicked my healing process into high gear.[60] It was hard, yet the results were spectacular.

People began asking me to participate on panels. The most powerful extinguisher of shame is speaking the truth, and I was happy to hand that key to other survivors. I now had a vision of how sharing this broken part of me could allow it to heal and, in turn, give others an example for their own healing process.

Because I was speaking publicly about my experiences, I decided I needed to tell my mother about what happened with Rusty so it wouldn't surprise her if it got back to her. I didn't share the ugly details, just that it was bad. Her response was not, "Oh, Laura, I'm so sorry that happened to you. It must have been terrifying. No one deserves to be treated that way. I wish you would have told me when it happened. I'm sorry I wasn't there for you. I love you." This is

---

60 Eye Movement Desensitization and Reprocessing (EMDR) is a psychotherapy treatment that was originally designed to alleviate the distress associated with traumatic memories. Therapist-directed lateral eye movements are the most commonly used external stimulus, but a variety of other stimuli, including hand-tapping and audio stimulation, are often used. EMDR therapy facilitates the accessing and processing of traumatic memories and other adverse life experiences to bring these to an adaptive resolution. https://www.emdr.com/what-is-emdr/

what I would have said to my own child if I'd heard that confession. But after thanking me for telling her, all she said was, "These things happen."

My mother's words were dismissive, but I didn't let them in at first. It wasn't until later, when I told Annie how my mom responded, that I felt the impact.

Annie said, "Oh my God, Laura, I'm so sorry she said that to you."

It was through someone else's eyes that I was able to see how I was suppressing the feelings of my mother's indifferent response. Then I could cry for the little girl in me who needed her mother's comfort in a moment of vulnerability. Sometimes I need permission to feel my feelings.

I'm not mad at my mother for that response. After considering it for a while, it makes perfect sense that she would respond that way, given her age and how she moved through the world as a young woman. She learned not to make a big deal out of such things, so my confession didn't strike her as unusual or worth a big kerfuffle. She'd spent a lifetime downgrading her own experiences, so it made sense for her to do the same to mine. If she allowed herself to see the ugliness of my harm, she would have to look at her own experiences and bear their weight.

I'm vulnerable to some specific triggers, which I can attempt to avoid, like choosing not to see certain people. But others come out of nowhere—a touch, photograph, face, color, smell, tone of voice or name can pop up anywhere. When triggered, the past and present co-exist, and it's hard to separate them. I remember one time I was in public and got a strong whiff of musky body odor. Because of what happened with McLean, that smell can cause a trauma response. On this day, because my protective layers had been stripped away by the demands of litigation, I was transported into fear mode by the smell of a stranger. I tried to brush it off. I entered a grocery store and started putting things into an empty shopping cart. In the middle of the frozen food section, I started shaking violently, but not because of the freezers—I was having a panic attack. The odor had stimulated a memory, and then my body, which couldn't separate the moment from the memory, ran with it. There is no "getting over" a panic attack. You have to move through it.

Fighting back tears and trying not to make a public scene, I left the cart in the middle of the aisle. I staggered out of the store to my car, unlocked it and got in. I sobbed uncontrollably for about ten minutes, then, with shaking hands, managed to call my friend Rana. She helped me by listening and being present to my experience. Sometimes it's the emotional witnessing from a fellow survivor that allows us to come back to the present moment. Because she is part of my healing community, she is one of the people who can see all of me in a way no one else can, even from two thousand miles away.[61]

~ Jumping Through Hoops ~

In the United States, our judicial system relies on something called due process—a vigorous interrogation of the facts. People accused of crimes are presumed innocent until proven guilty beyond a reasonable doubt. A criminal defendant has the right to cross-examine witnesses, call their own witnesses and even choose not to testify. A judge must instruct the jury that their silence can't be held against them. These are some of the fundamental principles of our legal system.

On the other hand, our civil legal system is seriously lacking in these "protections" when it comes to victims of sexual crimes. The

---

61 A natural bodily response to trauma is shaking, a symptom of stress and not a sign of weakness. When animals experience fright or physical harm, they can't internalize and process it psychologically as humans do, so afterward, they just "shake it off." Shaking can be a natural healing response. If this happens to you, don't be ashamed—embrace it as your body's way of taking care of you.

civil legal system is not trauma-informed and can inflict damage on people who seek justice through it.

A civil sexual assault case re-traumatizes the victim. In my case, I was repeatedly forced to relive traumatic experiences and suffered new harm throughout the process. And the question of whether I had been raped wasn't even in dispute. No one was saying they didn't believe it happened. The case was supposed to be about accountability—how and how much I was damaged and who was to blame.

Nothing strikes at the core of our humanity like a sexual crime or comes close to the emotional and psychological trauma of being raped. I have spent my life walking around in a body that's also a crime scene, doing my best to ignore transgressions done to me physically and mentally.

Coming forward meant eliminating my denial and embracing the full reality of everything that had happened. After that, I spent the next four-plus years jumping through legal hoops and having my experience meticulously scrutinized and sterilized—not by my own coping mechanisms or my therapist, but by CTC's lawyers. I was trying desperately to embrace my humanness while others fought to discredit it.

I knew the litigation process would be long and difficult. "The wheels of justice turn slowly," Jeff Anderson told me. He wasn't kidding. I first met Jeff in August 2015; he filed my case that December. I wasn't even deposed until May 2017. During the four-plus years of legal battle, I flailed around in an emotional storm as CTC's lawyers did their dirty work. I went through psychological and vocational evaluations for both prosecution and defense teams, which included a variety of tests, including measuring my IQ and assessing my personality type. They deposed me not once but twice. They sought to depose my friends and my husband and demanded I answer written questions about every personal detail of my past. Every time I had to face yet another set of information demands or litigation tactics, I was pushed back into the deep end of the trauma pool.

I swam around for years in the boundless waters of trauma. Meanwhile, McLean ignored the court's orders that he appear for his deposition and spent his days on the beaches of Cabo San Lucas, and CTC continued to ignore its tragic history without consequence.

JAA hired professionals to do the specialty interviews, including psychological evaluations. They were conducted by respectful experts. It appeared as though they understood how hard it was for me to talk about my trauma. They tried to cause as little discomfort as possible in a process that was wearing me down, which I appreciated. Yet there is a fundamental difference between what the lawyers and specialists do in litigation and what I had to do.

The experts do this legal dance every day—they're used to the gamesmanship, the waiting, the disappointments and endless paperwork. I had to go through that same experience accompanied by my trauma and my unpacked mental baggage. I had to take a leap of faith that my lawyers would guide me safely through it. I was, and still am, a victim of epic institutional betrayal, so trusting anyone was a big ask.

During the early stages of the discovery process, a party to a lawsuit must answer "interrogatories." This meant I had to write down everything I could think of that was emotionally or physically damaging throughout my entire life, even if I thought it was irrelevant. Everything.

My preparation included reviewing the old journals I'd kept while at CTC. I discovered events and feelings I'd completely forgotten, but there they were, written in my own hand. Ironically, I wrote these journals as an assignment Donahue had given us. Decades later, they were providing evidence of my harm and his guilt.

I came across a 1983 journal entry clearly stating that I had told my friend Stacey that Rusty had raped me. Yes, I had used the word "rape." *When had I stopped using that word?* I clearly knew what rape was when I was fifteen, but as an adult, I had stopped using that word, even in my thoughts. I'd always say "molested" or "sexually assaulted." Not raped. Rape is an ugly word for an ugly act. I don't like it, yet to avoid it defuses the reality. I've worked hard to reincorporate it back into my vocabulary.

My first psychological evaluation was scheduled for spring 2017. It was meticulous and excruciating. Both legal teams would have access to all of my medical files, so there was no hiding anything. I had to dredge up every little detail of my life and discuss it in full detail with the psychiatrist. I gave her the unabridged version of my life story, everything that had ever happened to me and how it had affected my life, all the way back to my memories as a small child. I picked through the debris with her, identifying the direct wounds and collateral damage from my childhood abuse. I discussed every family member—Mom, Dad, siblings, offspring. I had to talk about how my marriage had been affected by the trauma. I had to describe each of my rapes in full detail. Nothing was off-limits. It took two days to get through the interview.

Families can suffer through the process right along with the litigant as they're jumping through the legal hoops. There wasn't a system in place to help us navigate the trauma as it came up. Litigation brought painful things to the surface for me, and there was no way it wasn't going to infiltrate my life beyond the legal proceedings. For me, when a piece of my trauma would come forward in conversations with my husband, it was like he was trying to catch a fastball with no mitt. It stung. In retrospect, we should have been doing some therapy together, so he would have had support for the unique set of issues.

Preparation for my deposition in May 2017 was simple—take a breath, don't talk over the lawyer so the court reporter can get every word, answer the questions honestly, ask for a break when I needed one, and it was okay to say, "I don't remember." Jeff warned me it could be very arduous and emotionally taxing, but he and Molly Burke would be in the room with me. He said they would get back to me when they had a date scheduled.

One afternoon, Molly called me at work to let me know the deposition date was about two weeks out, which worked for me. I asked her who would be asking me the questions, who else would be in the room, and would the insurance companies be represented? I was trying to envision the deposition to help me prepare for it.

Molly said CTC's lead defense attorney, Theresa Bevilacqua, would be doing the questioning and might have another lawyer with her. Then she said something that ran my brain off the rails—McLean could be there too.

"Wait—what? McLean might be *in the room*?" My heart started pounding. "Are you fucking kidding me?"

Molly explained that because his name was on the complaint, he had the right to be there. And since McLean no longer had a lawyer, it was possible he would show up to represent himself. For legal reasons, he would have to be informed of the date and time.

I was heading for a major panic attack, and I stopped hearing her—my head was spinning. I went outside for fresh air, called Annie on her cell and told her what I'd just heard. The very thought of going through an interrogation about my rape conducted by the person who had raped me was surreal. My body shook as I paced around the park next to the Guthrie.

Then Annie asked a simple question that helped clear my head. "Well, what if I came too? Could I be there with you?" Moments like this, when my friends rally around me, are what made it possible for me to imagine the impossible. Thank God for Annie.

"I don't know," I said. "That's a great question. I'll ask."

I called Jeff. He said Annie could not be at the deposition, but she or anyone else could be at the office with me in a side room. I complained that having McLean in the room with me was outrageous and asked how the system could allow such a threatening thing in a sexual assault case. He explained that in criminal court cases, the defendant wouldn't be allowed to be in the room for a plaintiff's deposition. But because we were in the civil system, the defendant and his lawyer had the right to be in the room. It seemed that my rapist had more rights in that situation than me.

I spent the next two weeks in a constant state of worry, riding waves of panic at the thought of seeing McLean's face at my deposition.

When the day of my deposition came, I summoned my courage and drove to St. Paul. Annie had taken the day off to be with me, and a few other plaintiffs and friends were there also for emotional support. We gathered in a conference room on the third floor of the Guardian Building, far enough away from the room where the deposition would be held for me to feel safe. Though Annie was thoughtful enough to bring some healthful food for us to nibble on, my stomach was in knots and I couldn't eat. The lawyers had a plan for how to deal with McLean if he showed up; now we just had to wait and see if he showed up.

The start time came and passed, and McLean was nowhere to be found. I was utterly relieved. All I had to worry about now was cracking myself open emotionally, revealing the details of my life in a room full of strangers, all the while hooked up to a microphone and listening to the soft tapping of the stenographer sitting by my side.

~ Mediation ~

In civil court, the judge will insist the matter go to mediation before proceeding to trial. It makes sense—if every case that's brought forward went to trial, cases would be stacked up for years. Many things can be handled with skilled mediation, and it saves a lot of time and money.

We went into mediation in the fall of 2017, almost two years after my filing. Before the meeting, Jeff Anderson told me I had the right to request "non-monetary asks" beyond a financial settlement for damages. I brought a list to the mediation meeting. The main thing I wanted from CTC was financial support for community healing. I envisioned a conference facilitated by professionals who could help us heal our wounds. Connecting with a small group of CTC alums over the past two years accelerated my healing. I wanted the same kind of healing process for the whole community, and I wanted CTC to pay for it.

It was the first time I met Kim Motes, CTC managing director, and the first time I'd seen artistic director Peter Brosius in almost twenty years. I'd left the theater not long after the incident where a little girl had fallen into the orchestra pit. I thought about the conversation we'd had after that accident—*Who is advocating for the children here?* He had cried with me and seemed to understand something about the scope of harm that occurred at the institution he'd inherited. So why had he ignored that history?

Attempting to settle through mediation seemed straightforward. I'd tell my story, and they would listen; lawyers would haggle in separate rooms; insurance companies would piss and moan because they didn't want to pay anything. I learned that retroactive claims were covered even if the theater no longer held policies with that company. This insurance biz was a whole new world for me. Mediation offered the possibility of settling out of court. I was optimistic going in. I started to think it was going to be okay.

And then it wasn't.

The legal and insurance machines took over the process, and the humanity was sucked out.[62] The insurers had their own team of lawyers fighting me and the other plaintiffs alongside CTC's defense attorneys. Two teams of lawyers were attempting to squelch the claims of plaintiffs who were sexually abused as children.

On paper, it's the job of the insurance companies to cover you for unforeseen incidents, bodily harm or property damage. In reality, though, their job is to retain as much of the company's money for as

---

62 I'm going to say this out loud—most insurance companies are fucked up. *Can I get an Amen?*

long as possible and pay as little to the claimants as they can. They make millions per year in interest alone. Insurance company owners and their lawyers don't look at victims of sexual crimes as people requiring care—they see victims as potential deductions from their multi-billion-dollar profits. There's no room for the human equation in their boardrooms; it's a business transaction.

Insurers play a numbers game based on an arbitrary list of damages that dictates what a sexual crime may cost them. If there is sexual penetration, their loss is greater than if there was no penetration. The insurance companies have established metrics for liability and price tags on harm, and survivors must prove the worth of their claims. They might just as well strap the victim to a chair under a cold interrogation light and pepper them with probing questions such as:

"Did you Scream?" *No.* (Must not have been so scary.)

"Did they have a weapon?" *No.* (Must not have been forced.)

"Did it happen again?" *No.* (Two times would have been worse—much more painful.)

"Did you tell anyone?" *No.* (Must not have been that traumatic.)

Insurers do everything they can to downgrade the experience of victims so it won't cost them as much. The legal system not only allows it, the rules of court support it. The system is so slanted in their favor that if you even mention the word "insurance" in a courtroom, it's grounds for a mistrial.

What could have been a simple payment of liability damages settled in mediation turned into a long, drawn-out battle. Complicating it at the heart, I'm sure, was the #MeToo movement, the social reckoning and the increased number of suits against the Catholic Church and the Boy Scouts of America. More and more victims have been coming forward, finding their voices, breaking their silence. Child Victim Acts have been popping up in states across the country. The insurance companies are scared. They know what's coming, and though the CTC cases were relatively small in the big scheme of things, my case could set a precedent not just for the other plaintiffs against CTC but for every future litigant who could file an insurance claim.

~ No Boundaries ~

Round one of mediation had failed, so we kept moving down the long road toward the courtroom. The process of discovery was a forensic evaluation of my life. Defense attorneys can keep asking for whatever they want until the discovery stage closes before trial.

Jeff's advice was to hide nothing. "If you do, they'll make a big deal out of whatever you're concealing." This made sense to me, so I was forthcoming with every aspect of my life. I opened myself up to total scrutiny—medical records, taxes, work evaluations, school records. I cooperated with whichever expert they sent me to, and each of their requests landed in my body as a fresh attack. Some were little jabs, others were punches to the gut. The only area in which I wish I'd drawn the line was my therapist.

Jeff cautioned me in our first meeting, informing me to be careful about what I put down in writing. Anything I wrote down could end up in the courtroom. This gave me pause because one of my tools for processing negative thinking was to write down my thoughts on paper. My thoughts weren't something I wanted on display, and Jeff was now telling me that this practice of therapeutic journaling could cause me harm if I used it. I was processing everything verbally, mostly in the safe space of my therapist's office.

We have the right to withhold our medical files. Lawyers need permission from the court or the party in question to see those records. I had granted access to literally everything they asked for, and I could have said no to giving them access to my therapist and her notes. That was my single safe space where I could say whatever came to mind unfiltered. I'd been doing some extremely challenging work with her, doing EMDR, making huge strides in my healing, and saying "yes" would give the lawyers access to everything she had ever written about me.

Jeff stood by his regular stance of hiding nothing, so I agreed to grant access, and I regret it. Not because they found anything with which to attack me—they didn't. In fact, it may have even aided my case because my therapist's testimony helped the jury understand how I'd been affected, and she gave an excellent description of how trauma is stored in the brain. My regret was simply that the only person I had to protect the most fragile part of me was her.

My most damaged self is the child within me who needed protection, wanted caring and comfort. Now, that child was being asked to stand naked in a rainstorm. What I wanted was a mother's skirt to hide behind. What I got was the blazing light of interrogation and unrelenting pressure to expose myself.

The legal process is a frightening place for a vulnerable survivor of sexual crimes. The core of my wounded humanity was on display. My therapist's office was no longer my place of private retreat. To be so completely exposed, with not one single person to hold a purely safe space for me, was inhumane. My therapist's notes would be on display to attorneys for CTC and the insurers—even McLean if he wanted them—and a jury of my peers. Defense lawyers were now figuratively in the room with me for my therapy sessions. So, I stopped doing the trauma work and quit the most helpful therapeutic process I'd ever experienced, just as I was benefiting from deep healing. It was like capping a geyser.

By winter 2017, my entire world revolved either around work or the plaintiff group and its CTC issues. Running an understaffed department at work had its own problems, and when I wasn't keeping that wheel turning, I was dealing with the legal battle, processing the death of my father, addressing my own trauma or talking to other plaintiffs about the progress of their cases. I felt anxious and stretched beyond my limits, and I didn't know how much more I could stretch.

Tensions caused by the litigation were building at home. There was almost nothing I could discuss that didn't cause more stress, so I stopped talking about anything important. I was trying to keep the tension at bay, and conflict was something I had always avoided, to my own peril.

~ An Ending and a Beginning ~

When I was younger, I was able to neatly compartmentalize my trauma, take the memories and lock them away in mental boxes. I could ignore the low hum of energy, like an electric amplifier at the lowest setting. Slowly, over time, it got louder. I'd get blasts of power to that amplifier whenever my trauma was triggered, turning the volume up to ten for stretches of time, then down to a tolerable five after my body would regulate again. During the quieter years of my life, the internal noise had leveled off to a volume I couldn't ignore but was able to tolerate.

Litigation turned the volume up to eleven, and it stayed there.

Being assaulted so young caused me to identify myself as an object, not a human being with sexual autonomy. Those rapes made me feel broken and amplified my belief that I don't have much say in what happens to my body.

Throughout the years of legal action, I was forced to look at my life through a specific lens, to open those mental boxes and dig through the memories of trauma, picking up all the pieces so I could examine them closely. And through my deepening relationships with other CTC survivors, every time I heard a new story, it helped me understand my own. My false beliefs were being stripped away. I found truths that had long been buried. This cleared pathways in my mind, bringing order to chaos and an unexpected understanding of how I'd been altered came into focus. Everything changed.

It started this way. A few months before I ended my marriage, I'd had a conversation with a close and trusted friend admitting I believed I was bisexual. I had never said that out loud, but admitting it was the beginning of embracing my sexuality. I'd always assumed that my aversion to being touched intimately was solely because of abuse, but that private confession was a gateway to a larger understanding.

I sat with it for months, turning the thought of it over in my mind like a puzzle piece in my fingers as I looked for where it went, inspecting the curved edges and colors to see how it fit within the whole picture. Then it clicked into place. How do you pluck out a puzzle piece once it's filled a hole in the picture? There are no edges to grab, and there's no other place for that piece to go other than where it belongs. Everything started to make sense. A missing piece of my puzzle had landed, and now that I saw it, I couldn't un-see it. Was I having a different trauma response and was just searching for other reasons to not have to be touched? It didn't feel that way—it felt like an awakening.

The full story of how my marriage ended, and all the reasons for it, aren't for public display. I don't want to speak for Lee, and out of respect, I won't try.

The overly simplified version is that I told him I was gay and wanted a divorce, and it broke his heart. I was blunt, abrupt and clumsy. I can't go back and change the way I did it. I wish I could. The pain felt by my family when we divorced was incalculable, and I have profound sadness about causing so much anguish to people I care about. I also know in my heart it was the right choice.

I was attracted to boys when I was younger, which is a huge reason I married a man, but I had never felt the same way about the male body as I had about the female form. I had always chalked up my fooling around with a friend's sister as an experiment in discovering bodies—a lot of people do this when they're young. I never thought it meant I was gay. My friend's sister and I hadn't done much, really, but it was enough for me to know how comfortable it was, to remember the intimacy and emotional safety I'd felt with her.

I always considered my inner fantasy world with women as a way to be sexual in the present moment, not an indication that I should be with women instead of men. Later, the understanding I gained about my trauma experiences and the gift of hindsight helped me clarify my sexuality. It was like discovering an unopened gift hidden in the corner behind the Christmas tree. Late in my marriage—too late, I know—I realized it wasn't so much that I didn't want to be touched but that I didn't want to be touched by a *man*. Unpacking this incontrovertible truth was truly life-changing.

I was standing strong and grounded in my own body for the first time in my life. Allowing myself to fully own this reality gave me full agency over my body, and I felt completely, wonderfully, and entirely normal. I'd never experienced that before. It was miraculous—and also devastating. I spent every day of the next year crying. On one hand, I had tremendous gratitude for the joy of finding that miraculous gift and opening it. But I also experienced tremendous sadness because of what this truth did to Lee and our kids. I cried more that year than I did for the preceding fifty years combined.

Other obstacles had also obscured the reality of my sexuality. My development as a sexual being had occurred forty years ago. Being homosexual was socially unacceptable, though gay men were rapidly becoming mainstream. My first memorable awareness of normalizing homosexuality was seeing the gay character Billy Crystal played in the television series *Soap* in 1977. But there was no equivalent for women. To me, lesbians were butch chicks who hated men, cut their hair short, wore men's clothing and refused to embrace femininity. That wasn't me. I liked my long hair and makeup. I wasn't that into feminine clothes, but I certainly wasn't butch. And I liked girly girls, not butch girls. There was no cultural reference pointing to something I could identify with until Ellen DeGeneres came out in 1997, and by then, I was thirty years old and married with two babies.

Ellen was the first I heard of a "Lipstick lesbian." I had never liked the word "lesbian." I found it unappealing—not because I was offended by the thought of it—I had my nose in Dad's *Playboys* all the time—but the sound of the word seemed abrasive. "Gay" is light and fluffy. But "lesbian" sounds like a chainsaw.

I've never felt so comfortable being physically and emotionally intimate as I do with another woman. Bisexual doesn't seem to fit anymore, so I have to go with lesbian—but there's that chainsaw thing. The LGBTQIA community has many terms, but gay feels like the most fitting for me. I'm a gay woman.

After I left my marriage, my first intimate encounter with a woman was a coalescing of all my parts. It's not that sex with men was bad. It was *different*. With her, I felt whole, free to be myself—unabridged, authentic, unencumbered, sensual and completely safe. I wasn't pretending to be any of those things or trying to convince myself I was. I just was. I'd never felt that before. I'm so grateful to her for that.

That relationship didn't last. I'm a survivor of sexual violence no matter who I'm with, and I was still deeply affected by my trauma. I wasn't ready. Healing is a process. I can still find myself waking up feeling paralyzed, waiting for the morning birds to sing. Even my dog rolling in bed can trigger me.

During this transformation, I was heading into the hardest stretch of the litigation process. I could not tend to a new relationship. All I could do was take care of myself and gear up for the battle ahead.

Chapter Six
Journey to Court

McLean had ignored several requests, including a court order to be deposed. Jeff Anderson went before the judge in November of 2017 on behalf of one of his victims, asking for a default judgment against McLean. The judge agreed, declared McLean guilty and gave a judgment of $2.5 million in damages. It was a victory for certain, yet also laughable because there is no way she will ever be compensated for her damages. McLean had fled to Mexico with all of his assets, and no laws allow for the collection of that money.

In spring 2018, we made a second attempt at mediation. This time no clients were in attendance, just lawyers and insurance companies hashing things out. There was no progress, and the mediation failed again. At this point, we made the decision to go to trial. Previously, litigation had been about reclaiming power and centering the survivor. Now that we were headed to the courtroom, we shifted to battle mode, and I was at the center of it.

My civil complaint had been joined with Todd Hildebrandt's back in 2015. After the second round of mediations failed, Jeff decided our cases would be separated, and I would be the first to go to trial. The judge set the trial for a date in July 2018, but in response to a motion by the defense, it was moved to September

2018. The defense then argued for another extension. The date was moved to November. Those ballsy defense attorneys asked for a third extension, clearly trying to wear us down. This time the judge changed the trial date to January 2019 but said it was the last time he would grant an extension.

Every time the trial date was moved, I was devastated; the defense team's stall tactics were working, and I was wearing down emotionally. Then they made me jump through the hoops again— another deposition, another psych eval, more interrogatories. Their argument for this was that so much time had passed—*I wonder why?*—and because I had come out of the closet. My newly outed self had to place that fresh bit of incredibly personal information under the white-hot light. I felt so unstable I was even considering going into the psych ward at one point because I felt like I was losing my goddamn mind.

~ Seventh Round ~

Lee was called in for a deposition to give them his unique perspective about how I'd been damaged. Afterward, I was livid when I found out the insurance company's lawyers used bullying tactics—peppering him with questions about my rapes and personal elements of our marriage that had no place in the conversation. In the middle of the deposition, Lee was so angry with their line of questioning that he took off his mic and left the room— Jeff threatened to report them to the bar. Things were getting ugly.

This was the most difficult year of my life. The stress at my job was at its zenith, and I'd started smoking again after leaving the marriage. McLean, of course, was nowhere in sight, basking in the Mexican sunshine avoiding all consequences of his actions.

I was at an all-time low when the law office called me. The defense now wanted all my social media profile names. My back suddenly stiffened, and I told my lawyers to say, "No."[63] I rebelliously posted the following on my Facebook page:

August 8, 2018

An open letter to the lawyers who represent the Children's Theatre Company and the institution who continues to allow them to re-victimize those who have called on them to own their history.

When I received the request yesterday to reveal my social media accounts for the defense attorneys, my first thought was, "Seriously? If you aren't already watching my social media accounts, you are incompetent." My next thought was, "They're grasping at straws." I'm not sure why this mundane request was the thing that shifted me from a place of pain to a place of strength, but it did. And there is no turning back. The dragon is awake.

I have done nothing but cooperate with you in this process. I have answered your questions with honesty and with respect of the ones who have been charged with asking them. I have exposed the deepest, most vulnerable parts of myself numerous times in order to expose truths of a community that have been buried for decades. I have been calm in the face of your tactics to wear me down. But I say, "No more."

You made a mockery of the mediation process. You have had ample time to gather your information, and yet you have requested trial dates be moved, multiple times. What you are doing is harassment, plain and simple. The system allows for you to investigate and gather information through the process of discovery,

---

63 I might have also asked them to tell the defense attorneys to go fuck themselves, which my lawyers had the good sense not to do.

but you have taken this process to despicable lows. You have insulted a member of my family by going into territory that was unnecessary and unethical, and I have lost all respect for you and what you do. How do you sleep at night? You should be ashamed of yourselves. My family is off-limits. They have been hurt enough by this process. They have nothing to do with what happened at CTC. NOTHING. They will not be bullied again. How dare you.

Victims of sexual assault are not "crime scenes," we are people. Your inability to understand trauma is inhumane and unacceptable. Not only did you put me through the ringer, you did it AGAIN, demanding that I be reevaluated, re-examined, re-deposed, insulted my family and invaded my therapeutic process so you could find something to discredit me, a person who was raped as a child. It's no wonder people don't come forward to prosecute rapists because this process is almost unbearable. As a child, it would have been impossible. But that's what you count on, isn't it? Break the victim down so they will withdraw and go back into the darkness that kept them silent.

I have to admit, it was taking its toll on me. I felt as if I wasn't sure I could withstand the pressure. Well, I'm sorry to inform you that your tactics are backfiring. I am turning your destructive intentions into my own strength, into armor, and I have an army behind me. The other 16 litigants and I are not going away. We are resolute, and the allies of the survivor community aren't going away either. Time's up.

The Children's Theatre Company does not get to ignore their responsibility. History isn't an ala carte menu. You don't get to pick and choose which parts of your history to own. If you are going to own your

50 years, the Tony Award and the prestige that goes along with it, you damn well better own the fact that the first 20 years of that theater's existence was built on the emotional, physical and sexual exploitation of children. Let's be done with this so we can get on to the much more important process of healing a theater community that is deeply wounded.

Sincerely,

Laura Stearns
Rape Survivor

I felt like a prizefighter getting a second wind in the seventh round. Over the next two months, I got three tattoos. I'd never had one before, but the time had come. The first was a symbol for truth, which I put on my forearm so I'd have a daily reminder of my commitment. The second one acknowledged the difficult legal journey for survivors of CTC. It includes eighteen dragonflies—one for each of the litigants who filed suits and one that represents those who were abused but couldn't come forward. Beneath the dragonflies are two words: Peaceful Warrior. I carry the survivors of CTC with me, always. The third tattoo is a heron in flight, a reminder of my connection to spirit and a power greater than me. These images help me focus beyond my own personal quest for justice, to center the larger fight against those who perpetrate sexual violence and to remember that my story is part of something bigger. I've moved on from the role of victim to one of advocate.

~ Evidence ~

Seventeen lawsuits were brought by child victims from the Children's Theatre Company, and twenty-eight perpetrators were identified from the time between 1965 and 1986—fifteen of them between 1979 and 1984. Over a hundred child victims were identified overall. The number of cases filed includes only the victims who were willing and able to come forward during the three-year window of the Child Victims Act. It does not reflect the countless other victims who chose not to break their silence or weren't able to. These numbers also reflect only the perpetrators who were identified by victims willing to talk, not those who are still in the shadows. Nor do they reflect the number of students who were assaulting each other.

The environment at CTC in the 1980s was a cesspool of harm. A perfect storm developed from numerous dark elements—the cult of personality centering around John Clark Donahue, the way in which kids were groomed as part of the artistic culture, how Donahue used students' love of art as a tool to lure and control them, the nest of perpetrators who gathered in the safe haven of CTC, the complicity of many adults, the way in which the community failed to intervene, the lack of justice from a "system" that failed us, the ongoing reverence for Donahue and shunning of anyone who told the truth.

Some victims have described situations in which Donahue brought them to parties where they were trafficked to other men in attendance, and in some cases, Donahue and other staff members attempted to, or succeeded, in coercing children to participate in the filming of pornographic child abuse images. This is the dark underbelly of what was happening behind the scenes.

JAA collected a mountain of evidence unprecedented in Jeff Anderson's career, and it just kept growing. "I've never seen anything like it in forty years of doing this work," Jeff told me.

As we were seated in the conference room, Jeff said they had enough boxes of information to fill the entire surface of the huge conference table. Then he set his cell phone on the table using its size to illustrate and said, "This is the amount of evidence that will actually make it into the courtroom."

There are countless rules about what's allowed in court. Lawyers argue for what should or shouldn't be allowed, and the judge makes the final call. During the trial, evidence that seemed obviously relevant to me was rejected, and some things I thought were irrelevant were allowed. It became clear that only part of the true story was going to be told in the courtroom—a very small part.

In this case, we walked a tightrope. If we proved that those who were running the institution back in the 1980s knew what was happening, that would mean they had "intent" and engaged in "willful concealing of harm," which would take them out of their insurance coverage. Therefore, we had to prove only that they *should* have known, not that they *did* know.

We had enough proof to take down CTC completely, but we weren't interested in putting them out of business. This tightrope, however, made Jeff's job difficult—proving to the jury enough to get the point across, yet not too much.

~ Touring the Building ~

Jeff wanted to go into the theater to videotape areas of the building to give context to the jury, not only for my case but for subsequent trials if it came to that. Because I knew the building so well, he asked if I'd accompany the team. He wanted me to point out certain places, including the showers where Donahue abused students and a specific bathroom in which a plaintiff said he was raped. I agreed but didn't want an entourage.

On December 3, 2018, on a night when the theater was usually closed, Kim was to let us in; and because CTC had the right for a legal representative to be present, Theresa Bevilacqua would also be there. Though we all agreed to these conditions, the CTC team showed up not just with Bevilacqua, but also lawyers for the insurance companies. These were the attorneys who had treated my ex-husband so despicably at his deposition. I was furious; just having them present felt like an attack.

"I don't have to talk to them, do I?" I asked Jeff and Molly .

"You don't even have to look at them if you don't want to," Molly said.

So, I didn't. I pulled all my feelings inside, walked past them and tried to pretend they weren't there. For the most part, they were well-behaved, though Molly and I heard them making off-color jokes at one point, like improper guests at a funeral.

Going through the building after so many years was strange and difficult. I know people who won't even go to Minneapolis because of what happened to them at CTC, let alone set foot in the building.

We rode the elevator to the fourth floor; we visited the dance studio first. Memories flooded my brain—meeting Donahue for the first time at my audition for the school, seeing all those faces in the doorway of kids who would eventually become my friends, countless dance classes and auditions. I remembered exactly where I'd been standing when I botched the song for my audition for *Mr. Pickwick's Christmas*. I tried to compartmentalize as we moved through the building, describing what things had been like. I pointed out the locker rooms with the showers for Jeff so he could make a note of their location.

In the long hallway, I spotted a gigantic potted *monstera deliciosa*, a huge plant with large leaves. This plant had been sitting in that very spot more than thirty-five years earlier. It was large back then but now reached all the way to the ceiling. *If only plants could talk.*

Next, we visited the recording studio and then the Studio Theater, where James Earl Jones had visited our class. This space was less familiar because it had been turned into office spaces. We made our way to the lower floors via the stairway.

As I started down the steps, I recognized what was happening inside my body. My coping mechanisms had kicked in. My body was dysregulated, and I was emotionally dissociated. From the outside, I looked calm, but my legs were shaking so badly that I tightly gripped the railing so I wouldn't fall. I whispered to Molly that I was having trouble, so if I tumbled down the stairs, she would know there was a reason for it.

One flight down, I pointed out the bathroom in the hallway outside Donahue's office, the one Jeff had asked about. Strangely, the grand staircase that used to lead down to the main lobby was gone. I wondered why it had been removed.

Then we entered Donahue's office—it was empty but for two chairs. The windows overlooking the stage were boarded up. The striking inlay wood pattern on the floor was the same as several other rooms in the building. Sadness and anger began to swirl inside me, and then I felt the familiar shutting off of emotions. I wasn't going to cry—my body wouldn't let me, not there.

The room was eerie—I had heard many stories about abuse in that office and that there used to be a keyed lock on the inside of the door that had no keyhole on the other side. This meant that Donahue had the ability to lock the door from the inside, making it impossible for someone to enter the office unannounced or for someone to leave without the key. The current administration wasn't even using it for storage. Seeing it like that, empty and void of purpose, told me they knew this room was filled with bad energy. They didn't use it because they didn't feel comfortable putting anything in it.

Then I realized why they'd removed the staircase from the lobby—they didn't want people to go anywhere near that office.

We walked through the theater itself, backstage and down to the basement dressing rooms. Memories followed me like ghosts. I half-expected to see the gigantic cast photograph on the wall of the green room, but it was gone, likely in a landfill somewhere, buried like the rest of the history.

After the exhausting tour, I went to bed and slept hard. For the next several days, I walked around dissociated from my emotions. I called in sick and was incapacitated for an entire day.

An ironic sign from an old set hanging in the scene shop at CTC,
taken during my tour of the building: *Speak the Truth or Perish.*
Photo: Laura Stearns

~ No Relief ~

Jeff Anderson told me he doesn't typically let plaintiffs be present
for the entire trial— he wants to prevent re-traumatizing his clients.
He prefers to have plaintiffs only in the courtroom for their own
testimony. I was committed to being there. I wanted to hear my
friends speak the truth out loud in a courtroom. He said he'd think
about it, but I was insistent. Still reeling from the CTC tour, I
did more trial prep with a focus group comprised of anonymous
people from the community who listened to the evidence and my
testimony and then provided feedback to the legal team. Apparently,
it's standard practice. When I finished my part, I left the room, and
Jeff stayed with the mock jury, so he didn't see me go into a side
room and plummet into an emotional spiral. I wanted to debrief
with him, but he was in the focus group room pointing at charts.

I perform well in front of an audience, so Jeff couldn't see how
rattled I was. This is one of the places where attunement on the

part of my lawyer would have made a huge difference in keeping me centered emotionally and mentally. What appeared as a little thing, walking me out of the room and seeing if I was okay before plowing forward with the practice session, would have made a huge difference in the overall emotional weight I was carrying as a plaintiff and survivor. Small misstep on his part—huge impact on me.

After all these stressors, I needed a break. I gave myself the gift of a week-long vacation to visit friends in California over the new year. A few days in, I got a call from Jeff asking me if I'd be willing to go and see a Los Angeles expert in trial preparation who happened to be available that week. I'm a practical person, so instead of saying, "I can't believe you're asking me this. I'm on a *vacation* to get away from this shit," instead, I said, "Sure, what time?"

Because life keeps moving, I still had to live in the world when I got back to Minneapolis. Everyone was going about their business, but I could barely get out of bed. I was emotionally fragile and operating on automatic pilot, trying to keep myself fed and get my work done. I went shopping at Target and, in the middle of the store, had a panic attack. I was overwhelmed by the number of things surrounding me—*too many things*—and the noise of the shoppers was a disorienting cacophony. I left without purchasing anything.

Two hours later, I got a call from Jeff telling me he wasn't going to allow me in the courtroom for anything but my own testimony. He said he didn't want me exposed to the potentially damaging environment of the courtroom. But the real reason my lawyers neglected to inform me of my legal right to be at my own damn trial was because the courts are biased in favor of the insurance companies and their compassionless pricelist for damages from sexual violence.

Because Rape Culture trivializes the damage to victims of sexual abuse, Jeff believed that if the jury saw me as less than completely destroyed by my trauma, then they would be less likely to believe I had been significantly damaged. If I had ended up in a mental institution or taken a blade to my wrists, apparently, that would have demonstrated tremendous damage.

Jeff didn't want the jury to say, "She looks fine to me. So what's she complaining about?"

I had beat the shit out of myself for decades and become a nihilistic perfectionist instead of a drug addict, but on the outside, I looked like a success, so I must not have been damaged.

I had no interest in hearing defense witnesses and the lies I knew they would tell, but I wanted desperately to be there for my friends and to be a witness to the unfolding of the truth. I'd drawn strength and focus over the years of preparation, knowing that the true history would be revealed and I would get to see it, so I was absolutely gutted by the decision to keep me out of the courtroom. It was like being the chief engineer of the space shuttle and being told, "You're not allowed to watch the take-off. Furthermore, no pictures or video will be taken, so you'll just have to imagine it. You'll be able to read about it, and the people who are there to witness it will tell you what it was like, but you don't get to see it."

In a nightmare that night, I was lying on my bed and Molly was sitting on the end of it looking in the other direction. I was being raped, unable to say a word, and she was oblivious to it. I woke up crying uncontrollably.

I was extremely angry at Jeff, but I felt like I had no choice in the matter. I seriously considered going into the courtroom in disguise. I had access to everything I needed at work—clothes, wigs, makeup. I could even have gone as a man. It would have been brilliant—or a complete disaster. What stopped me was the fear of getting caught in full disguise going through security. *Excuse me ma'am, would you mind stepping to the side?*

On the Saturday before the trial started, Jeff called me. He told me there was an offer on the table.

I had questions. "What will happen to the evidence if I settle? Will it go into the public record?" No.

"In your opinion, if I settle, is it likely the other cases will settle too? Will the outcome of my case set a precedent?" Jeff believed it would.

"What happens if the other cases settle out of court—will the evidence go into the public record?" No.

"Will the truth about what really happened be fully revealed without that?" No.

"If we go into court but decide to settle out of court before the trial ends, what happens to the evidence—does it go into the public record?" Yes.

Jeff also said that CTC would not be willing to admit any wrongdoing publicly or release any of the evidence that had been collected so the larger story could be known. My decision was clear. "Then I guess I need to walk into that courtroom," I said.

And that was that. I turned down the offer so the truth could be told.

~ Walking into the Room ~

The first day was for jury selection, so I couldn't attend. I went to work thinking I could just go about the business of my life, but I was completely distracted and too emotional—and that was just the first day. I felt it would be irresponsible for me to just disappear from my job, but my assistants told me they could handle everything. They were right, so I told my boss I needed some time off for my mental well-being.

I left work and went into full-time self-care, something I almost never do. It felt weird, but my body was screaming at me to take care of it, so I tried. A couple of days later, I got a bouquet of flowers from my "Guthrie Family" wishing me well.

Just one article appeared in the *Minneapolis StarTribune* announcing the start of the trial.[64] After that first day, only one news

---

64 Rohan Preston, "First Trial Begins in Children's Theatre Suits," *Minneapolis*

segment was broadcast on a local news channel. Then—a deafening silence until the trial was over. Judge Francis McGill had said he didn't want a media circus, so Jeff Anderson couldn't rally the media.

Jeff didn't argue the issue. This contradicted his earlier exhortations to get Court TV in the room, which I was all for. As it happened, the largest theater for children in the country was in a courtroom charged with nurturing a nest of pedophiles who had sexually abused countless children—and no one was paying attention. I guess it was old news; it had happened so long ago. Not one reporter was assigned to the courtroom to cover the trial.

The trial lasted from January 14th to the 31st. I took the witness stand on January 24th and 25th. Other than the eight hours I spent testifying, I was home, trying to distract myself and wondering what was going on in that courtroom where my life was being debated. Annie sat with me most days so I wouldn't be alone. She'd bring her guitar, and we folded a lot of origami.

At the end of each day, Jeff called with updates on the proceedings, and people who had testified or were scheduled for the next day would come over. We commiserated; we found solace in each other's company, laughed and cried. It was helpful, but I still felt deprived of my rightful seat at the table and being present for my friends as they bravely spoke the truth.

One evening, as a group of us sat in my living room, we shared some of our stories with each other, and one of the litigants shared a name I didn't want to hear. I'd heard so many names of perpetrators over the years, but this one hit me in a different way because it was a well-known member of the community. I crossed the room and hugged my friend as the reality of it sank in. I said the words I doubt he will ever hear from his abuser, "I'm so sorry."

Jina and Melissa both testified and had named McLean in their own suits. Rana had escaped his attempts at assaulting her, though she testified about it as well as the abuse she endured at the hands of others. These brave women, and the other former students who testified, were critical for laying the foundation of the culture of complicity at CTC. They stepped forward on my behalf.

I wanted something in the courtroom to represent me. I asked the assistants of the legal team if they would help coordinate the passing of a personal totem for each witness to hold while on the stand. They agreed, and I chose a beautiful crystal and stone amulet made for me by my dear friend Rhiannon. It had been in my purse for more than a year—in my pocket on especially difficult days—as a totem of protection and a reminder to take care of myself. The small stones and crystals—spun easily between my fingers—were connected to a brass ring by wire. It had great meaning to me and was the perfect size for this purpose.

Some evenings it came back to me at home, clenched in the hand of the person who had testified that day so I could hold it and feel connected to the collective effort. Then it would return to the courtroom for the next day. This gesture on behalf of the witnesses and the legal team helped me immensely.

I held the amulet while waiting to testify on the day I was called to the courthouse. I could feel the energy of those who had held it while testifying before me. They were with me—but something was missing. I grabbed a pen and wrote on a napkin some names of people I knew had been abused but hadn't come forward. I wanted a tangible reminder of them with me too.

Sitting in the hallway, I recalled that Jeff had suggested I allow myself to be the most vulnerable Laura, to remove the camouflage that kept my wounds hidden. I knew the only way to do that was to let the fullness of the damage inside me come to the surface so I could feel it without any buffer. And that's what I did. I felt it all. I looked at my shaking hands, amulet in one, napkin with names in the other, took a deep breath, stood up and walked into the courtroom.

I had asked some friends to be in the courtroom with me when I testified, including Shanan and Rhiannon. I could see them as I entered the room. I had asked everyone who had testified to describe the room to me, and it was what I'd expected. As I walked toward the judge, everyone watched me. A friend told me later that I looked regal as I floated through the room—that's not how I felt. *Don't judge a book by its cover.*

The amulet Rhiannon made for me that provided the link between the witnesses. Photo: Laura Stearns.

I was sworn in, and as I sat down, I looked at the jury. At that moment, I was grateful for all the work I'd done with the trial expert in Los Angeles. She had told me those people were there for *me*, to witness my story, to listen. All I had to do was invite them to be with me through my eye contact and by truthfully answering questions. I was instructed to look directly at them, not the lawyers, when giving my answers. Because of this advice, I didn't see them as adversaries but as supporters. Most of them reciprocated by looking directly into my eyes—a couple of them looked bored. After my years in theater, I knew to ignore the snores you might hear from an audience member, so I wasn't thrown by it. I focused on those who engaged with me and didn't worry about the rest.

With the prior supporting witnesses, Jeff had already established the culture of grooming at the theater, so I didn't have to testify about that. Lee and my therapist had testified earlier that day to share their perspectives of how my life had been affected. Ellie also testified on my behalf and told of the written account I'd read to her about being raped by McLean, how I'd burned it and sent it down the river. My role was to talk directly about McLean's grooming, the rape, and how destructive it had been to me.

For a sexual assault survivor, a courtroom is no place for justice. It's a wounding room—a place where victims are re-victimized and skilled adversaries dissect the experience of survivors who cannot defend themselves because to do so characterizes them as a fighter, not a victim. We victims need to look and act the part. Survivors are shackled to their pain, and there is no moment when they can stand up and let out a primal roar of self-protection. They need to keep the most vulnerable pieces of themselves exposed to that blazing hot light.

In a murder trial, the focus is on how heinous the act was, not how dead the victim is. If it's a trial for armed robbery, the focus is on the act of robbery and the value of what was taken, not the person who was robbed. You never hear, "Are you sure you didn't do something to make that person believe you wanted them to rob you?" No, people steal things, and when they're caught, they suffer the consequences because we understand the value of tangible things—like money and property—and disavow things we don't understand—like the physical and psychological cost to victims of sexual violence.

I was robbed of my birthright to healthy intimacy and a sense of agency over my own body.

Trial for a sexual assault survivor is about exposing hidden scars, which are poked and prodded and made to bleed again. If you don't bleed, you must not be hurt. If you didn't end up in the psych ward, you must be lying when you say you felt like you were going crazy. You can't let the jury see you strong if you're trying to show them how broken you are. It's not about justice; it's about how the insurance company's lawyers "rate" your damage.

When seeking emotional and psychological damages in a civil case, everything is on the table. That is, the defendant is allowed to blame my damages on anything and everything that ever happened to me—my family life, the other rapes, my marriage, my history of depression—anything that could be used to decrease CTC's responsibility. The defendant is looking to distract and deflect attention away from the actual cause of harm. While this is the defense attorney's job, a lawyer's job, it is despicable from the eyes of the person who suffered the harm.

Most of my testimony is a blur. I dissociated while giving it and have blocked most of it. I've read the transcript, but I don't remember saying the words. What I remember most is looking at the list of names—I'd set the napkin on the counter in front of me—and the feel of the amulet in my hand.

Jeff asked a lot of questions, and I answered them directly to the jury as instructed. When I was cross-examined by Bevilacqua, who had conducted both of my depositions, I was required to describe every single one of my rapes in full detail. When pressed for the names of my other abusers, I looked at the judge and said, "Do I really have to say their names? How is this relevant?" He wasn't unkind in his expression, in fact, he looked a bit uncomfortable, but in the end, I had to say their names.

At the end of her cross-examination, Bevilacqua quoted something I had said to Wendy Lehr in a conversation with her and her husband Gary Briggle after I'd filed my case. They had told me how sorry they were about what happened with McLean and how they had no idea "those kinds of things" were happening at CTC. I had said that I understood how she could have "not known" about what Donahue was doing.

What I meant by this comment was I understand willful ignorance—the ability of a person not to see something or to ignore things that are right in front of them. I was not letting her off the hook for putting blinders on; I was saying I understood that she could have them. But Bevilacqua used my own words against me, insinuating that even I—the victim—understood how Wendy was not aware of the abuse happening at the theater. She made me look like a liar for bringing this whole thing into a courtroom while knowing the theater wasn't responsible.

When I tried to articulate what I meant, it came out all jumbled. I'm not sure the jury got my point. I wished I had practiced answering questions in cross-examination during my trial preparation—the focus was always on telling the truth, never role-playing how to respond if I was being bullied during questioning. Another misstep.

There were other female students who had been assaulted by McLean, one of them violently over a period of about a year, yet they were not allowed to testify. We were told it was because their abuse had happened after mine. And yet, Judge McGill allowed the current CTC Managing Director Kim Motes to take the stand and talk about how great the theater is today and list all the policies they now have in place to protect kids. Her testimony referred to developments that occurred after my rape. CTC's current reputation and policies are completely irrelevant to what happened thirty-five years earlier.

It felt unfairly contradictory, allowing them to flaunt the righteousness of their present actions, yet I was forced to describe rapes that happened to me after CTC, and had nothing to do with McLean. It was a great strategy—to give the jury a reason to feel bad for CTC and to blame my significant trauma on what happened after I left.

After regarding a photograph of me at the age of fifteen that was shared on a projector, Bevilacqua looked at the jury and said, "She looks a lot older than fifteen." This coming from a female lawyer in the year 2019 is infuriating. She might just as well have added, "Clearly, she had it coming." This kind of dismissive comment about a victim of child abuse is one of the many ways our legal system perpetuates Rape Culture.

When I finished testifying, I quickly exited, followed by several people. I was in a thick fog. I started to cry and walked toward nothing specific, just away from the pain of what I'd experienced. I could hear people saying I did great, but my eyes were searching for something—I didn't know what—and then they landed on Todd. I had no idea he would be there to catch me when I left the courtroom and didn't know how important it would be to have him there. I rushed into his arms and sobbed. There were other survivors there too, and we held each other and cried in that hallway.

~ Unearthing ~

The trial continued without me. I spent the following days unable to sleep for more than forty-five minutes at a time, and then with the TV volume up to obliterate the noise in my head. (Sorry, neighbors.)

I didn't get to see anyone testify. However, I did read the transcript of the trial, watch depositions and study evidence while researching for this book. Volumes could be written just about the things discovered through the litigation process, Donahue's escapades and how the Children's Theatre Company chose to handle it. It's difficult material for me to look at, and at times research for this book felt like self-flagellation, immersing myself in the trauma pool on purpose.

The following former CTC employees and board members willingly chose to go into the courtroom and testify for the defense at my trial:

- Wayne Jennings—former director of education for the conservatory school

- Jay Bush–former general manager
- Winthrop Rockwell–former board member
- Jon Cranney–former artistic director
- Mary Winchell–former stage manager
- Wendy Lehr–former company actress and teacher

Even if these defense witnesses did not intend to be hurtful to me, they were. Someday, perhaps I won't be angry, but right now, I hold my anger as a shield. It's an act of self-preservation, a gift to myself to no longer be willing to put my mental wellbeing at risk in order to uphold someone else's false reality.

I do recognize that some of these people experienced trauma at CTC as well, in a variety of forms. Donahue was an abusive megalomaniac as well as a pedophile, and he left many damaged people in his wake. Still, of those who testified for the defense of CTC, I can't easily let them off the hook. Donahue and Frank McGovern did not appear in court, but disturbing clips from their depositions were played for the jury during the trial.

The following information is part of the public record, evidence presented at trial and depositions taken by JAA:

John Clark Donahue

Donahue was McLean's boss, the person responsible for overseeing him as an employee. A section of Donahue's deposition from 2017 was played during the trial;[65] he wasn't called into court because of his health. Jeff Anderson asked Donahue if he was aware of McLean's abuse of me and other female students:

> *Donahue: Well, I'm not…to the extent that I paid any attention, I wasn't paying attention to that, you know, the drama of his…romance, if you will, at all, I was*

---

65 Video Deposition of John Clark Donahue, timestamp 13:00:32, given January 24, 2017

paying attention to how he was acting in the plays.

Anderson: Who was supposed to be paying attention to the drama of his romance with those, with those girls?

Donahue: The girls themselves, I suppose [he laughs].

Anderson: They were minors, weren't they?

Donahue: I don't know, uh, I don't, that they'd, I'm not saying that I knew anything about that, I didn't. But, ya know, [swatting his hand and acting as if he is one of the girls] "Hey, don't touch me."

As if saying "don't touch me" would have been enough to deter an act of sexual violence. It's disturbing to watch. I have to say, though, his comments were, sadly, fully in line with who he was. He was the leader of the pack, the one who set the precedent. And his attitude shows exactly what it was like there.

The collected evidence identified a total of twenty-three victims of criminal sexual assault by Donahue.

Wendy Lehr

In Wendy Lehr's deposition from October 24, 2018,[66] my lawyer Molly Burke asked her about statements that had been given by former students stating they'd told Lehr about Donahue's abuse or they knew she was aware of what he was doing. Some of them have told me this as well.

> *Burke: Do you have any sense, in your experience, about why any victim of child sex abuse at Children's Theatre would say that you had information about abuse at the theater?*
>
> *Lehr: I, I would think it was a misapprehension.*

---

66 Video Deposition of Wendy Lehr, timestamp 12:13:31, given October 24, 2018

Burke: And what do you mean by that?

Lehr: That they thought it was true, but it wasn't true, and it could be, speculation, a kind of paranoia?

She could just as easily have said she didn't know or remember any such confessions. Instead she chose to insinuate that these survivors are crazy. If you're one of the people who told her you were being abused, I want you to know—*you are not crazy.*

Frank McGovern

A clip of Frank McGovern's deposition was played at trial.[67] According to him, he barely knew the names of any students, we didn't hang out in his office, none of us lived at his house—we were basically erased by him, even his girlfriend of five years who lived with him. He said "no" to every single question I knew was a "yes." His cavalier attitude while spewing this garbage was gut-wrenching to watch because of our personal history.

Jason McLean

McLean never showed up for any of his scheduled depositions and ignored a court order to appear. He didn't testify at trial, but there was plenty of evidence presented in the courtroom in his stead.

It was not uncommon for McLean to act inappropriately with girls backstage. He didn't hide it. A former student testified that during *The Cookie Jar*, he would harass the teenage girls, licking their necks and manhandling them. She went to a stage manager to complain and was told the behavior wasn't okay, but the stage manager did nothing to stop him.[68] It was up to the student to take the report further to get him to stop. McLean was eventually told to stop by management and to apologize to the girls, which he did,

---

67 Video Deposition of Francis McGovern, given November 8, 2018
68 Stearns v. CTC No. 27-CV-15-20713, testimony of Marta Hartman, trial transcript, pp. 48–53

but the behavior only stopped with the girl who had complained. He continued to harass other girls.

In trial exhibit #136, the Memorandum of Understanding dated October 22, 1984, presented by Interim Executive Director John B. Davis and signed by McLean when he was re-instated in the acting company, states: "His [McLean] social contact with actresses under the age of eighteen and female students of the Children's Theatre and School shall be confined exclusively to officially sponsored Children's Theatre Company and School events at which time(s) he will exercise great discretion in terms of engaging in private conversations with students."[69] This piece of paper was meaningless to McLean, and he continued to abuse female students right up until his dismissal in January 1986. It was completely improper to have such an agreement and not warn anyone that McLean was a threat. CTC failed to supervise McLean and continued to give him unlimited access to and authority over female students.

Side note: This letter is proof that CTC was fully aware of the change in the age of the consent statute from sixteen to eighteen years old, so when Fogelberg was caught in spring 1985, he should have been reported and prosecuted, not simply fired.

A former apprentice testified at trial that McLean and a few other adult staff members would discuss which girls in the school they intended to "deflower." In his deposition, company actor Gary Briggle tells about McLean bragging to him about his sexual conquests. "I like to be the first," he told Gary. Though he confessed in his deposition that he thought it was a disturbing comment, apparently, Gary didn't seem to think it was worth reporting.

During the conversation I had with him and Wendy after I filed my lawsuit, they told me that when they found out McLean

---

69   Stearns v. CTC No. 27-CV-15-20713 trial exhibit #136, Memorandum of
     Understanding between McLean and interim Executive Director, John B.
     Davis, signed October 22, 1984

was being investigated, they went to him and asked him if there was any truth to the rumors. McLean denied it, telling them he'd done nothing wrong. They chose to believe him even though Gary had heard him bragging about such things. Gary also describes how in the summer of 1984, while he was working at a theater in Florida, McLean called him and asked to stay with him there while he was being investigated by the BCA. Gary said "yes," and McLean went "on the lam" in Florida.[70]

Jon Cranney and Jay Bush

McLean, who had stayed on staff at CTC after his reinstatement in the fall of 1984, continued to abuse several girls at the school.[71] New CTC Artistic Director Jon Cranney claimed he found out McLean was "breaking the rules" with students and he fired him, and admitted under oath that he didn't report him to child protective services.[72] McLean claims he wasn't fired but chose to resign and presented Cranney with a resignation letter. In his letter, McLean cited his reasons for leaving were rumors and innuendo about his "easy rapport" with students, and he requested a severance package which included the theater to pay off any fines to Actors Equity, the continuation of his salary and benefits through the end of the season, agreement not to contest his unemployment insurance claim, erasure of any and all negative citations regarding the "ethics of my behavior with students that may appear on my employment record with CTC," and "the striking of any and all negative remarks which may appear on the records of students appertaining to me."[73] General Manager Jay Bush agreed to all of it in writing. McLean

---

70 Video Deposition of Gary Briggle, transcript pages 81–84 given October 24, 2018

71 Protected victim statements and depositions with Jeff Anderson and Associates

72 Stearns v. CTC No. 27-CV-15-20713, testimony of John Cranney, trial transcript, pp. 1623–1633.

73 Stearns v. CTC No. 27-CV-15-20713, trial exhibit #139, resignation letter of McLean, dated January 15, 1986

wasn't reported to the authorities for his behavior. Evidence shows that Bush also was aware Donahue might be abusing young boys as far back as the mid-seventies and chose to do nothing about it.[74]

These men were mandated reporters—if they knew or had reason to believe something was happening between McLean and students, and children were being harmed, they were obliged to report him—not fire him, agree to his demands and pay him off. They basically colluded with McLean to hide his crimes. Maybe the fact that Jennings and Creeger got off the hook two years earlier for failing to report allowed them to feel they didn't have an obligation to protect kids, that it was more important to get rid of the problem quietly to not draw negative attention to the theater again. So once again, McLean wasn't held accountable. This is a critical moment in the continued strategy at CTC to bury the truth and sacrifice the well-being of children.

Wayne Jennings

Wayne Jennings, the director of education for the Conservatory School, who was indicted by the grand jury in 1984, was the one who provided training to the academic staff on mandatory reporting, yet no training was ever given to the theater school staff or the acting company.[75]

Mary Hallman, a parent of a CTC student, testified at my trial for the prosecution, stating she went to Jennings on two occasions in 1982 and told him that she knew of specific children who were being abused by Donahue. Jennings told her he didn't feel there was cause to do anything. Hallman considered this an unacceptable answer, and when she pressed Jennings, he was dismissive and

---

74 Stearns v. CTC No. 27-CV-15-20713, testimony of Janet Warren, trial transcript, p. 1748

75 Video Deposition of Wendy Lehr, timestamp 11:27:48, given October 24, 2018

called her "a bored housewife."[76]

Another parent, Ina Haugen, testified at my trial as well. She had told Jennings she knew of Donahue's inappropriate sexual activity with boys in the spring of 1983. Jennings, instead of going to the BCA, went to Donahue and told him about Ina's accusation. Donahue denied wrongdoing and wanted to know the names of the students, which Ina did not provide.[77]

Additionally, Ina Haugen was part of a parent's group and recalled a written statement from one parent survey in spring 1983 where the parent complained about the education their child was getting at the conservatory school. "My child doesn't know anything about Medgar Evers," it read, "but they know everything about John Donahue's sex life."

Right after Donahue's arrest, while sitting at her dining room table with a group of other concerned parents, Haugen received a phone call from someone at the theater telling her not to talk to anyone, like the press. Haugen told me, "It totally changed my view of news and news reporters because if we don't talk to them, they don't get the whole story." After that call, Ina became one of the most outspoken parents.

"I trusted them to take care of the kids," Ina recalled to me in a conversation. "I'll never get over how betrayed I felt, how betrayed I still feel, and with that comes the guilt you feel as a parent."

Our parents had assumed we were all in good hands.

Items of note

- A former student testified that a local liquor store allowed students to charge liquor on the CTC charge account if

---

76 Stearns v. CTC No. 27-CV-15-20713, testimony of Mary Hallman, trial transcript, pp. 57–60
77 Stearns v. CTC No. 27-CV-15-20713, testimony of Ina Haugen, trial transcript, pp. 63–71, and eyewitness statements

they were wearing a grey CTC T-shirt or sweatshirt with the company logo on it—a standard part of the uniform—which would allow them to avoid showing any form of identification.[78]

- While reading my trial transcript, I came across an argument between counsel and the judge regarding evidence the prosecution wanted to present. In 1982 a CTC acting company member had sent a letter to a former girlfriend of McLean's informing her that she was aware McLean was having sex with a thirteen-year-old student. The former girlfriend was willing to testify at my trial regarding this exchange, even came to the courthouse, but wasn't allowed to testify because she no longer had the letter.[79]

- After his arrest, Minneapolis city records show that Donahue transferred the deed of his home to the Minneapolis Society of Fine Arts, the entity that had sold him the home for one dollar and owned the property on which the theater was built.[80] Why would MSFA protect Donahue's house? The records show that MSFA transferred the deed back to Donahue in 1986. When I first saw this document, I assumed the transfer would make it so his home would not be at risk in the multiple civil suits he had filed against him, but the civil suits were settled in 1987. This whole transaction is suspicious. I don't know what it means, though it does show the roots of connection to the MSFA and the Minneapolis Institute of Arts go deep. I showed this public record to

---

78 Stearns v. CTC No. 27-CV-15-20713, testimony of Karen Hagen, trial transcript, pp. 85–87

79 Stearns v. CTC No. 27-CV-15-20713, trial transcript conversation between council and Judge McGill, pp. 480–484

80 City of Minneapolis Block 6 Record, ADN 17090, GEO Galpin's Addition to Minneapolis, and State of Minnesota Department of Taxation Form 7-M, #3992242

investigative reporter Brandon Stahl in 2019. He found it compelling and looked into it but was unable to do a story about it because he ran into "roadblocks." He wasn't specific about what those were.

- In 1984, editor-publisher Tim Campbell of *The GLC Voice* wrote a feature article in support of Donahue, advocating for the views of the Man-Boy Love Association (MAN-BLA).[81] But he was not the only one who voiced support for this obscene affiliation. According to the eyewitness account of executive assistant John Humleker, a company member went to the office of executive director Sarah Lawless on several occasions, telling her CTC should publicly declare its support for MAN-BLA.

Additional perpetrators

A total of twenty-eight perpetrators were identified between 2015 and 2019 during the investigation for the lawsuits. Not all of them were named in official court documents but appear in protected victim statements. Many of these men were victims of Donahue when they were children and went on to perpetrate against others, continuing a cycle of abuse. Others I would consider serial abusers who suffer from some form of pathology. All of them committed crimes.

I decided not to name specific perpetrators who don't intersect directly with my own story. Their victim's stories are not mine to tell. However, I will say this: I have a sliver of hope that someday these abusers will come to a place where they truly desire to heal the wounds they caused. With highly skilled facilitation from people with expertise in the powerful process of transformative justice,[82]

---

81 Deborah Caulfield, "The Scandal at the Children's Theatre," *LA Times Calendar*, July 22, 1984, p. 4

82 Transformative Justice aims to transform the conditions that enabled the

there are those of us who would be willing to participate if the desire for healing was authentic on the part of those who caused harm.

As I read transcripts and watched depositions, it was extraordinary to see the level of denial and outright lies that came from the mouths of people I'd always loved and considered friends and mentors. Those who won't look at their own participation in the institutional betrayal, direct abuse or enabling of abusers, hold themselves in their own prison of shame and denial by not acknowledging the truth. It's troubling that every single person who was an adult at CTC when Donahue was in charge chose to continue lies and not do the hard emotional work of looking honestly at their own participation in protecting the institution and silencing victims.

~ The Verdict ~

Closing arguments were presented on January 30, 2019. I heard them later because I asked Jeff Anderson to present them to those of us who weren't allowed in the courtroom or couldn't emotionally bring themselves to be there. In his argument, Jeff pointed out no fewer than twenty-three moments in which the Children's Theatre Company could have made a different choice to protect the children instead of the institution and chose not to.

On Thursday, January 31, 2019, we got the call from the court's clerk that the verdict was in. Jeff was in high-energy mode, feeling good about how everything had gone. I was in a daze. Other plaintiffs and a few of my close friends met us at the courthouse.

I watched the jury enter. They were looking at me with compassion. Jeff had told me that if juries look at the plaintiffs, it's a good sign because it means they sided with them. If they don't, it

---

harm, at the same time as facilitating repair for the harm, by cultivating accountability, healing, resilience, and safety for all.
https://www.sace.ca/learn/transformative-restorative-justice/

means they sided with the defense. I took their demeanor as a good sign. I held Molly Burkes's hand under the table as the verdict was read.

The way the instructions were given to the jury was confusing. It wasn't like in *Law and Order* when they give a straight-up guilty or not guilty verdict, and the credits roll. The jury had two main questions to answer and then a bunch of yes's or no's regarding damages.

To the question of CTC's negligence, they answered "yes." Tears of relief streamed down my face—that one word said it all. Then they read the answer about liability. The answer was no.

Molly squeezed my hand—something was wrong, though I didn't know what. Then they read a bunch of other things about damages, and finally, I received a judgment of $3.68 million dollars.

I didn't understand what had just occurred. I knew there was success because they had said yes to the question of negligence, but my legal team was somber. I stood up to leave, following Jeff. As we passed the defense table, Bevilacqua said to Jeff, "Congratulations."

Jeff quietly said, "Thank you," and kept going.

Outside of the courtroom, I rushed into the arms of my fellow survivors. We huddled there, crying together in a group hug, overwhelmed with emotion. Hearing the acknowledgment of negligence spoken out loud was groundbreaking for all of us. When we finally broke apart, I turned to Jeff and said, "What in the hell just happened?"

"We're still trying to figure it out," he said, then turned to confer with the team.

What? Is he fucking joking? He's the lawyer. He's supposed to know what's going on. The lawyers were scurrying around, talking quickly and quietly amongst each other—yet they were congratulated by the defense. The jury was smiling at me; a large number for damages was spoken out loud, yet nothing was making sense.

Finally, Jeff came over to explain. The judge had decided to give the jury two initial questions to answer—the question of negligence and liability were presented separately. Typically, this is presented as one question, so if you're found negligent, you're also liable. The jury needed to say "yes" to both questions for the verdict to be a complete win for us, but they only did so to the first question.

I discussed this later with a district court judge, and she was astonished that the questions were separated. That was Judge McGill's call—and it greatly favored the insurance companies, not me, the victim. Children's Theatre was found negligent but not found liable. The judgment of $3.68 million had been assigned solely to McLean, which meant CTC wouldn't have to pay a single penny for its negligence. The insurance companies had won.

Justice wasn't served for us. McLean can't be arrested for raping me and other children because the criminal statutes have expired. He got away with his crimes—again. There's a snowball's chance in hell I will ever see a dime from him, nor will any of his other victims who received summary judgments because he is a fugitive in Mexico. There is now more than $8 million in judgments against him.

Jeff didn't win the liability argument in court—it was nearly impossible to do so under the restrictions to keep CTC covered by insurance. This isn't because CTC wasn't liable—the mountain of evidence proves it was. We could have put the theater out of business if we had wanted to.

There were, however, some good things that came out of the trial. The number that the jury came back with was big—more than twice what the insurance company offered before the trial. My case was one of the more straightforward ones. Others had the potential for higher damages because of the severity or length of time they were abused, so if the other cases went to trial, they could very likely receive higher numbers.

Also, we absolutely celebrated the verdict of negligence. It was an important moment because it validated the experience of all those who were abused and shined a light on the abusers and those who looked the other way. It upended the barrel of denial for those who didn't want to believe what happened.

Jeff held a press conference the next day stressing the importance of the negligence verdict. I sometimes wonder if the media would have paid any attention to the outcome if he had not done that. The headline made the front page of the local papers, but CTC had gotten away with a slap on the wrist—which is more than before, so that's a small victory. I walked away with what I considered an unsatisfying tie.

During testimony, one of the defense experts, Janet Warren, revealed to Jeff for the first time the existence of a list of hundreds of perpetrators held by the Boy Scouts of America.[83] He told me later it was because of my case that he was able to use that list to show the negligence of that organization in the same way he'd been doing with the Catholic Church for decades.

He said I can be proud of that, and I am.

---

83 Stearns v. CTC No. 27-CV-15-20713, testimony of Dr. Janet Warren, trial transcript, p. 1696

Writing about this whole litigation experience brings it all back. I don't know about you, but I could use a break. When I'm stressed, walking helps me regulate my body. I often take my dog Wilbur for a walk when I'm feeling this way. He's an excellent distraction, so, before we move on, here's a picture of him watching a cheetah running on TV. And yes, he really is this cute.

Chapter Seven
The Aftermath

After the trial, I was exhausted, barely having slept for two weeks. It was the dead of winter, and I was living alone, just me and my cat. The emotional rollercoaster of the past four years had taken a huge toll, yet I didn't feel like I could rest. I went from trial straight into a week of technical rehearsals for the next show at the Guthrie, of which I'd missed the last two weeks of prep. I had zero time to process anything that had just happened—going from one fire into another.

The press conference after the trial was somewhat satisfying because I read a statement and said some things out loud that I wasn't allowed to say in the courtroom. But, of course, the choice of quotes or soundbites the media decides to use isn't up to the person who says them. I tried to get a few reporters to take up the story and tell the fuller history of what had happened at the Children's Theatre Company, not just the outcome of the trial, but I wasn't having much success. By then, it was ancient history. Editors and producers don't want old news, and this story didn't seem relevant to anyone but those of us who had lived it.

Donahue died not long after the trial, and it sent ripples of emotions through the alumni community. Some people wanted to honor him; some wanted to dance on his grave. I struggled with holding the multiple truths that swirled in me. I wanted to stay connected to the joy and appreciation of what I learned at CTC, which Donahue represented, but knowing how much harm he had caused to so many people made me rageful. Today, I don't celebrate the man or dance on his grave. I hold his victims in my heart, and damn the memory of him.

~ The Missing Report ~

In May 2016, Jina filed a report with the Minneapolis Police Department against McLean for his abuse and involvement in trafficking her back in the 1980s. The statutes were different in her case than they were in mine, and it allowed her to file a criminal report.

In her videotaped report, Jina described how she was drugged and used in pornographic filming of child abuse directed by Donahue. Jina provided physical evidence, copies of still images from a pornographic film of her as a child that had been discovered on the internet back in the 1990s. She kept the originals.

Her filing opened a three-year window for investigation, so it became our only hope that McLean could be criminally charged.

By spring 2019, shortly after my trial, the deadline for the investigation window was approaching. This prompted JAA to reach out to the Hennepin County Attorney's Office (HCAO) regarding the investigation's progress. The district attorney's office had no idea what they were asking about. Typically, a report like Jina's is sent to the district attorney for investigation, but no report had been submitted to them.

Jina's official police report, which had been videotaped, had never been given to the HCAO. There was a record of her giving the report, which prompted the opening of the three-year window, but the videotape, evidence, and written report were never filed with the district attorney. In fact, they are all missing from her file and are nowhere to be found.

The person who conducted the interview no longer works for that department. The investigation window was officially opened, and the clock started ticking, but no one was investigating. The assistant district attorney apologized, even though she claimed it wasn't their fault that the report was not submitted to them. There was little they could do.

The five of us who had filed suits against McLean were interviewed at the HCAO. An assistant to the district attorney and an investigator who had knowledge of child trafficking and pornography rings from his earlier days on the police force asked us questions. Unfortunately, in the end, no criminal charges could be filed against McLean.

We were infuriated, but it wasn't exactly a surprise that another obstruction had appeared regarding Donahue's involvement in trafficking. Human trade is a billion-dollar business, and as psychologist and trauma therapy expert Dawn McClelland said in an interview with reporter Marianne Combs, "The sex trade is incredibly organized. It's why we can't shut it down." In 2015, Minnesota recorded the third-highest rate of human trafficking in the US. I'm not a conspiracy theorist, but it's hard to deny that something untoward has been going on for decades with children in Minneapolis. Maybe a reader of this book can pick up the trail.

~ My Gloves Finally Came Off ~

Jeff Anderson called one day in May 2019 and informed me about a post-trial hearing that had been scheduled. The prosecution and defense would be arguing a few legal points in front of Judge McGill. Bevilacqua would be there too. I was curious about the process, so I decided to attend.

The hearing was in the same courtroom as the trial but with no jury, projector, piles of paperwork or onlookers. Jeff argued for post-trial motions, raising issues about causation and superseding cause.

At trial, Jeff had argued that the cause of my harm was, in part, the culture that normalized the sexualization of children at CTC, and this culture had been established by its leader and upheld by other adults on staff through their compliance and enabling. I was made more vulnerable because of the complicit culture, and McLean had direct access to me because he was a teacher, and I had to work with him in shows. Bevilacqua had argued there was a superseding cause, meaning something else was entirely responsible for my abuse—McLean had acted on his own, the rape happened at his home, and the theater had nothing to do with it.

Jeff also argued that the questions of negligence and liability should not have been separated by the judge in the instructions to the jury. Jeff told me this wasn't likely to sway Judge McGill because it would require him to admit making an error, which judges don't like to do.

Separating the questions had enabled Bevilacqua to argue that CTC wasn't liable for my harm because the rape hadn't occurred on CTC property but rather at McLean's home a block away. This argument completely cast aside the fact that I was required to be in the presence of McLean, who had a position of authority over me as a teacher and a staff member, and that I was sexually groomed by McLean at the theater, not at his house.

If we follow Bevilacqua's logic, the Catholic Church wouldn't be responsible if a priest molested an altar boy in the park down the street instead of in a chamber behind the sanctuary, even though the altar boy's relationship with the priest was due to his job as an altar boy, which had given the priest access to groom and manipulate the child.

Bevilacqua had one thing to present to the judge, a request for Taxation of Cost. This rule of court gives the prevailing party in a trial permission to demand the losing party to pay for a portion of the winning party's trial fees. Typically, this is applied in corporate cases where two businesses sue each other, and the winner tries to

neir offense
nice.
theater. Mine
rk others had
long.
dea of calling
t's something
it, and I can't
theater and
ice, but this
behalf.
and publicly
ne, the media
get people to
d newspapers
y filmmaker,
end, I'd have
is story more

en peacefully
matinee. My
this, however,
nd a group of
munity, were
had a couple
ent and held
greed to keep
e spoke to us.
nity standing
professionals
eater, making
survivors. It
er community

the winner's legal costs. It's a way the
nd plaintiffs to stick it to each other

because the theater wasn't found
the winner; therefore, she was
w CTC to "tax" me for a portion

hed Bevilacqua ask permission for
negligent for my harm, to present
vor—a bill to pay almost $300,000
his ruling for another day.

ked Jeff to explain the details of
erstood the mechanics of it, the
were attacking me financially to
other plaintiffs. "If you lose in
ut of your own pocket." It was a
likely instigated by the insurance
rvivors of CTC but all survivors
can be used to bully and silence
using the system to find justice.
arsenal in sexual assault cases.
ave to be run by CTC before
?" I asked.
o check with their clients before

and said, "Well then, my gloves
te."
expose this scare tactic by CTC
c boycott of the theater.
dn't know anything about the
a had requested it without their
ade the decision. Maybe it was
rs. All I know is that they tried

to get me to pay an outrageous amount of money for t
and it was the end of my patience. I was done playing

I'm not the first one to have called for a boycott of the
just got the most attention. I'm grateful for the groundw
done, and I'm so sorry their protests went unheard for so

Being an introvert in an extrovert's clothing, the i
attention to myself in that way was uncomfortable. But
I've learned to do because what I have to say is importa
let fear stop me from saying what's true. My years i
ability to speak in public have helped me raise my v
personal attack motivated me to speak out on my own

I posted a blog about the Taxation of Cost
requested an immediate boycott of the theater. This ti
paid attention—nothing like a little real-time drama to
pay attention to the past. Television, radio stations an
finally took note. Norah Shapiro, the documenta
proposed a project about the history of CTC. In the
to say the Taxation of Cost stunt backfired by giving t
attention than if CTC had been found liable.

For months after the trial, another plaintiff had b
protesting outside the theater before every Saturday
energy had been so depleted, I hadn't joined her. After
I started demonstrating every week. The boycott grew,
us, both plaintiffs and members of the larger theater cor
there every Saturday through the summer. We often
dozen protesters, sometimes only a handful, but we
our signs and answered questions from passersby. We
our signage age-appropriate and only spoke when peop

Having other members of the theater commu
with us was very empowering. Actors and other theate
started publicly refusing auditions or cut ties with the t
it clear they didn't approve of how CTC was treatin
was the first time I felt like anyone in the larger theat

cared that kids had been sexually abused there. Something was shifting. People were putting their own jobs on the line for us.

Some committed Twin Cities groups buoyed us up through this time. A group of performers and teaching artists, who called themselves "Standing with CTC Survivors," created a video demanding that CTC change its tactics with plaintiffs. An artist community council attempted to get CTC to act with integrity and accountability. Other theaters in town made public statements supporting survivors, and hundreds of people signed their names as allies of the efforts. These compassionate humans inspired me and kept me afloat—they showed up for all of us.

After the boycott was underway, I tried to get *American Theater Magazine* to pick up the story. Awareness of sexual harassment and harm in the arts was starting to get a lot of attention because of the #MeToo movement, so the time seemed right.

Even though the CTC story was one of the most scandalous in American theater history, and the new development was current and happening in real-time, the editors were hesitant. They told me they already had a story in process for the September 2019 edition and didn't want to do another one. They asked to interview me as one of several subjects for that article, a piece about #MeToo in the theater. I agreed—at least it was something. A micro-version of my story appeared in the magazine with five other people from across the country who talked about the different ways they had experienced sexual harm in theater.

After the #MeToo article ran, I tried to get the magazine to do a feature story about CTC. I gave up when I was told they wouldn't do such a story about one of their contributing theaters. *Ahhhhhh, there it was—money.* The magazine would point out abuse by individuals but not institutions that paid for ads in their magazine.

I'd met Minnesota Public Radio reporter Marianne Combs at the press conference after the trial. I remember seeing her sitting on the floor, close to the podium, looking up at me with microphone in hand. She had the most compassionate expression of any reporter in the room. When she approached me about doing an interview for MPR, I was all in.

At first, Marianne was covering the boycott, then wanted to do a series that would go deeper into our stories. I was ecstatic. Yes, finally, people were paying attention. Marianne and her team did an extraordinary job. They sought out training to be trauma-informed, taking care to do no harm as they worked. The series ended up being seven installments called *Innocence Lost*, now archived on the Minnesota Public Radio website.

While protesting in front of CTC, people often drove by and honked in support of our efforts. One day, however, a guy in a pickup drove by and yelled out the window, "Get over it!" I yelled back, "Get trauma-informed!"

One of the teaching artists told me about a father who had reached out to her, scolding her for protesting CTC. His own son had gone to a summer school program there a few years earlier, and the father declared it as "the most wonderful experience of my son's life." He didn't like that we were condemning a place that was loved by his own child. I'm truly happy that his son's experience there was so wonderful—that's how it should have always been. Does that mean, though, that because someone had a good time there, we shouldn't shed light on injustice?

During one of the protests, a grandmother stopped to ask me why were we picketing? As I talked to her, I kept my description benign because her grandson was with her to see the show. I explained that children had been harmed there, that the theater had been found negligent at trial, and then summarized the Taxation of Cost stunt.

She grew sad and said she didn't feel comfortable going into the building. She looked at her grandson, who was about eight, and asked, "Would it be okay if we did something else today?" The boy looked at me, then at his grandmother and said, "Sure." She wished me well, and they headed back to the parking ramp.

I was so moved by her decision to leave. I began to cry when I saw her sitting in the grass and talking to her grandson, pointing at the building and gesturing to us on the picket line. I could tell by the great care she took and the way he listened that she was explaining why they weren't going to see the play. I was so proud of that grandmother for being willing to stand in her conviction, doing the right thing and gracefully modeling that behavior for her grandson.

That same day, a girl about thirteen years old walked by, and I heard her ask her father, "Dad, what does 'Break the Silence' mean?" I don't know how he answered, but the fact that she asked him helped me know we were doing something right. It's exactly the question she should be asking her father, and hopefully, he gave her a good answer. If he didn't, perhaps her own curiosity led her to find the answer elsewhere. The concept of speaking the truth about sexual violence was now on her radar, and that's the kind of knowledge that can help her avoid it or get help if it happens.

Breaking the Silence means speaking the truth about sexual violence, saying what's true even if you're scared. It means not allowing fear to stop you from having a voice or allowing things that should be spoken to go unsaid. It means not suffering in silence and throwing down the shackles of shame that keep you chained to it. It doesn't require a monumental, courageous act. It can be telling one person about something that's painful, and you've kept to yourself or feared what might happen if you said it out loud. It means honoring your own narrative.

I spent much of my life not saying what was true for me in big and little ways. I grew up in a culture of "Minnesota Nice"[84] and "If you don't have something nice to say, don't say anything." I'm still learning how to break the habit of discounting what matters to me for fear of upsetting the status quo.

---

84 A local cultural reference to the way those brought up in Minnesota are taught to be "nice" above being honest, and to pretend to be OK with something even if you're not.

At a boycott protest in front of Children's Theatre Company, Summer 2019

~ Exposing the Insurance Companies ~

Insurance executives had paid close attention to what happened at my trial, even if the media didn't. The fact that my jury awarded more than double what the insurers had offered was eye-opening for them. They got away with not having to pay by sticking McLean with the bill, but that would not be a winning strategy in the future. The cases coming at them now could put abuse squarely in the building, and the defense would not be able to argue superseding cause.

And Jeff had learned a lot from my trial, what worked and what didn't. The insurers knew they could lose big in the courtroom, and it would cost them a lot more than settling out of court.

During the summer of 2019, a new mediator was brought in, and a few settlements occurred, though only for male students whose abuse occurred before 1980. The women with cases from the 1970s did not get settled. The remaining unsettled cases included one filed by a man for abuse in the 1980s and all of the women's cases.

My feminist hackles went up. Why were the males getting their cases settled earlier? A male plaintiff shared with me he believed they were getting the Donahue cases out of the way. He pointed out it wasn't about the 1970s versus 1980s or men versus women. But one of the unsettled cases from the 1980s was a male victim of Donahue, so that didn't make sense to me. Why wasn't his case settled too?

It seemed like the insurance companies involved in the earlier years were able to come to an agreement, but the different insurers in later years were not. But then, why weren't the girls from the 1970s settled? None of it made sense—it just felt wrong. Once again, women were being set aside. Rape culture at work—deal with the boys, because…well…boys. The girls can wait. I changed my signage at the protests to call attention to the imbalance.

I also took a stab at publicly exposing the ways the system protects the coffers of the insurance companies, not people who are in pain. I told Jeff I was going to do it, and he said he'd never seen anyone do that before, but…why not? After a few days, he encouraged me to let it go. I'm not sure why, but I remember at one point he referred to a conversation he'd had with Bevilacqua in which she had asked him to "call off his dogs." *Really? Sexual assault survivors are dogs now?* I'm guessing my loud mouth was making his job harder, so I let it go for the sake of the others who were in mediation.

The fact that some of the settlements had been completed was a sign that the end was near. But not for me. I wasn't being brought to the settlement table. No one in the plaintiff group wanted me to be left behind, but I was. As far as the insurance companies were concerned, I'd had my day in court—and lost.

~ Reparations List ~

Most of the plaintiffs had also presented non-monetary requests at their first mediations. For me, these were a central element of our quest for justice and desire for community healing and reparations. I wanted the theater to engage in actions that went beyond an insurance claim. The community was hurting. The legacy of harm would still be there when the settlements were signed, and that wasn't okay with me.

A group of us got together and wrote down a list of the things we wanted as reparations for the community to be presented to the Children's Theatre Company. Emotions were high. So much energy had gone into breaking the silence and speaking the truth, and CTC still wasn't being held accountable for its part.

Mediations were coming to a close, and the final cases were being discussed. This stage of the litigation process was so confusing to me. I wasn't being included in the conversations, and it felt like everything was moving too fast; at the same time, nothing was moving at all. I'd never done this before. I felt so powerless, and not knowing if the needs of the larger community would be addressed as final settlements were happening was destabilizing. There were things at stake that were more important than money.

In the end, I was brought back into the conversations. CTC could see that the larger theater community supported me and knew I wouldn't back down. We were in the window of time where we could file an appeal, which could drag on for years. CTC didn't want that—it was bad for business and their reputation. I'm not at liberty to reveal details of how the talks concluded, but I can say we did not pursue an appeal.

After the settlements were completed, CTC did agree to most of our collected list of requested reparations. These are referred to as "non-monetary requests," even though many of them require funds to accomplish. I'm grateful that CTC was willing to agree to these reparations, but few have been accomplished at the time of publication.

The following is a list of what was agreed upon:

- Public apology by Children's Theatre Leadership: Plaintiffs wanted a public apology to the survivors, former students and community.

- Survivors' Fund: The collective request from the plaintiffs was for CTC to support the creation of a Survivors' Fund. CTC agreed to donate $500,000 as seed money for the fund.

- Training for CTC Staff in Child Abuse Prevention and Trauma-Informed Practices: The plaintiffs requested that CTC review its training processes with an eye toward understanding that even if no child is being abused under their care, one in five children are victims of sexual abuse, so all staff should be able to recognize and assist children who are potentially reaching out for help.

- Resources in Show Programs: In the same way that the staff is being trained to understand that children performing or attending classes at CTC may be at risk in other areas of their lives, it was also requested that a point of contact for resources for potential victims, such as the Rape, Abuse and Incest National Network (RAINN) hotline, be placed in CTC's programs.

- Board of Directors Training: Understanding that staff training is not complete without board training in these areas of concern, the request was made to provide specific training for board members.

- Board of Directors Survivor Recruitment: A request was made to include voices of sexual assault survivors on CTC's board of directors, with a recruitment goal of two survivors (preferably childhood survivors) and/or career specialists appointed to the board.

- Opening the University of Minnesota Archive: The CTC archive has a seventy-five-year restriction placed on all contents related to John Clarke Donahue's years at CTC. Plaintiffs requested that this restriction be lifted and all alumni members be given access to the archive without prior approval from CTC.

- Acknowledgment of History on the CTC Website: It was requested that CTC create a page on its website dedicated to the acknowledgment of the early years of the theater's existence and the harms that occurred during that time. For trauma survivors, public acknowledgment of this history is crucial for the process of healing. Additionally, we want alumni-survivors to be able to find access to resources directly on CTC's website. There was also a request to include an ongoing acknowledgment of the theater's history of abuse in their programs.

- Community Support of CTC Alumni Healing: The plaintiffs also wished to have platforms to heal as a community and not just individually. What happened at CTC in the 1970s and 1980s caused community trauma. Some alumni may find it helpful to heal in the community as well. CTC has agreed to help support these alumni-driven efforts financially and is willing to participate if requested in whatever way would be supportive and useful. Plans include community-based opportunities designed with support from qualified professionals trained in complex community trauma and a survey of the alumni community to help determine current needs.

- Opportunities for Parents to Be Involved: We believe that communication with parents is imperative for the safety of children. CTC has parental involvement policies in place, but we believe it's important to further investigate how parents can be invited to be more actively involved in their children's participation in shows and their education at CTC.

- Memorial Placement on the CTC Campus: The request was made by plaintiffs that CTC not oppose future motions toward creating a survivors' memorial on the larger campus of CTC, Minneapolis Institute of Art and Minneapolis College of Art and Design. While no plans are in process right now, CTC has committed to withholding any objection to such a project in the future. Both sides acknowledged that the content would be age-appropriate for CTC audience members.

- The Space Formerly Occupied by John Donahue's Office: This space was the location of much abuse. The intention is to find a way to permanently acknowledge the impact of this difficult past while creating a space for positive experiences and community healing.

I don't believe any of us who brought cases forward against CTC for the harm done to us as children received true justice through the courts. But there is one thing I celebrate that makes it all worth it—the truth is finally being told and is continuing to be told by people like reporter Marianne Combs and documentary filmmaker Norah Shapiro.

The Twin Cities theater community has stepped up by coming together with me to create the Minnesota Theater Accountability Coalition (MNTAC). As a community, we wrote the Minnesota Theater Foundational Standards for Safety and Accountability, a document I believe will be an amazing legacy of safety and accountability for theater-makers, educators and students everywhere. Hopefully, the work we've done will be used as a template for others. For more information on these initiatives, please visit MNTAC.org.

I have gratitude for Jeff as well as deep criticism of how he handled the CTC cases. If perfectly handling a case is the goal, he and his team didn't achieve it. There were major missteps, and too many people got hurt. I don't think this was for lack of caring, but rather the lack of a trauma-informed education. The process could have and should have been less painful for me and the other plaintiffs and our families. He and I have spoken at length about my concerns, and he is aware of the contents in this book. We are still on good terms. He's taken to heart things I and other plaintiffs have told him and incorporated new policies and practices because of it. I believe this dialogue has changed him and his firm for the better. And I'm grateful for his continued support as I move forward in my work as an advocate for survivors.

As difficult as these years have been, they've allowed me to reclaim parts of myself, to take back the power that was stripped from me as a child. My litigation took four years and four months to complete. During that time, my life was turned upside down, and I was repeatedly re-traumatized by the requirements of the legal process—and I'm still glad I did it. As a result, my life is now exponentially better. I sleep better at night, and I wake up every day grateful for the life I'm living.

~ Changing the Statute of Limitations ~

In 2016, I met a woman named Sarah Super, an outspoken advocate for survivors of sexual violence and a survivor herself. This young woman has done some spectacular things in her few years of leading the cause, promoting the Break the Silence movement and spearheading an effort to create the nation's first public memorial for survivors of sexual violence in Minneapolis. She reached out to me after I'd filed my case, and we became friends. After my trial, she asked me to join her in an effort, along with another local activist survivor Asma Nizami, and State Representative Aisha Gomez, to get the Minnesota State Legislature to remove the criminal statute of limitations for sexual abuse from state law.

Sarah asked if I'd be willing to be one of three survivors to present my story to the Public Safety Committee. I leaped at the opportunity. I knew changing the statute wouldn't help me put McLean in jail, but if I could help change the law for others, I was all for it. Testifying in front of the committee would be simple compared to what I had already gone through.

The bill we fought for did not pass that year—or the next. In 2021, the bill was introduced again. The committee wasn't hearing testimony, I think partly because of COVID19 restrictions, though in March 2021, I was able to submit a letter that amplified my previous testimony, which was still on record. Both the House and the Senate approved the elimination of the statute of limitations for sexual violence from Minnesota State law in 2021, and with unanimous support, the removal of the statute was written into law on September 15. Asma and Sarah are heroes to me, as are the 2021 legislators. I'm honored to be part of that legacy.

Memorial bricks I purchased with the support of the community in
honor of CTC survivors for the Memorial for Survivors of Sexual
Violence at Boom Island Park in Minneapolis.

Chapter Eight
Mending

On November 3, 2019, the headline on the front page of the *Minneapolis StarTribune* read: CTC Tragedy's Final Act. The story mentioned the "decades long ordeal" being brought to a close. This declaration was just plain wrong. It's an end of an "act," yes, but certainly not the *final* act. It's more like an intermission. The attempt to heal the community was just beginning, so to say "final act" was not only premature but dismissive of the enduring pain and collective efforts for community healing many of us have dedicated much of our lives to.

Headlines from the *Minneapolis StarTribune* 12/2/15, 2/3/19 and 11/3/19.

For me and those who suffered sexual abuse at the Children's Theatre Company (CTC), this will never truly be over because that's not the way trauma works. It can get better, but it doesn't go away. Yes, settlements happened, and the legal battle was over, but that just allowed us to move into a different phase of the healing process. For some, that meant detaching themselves from everyone involved in the legal battle. A few of the CTC plaintiffs I was in contact with almost daily haven't spoken to me since. The re-wounding of the litigation process caused a fracture within our group that may never mend. I carry sadness about that every day.

~ Apologies ~

Jeff Anderson convened a press conference at his office to announce the last of the settlements with CTC. Kim Motes was invited to attend, which allowed her to address one of the items on our list of reparations—a public apology to all the children who were abused. Previous CTC videotaped statements had been a mockery of healthy communication and were not useful for community healing. Having Kim in the room could show clear intention and authenticity of the words. I wasn't interested in another video apology that fell flat. I wanted one to my face, viewed by everyone.

Kim made her apology and declared a new, more inviting stance, claiming that CTC had changed and was now "trauma-informed" and "survivor-led." The organization, she said, was now educated on how to be present to the needs of trauma survivors and the impact of harm to the larger theater community. In response to another one of our reparation requests, she announced they would appoint sexual assault survivors to the CTC board of directors, so it would benefit from that perspective. It was a start.

Jina was committed to accomplishing a CTC Survivors' Fund from the start; it meant a lot to her. It was agreed Kim would announce that CTC was giving $500,000 in seed money to establish the fund. It was a show of faith to CTC that we were willing to work together to accomplish the additional requests. I agreed to rescind my call for a boycott—my own gesture of good faith. I expressed my hope that CTC would use this opportunity to move their institution's legacy from one of harm to one of advocacy. I knew this was a risk, but I focused on my hope that systemic change at CTC was possible because if it happened there, it could be an example for other institutions that had caused harm.

We reached out to the other plaintiffs who were willing to discuss what to do with the funds. The end of the litigation process had marked the end of involvement for most of them. It was so painful that many of them walked away for their mental well-being. Most of them declined future participation, but a few said they would think about it.

Jina and I began to work on the list of reparations with Kim. The first few meetings were polite but tense—we discussed what the legal process had been like, attempting to lift up the human aspect. We talked about how hard it had been on our families and our relief that it was over. We started to chip away at the reparations list, quickly agreeing on an ad in which the RAINN hotline would be included in every program. Plans for CTC staff and board training soon followed. These things were easy to accomplish.

We discussed the Survivors' Fund, but it was moving slowly because it was more complicated than just writing a check. CTC was willing to provide the funds, but we had no structure in place to manage the money with accountability and no concrete plans for how to distribute it. We decided not to rush—we had their public commitment to provide the funding, so we started envisioning what it could look like.

Artistic Director Peter Brosius began joining our weekly conversations, and it felt like we were building a working relationship that could move us toward trust. Kim and Peter continually spoke in a manner that showed they had learned something about how to engage with trauma survivors. They weren't perfect at it, but we didn't expect them to be.

We met regularly to discuss the progress of the list. Kim would make a note to check various things, the archive in particular, and then update us later. But she never had updates about the archive. "Oh, right…" she would say when we asked about it, and then quickly scribbled a note.

Kim and Peter spoke a lot about how tense the atmosphere was within the theater. Those who were happy and loyal employees of the current administration didn't understand why the teaching artists had taken a public stand to support us. Some probably saw us as money grabbers or considered what happened ancient history that was irrelevant. They wouldn't accept the idea that the theater itself, even their own paychecks, existed because the theater's survival back in the day was more important than the children who had been exploited.

The teaching artists wanted to ensure that CTC would take their history seriously and treat survivors with respect, believing it was even more important to do the right thing in the here and now and not cause more damage to people who had been hurt as children.

These two groups were standing up for what they believed was right. I didn't like the thought of these hard-working theater-makers and educators battling each other, and I wanted to help.

Most of the staff members who were angry with us had absolutely no understanding about the buried truth, and Kim and Peter were not freely sharing that information. I didn't think it was fair to judge people who were making decisions based on limited information and half-truths. Jina and I offered to help the theater with this internal struggle by meeting with people and answering their questions.

In February, Peter and Kim invited us to meet with a group of teaching artists. The morning of the meeting, fearing it might be uncomfortable for Jina and me to go to the theater, Kim changed the venue to a more neutral setting. This gesture was appreciated and a sign that she was starting to think in a different way. Maybe that trauma-informed training was starting to kick in.

People were milling around when I arrived. Jina wasn't feeling well and couldn't attend. I greeted Kim and Peter with a handshake and took a seat. The conversation that ensued was difficult. It was obvious how deeply the administration and teaching staff mistrusted each other, but I felt a general willingness to attempt coming together.

People spoke authentically, and there was space for listening. Seeing how hard it was for this group to speak to Kim and Peter was telling. I could imagine how difficult it would be to bring other members of the staff into the conversation.

Maria, one of my old Conservatory School friends, was there. She had been the director of the Bridges Education program at CTC for many years and was one of the only people on staff who had ties to the Donahue years. Toward the end of the meeting, she and I had a very emotional dialogue. Both of us cried as we talked about how painful it was to witness the damage done to children and the fierce denials made by those who had ignored what was happening. When the meeting ended, she and I embraced in the middle of the room and cried in each other's arms for several minutes, oblivious to the people around us.

When most people had left, I started saying goodbye to Peter. I put out my hand to shake his, and he pushed my hand aside and gave me a hug. Had I wanted a hug, I would have offered open arms. I'm not one to make a scene, so I didn't push him back—which was what I wanted to do. I accepted the hug and said nothing about it, like a good upper-midwestern girl.

At our next meeting, I decided to forgo my typical "Minnesota Nice" upbringing and share openly with Peter what that moment was like for me. I reminded him of what had happened, that I'd extended my hand and he pushed it aside. "Do you realize that you removed my agency of choice completely at that moment?"

He looked at me ruefully, knowing I was right.

"I know you did that because you were moved by the rawness of what was shared at the meeting," I said, "and by my emotions and Maria's. But you robbed me of my choice to invite you into my personal space."

To his credit, he understood and apologized, saying, "That didn't occur to me. I'm sorry."

"It's okay," I said, "I know it didn't occur to you, which is why I'm telling you now." The process of learning to be trauma-informed isn't perfect. People make mistakes. It's how you deal with it that matters.

~ CTA Wellness ~

In late February, Don, another plaintiff and former classmate who had also testified at my trial, began working with Jina and me on the list of reparations. We continued to negotiate with Kim and Peter. The biggest question was how to handle the Survivors Fund. We saw two options: hand it off to a third party to administer or run the fund ourselves and have more say in how applicants were caught emotionally by people answering the phones.

After much discussion around the complexities of our community harm and research to see how to best serve the community, we decided to create a nonprofit that would hold and administer the fund. It would be run by those who'd fought to create it—former plaintiffs. We tried to enlist others to participate on the board or an advisory committee. Some were interested in advising, but no one else wanted to join the board, so our nonprofit was born with the three of us serving as the board of directors. We called this nonprofit the Children's Theatre Alumni Wellness Fund, now known as CTA Wellness. Its mission is to connect alumni with therapeutic support services, to help find providers and to pay directly for needed services for our alumni from the Donahue years.

Just as we were getting a handle on things, COVID-19 threw a planet-sized wrench into the process. Everything came to a screeching halt. For a while, we weren't sure there would be a fund to manage because we didn't know how the pandemic would affect CTC. Theaters around the world were empty and would be for the foreseeable future.

After a few weeks, we met Kim and Peter via Zoom, and our newest board member, Don, joined us. We learned that CTC was still committed to the reparation conversation, even in the face of a global pandemic. As a board, in a gesture of good faith, we offered to let them pay the $500,000 in installments. They gratefully accepted. It took many months to create a payment agreement, but it did happen eventually.

To broaden the perspective of our board, we convened an advisory committee made up of former plaintiffs and students and conducted online meetings. The presence of these committee members and the guidance from professionals in the field of complex community trauma made the final Survivors' Fund better than anything we could have done alone. Dawn McClelland, one of our professional advisors, provided invaluable guidance to our group and helped us find ways to take care of ourselves and each other as we did the work.

Our main objective was to set up the administration of the fund application process and what the fund would cover. Our meetings were often emotional as we addressed old community trauma at the same time we experienced the global trauma of the pandemic. And then George Floyd was murdered in Minneapolis, and our city was literally on fire for weeks—it felt like the world was upside down and spinning backward. Our group meetings became important touchstones on multiple levels because we were looking at and experiencing trauma through so many lenses.

It was complicated work, and just being in each other's presence could be a trigger for any one of us. We were bumping up against each other's trauma through the entire process, every time we gathered, there were emotional landmines that could potentially go off, and every time it happened, we stopped and addressed it. Dawn helped us navigate through them, teaching us about trauma and how the body dysregulates, so we no longer have access to our most resourced selves.

While working through these issues together, some of the largest leaps in my healing happened. I found unexpected things that also needed to be addressed in my personal life that never would have surfaced alone in a therapist's office.

Building trust within the group was paramount to its success. The complexities of our group dynamics, and the ever-constant desire to avoid causing harm to each other, made the work proceed very slowly. We were committed to doing it right, not fast. Our motto was: We move at the speed of trust, and trust is built with consistency over time.

The COVID-19 lockdown was extremely stressful for me—I had to put my twenty-year-old cat down, so I was completely isolated except for the short weekly visit with my mother to fill her pill boxes. She was in a senior living facility, still independent though needing more care because of her mental decline from Alzheimer's. COVID visiting regulations were strict. I was the only one in the family allowed to enter the building because I oversaw her medical needs. The residents were told to stay in their apartments. I could see how lonely she was.

Just when I thought things couldn't get worse, Mom's health took a bad turn. The stress of isolation had increased the rate of decline in her cognition, and it became obvious she needed to be in memory care. We knew that doing so would basically be saying goodbye to her because of all of the restrictions, so my family chose to move her to my oldest brother's house. I "podded up" with him and my niece to help care for Mom.

Something had to give. The emotional stress threw me into a tailspin, and I decided to step away from the board temporarily.

Fortunately, Rana had decided a few weeks before to move from our advisory committee to the board of directors. The work continued while I attended to my ailing mother.

By summer's end, the official applications for the non-profit had been submitted, and conversations about designing the fund were in full swing. I returned to working with the group in the fall and learned there had not been much contact with Kim and Peter. When we finally connected with them, they told us how much stress they'd been under because of the pandemic, which was understandable. We started scheduled conversations again.

~ Institutional Harm ~

In the post-settlement months, we had tried to lay a foundation of honesty and trust with Kim and Peter. They listened to our stories, told us they cared about our well-being and expressed a desire to do the right thing. Their words sounded good. Then we found out what had been happening behind the Children's Theatre Company's closed doors.

On October 1, 2020, we learned that CTC had appointed its defense attorney, Theresa Bevilacqua, to its board of directors during the summer. I felt like I'd been sucker-punched. After the shock of it dissipated, the emotions gushed in. The pain of the litigation process rushed back into my body. This woman had set the tone for CTC's legal defense, insisted I go through the extremely re-traumatizing steps of the litigation process twice, had personally deposed me both times, and had filed the retaliatory motion for Taxation of Cost against me.

Kim, Peter, and the CTC Board not only failed to honor our request for sexual assault survivors to be on the board of directors but added someone who was the polar opposite of what we had asked for. They couldn't have picked someone more offensive.

I sobbed on the phone with Maria, trying to make sense of why they would do such a thing. It felt like a hostile maneuver, a huge "fuck you," and I questioned why I ever decided to work with them on reparations.

Maria said I wasn't wrong to have tried to see the best in people, to believe that change was possible. But at that moment, my willingness to attempt to educate people who would do something so vile felt like a failing, not a strength. My efforts to help guide them to best practices seemed now like a fool's errand, and I was the fool.

In addition to this egregious offense, Kim and Peter hadn't been forthcoming with information regarding the status of the seventy-five-year restriction sealing the CTC archive. Public archives for art institutions are common, and the University of Minnesota houses several, including this one.

Apparently, sealing certain archived documents like board notes is common for a time, usually ten years or so, but a seventy-five-year restriction is unheard of. For some perspective—the documents of the FBI and CIA investigation of JFK's assassination were released less than sixty years after the event. This begs the question: What is in that archive that is so threatening to CTC?

We had asked Kim and Peter dozens of times what exactly was in the archive and why it was restricted. We asked that it be opened to CTC alumni. Every time we asked, they said they didn't know anything about it and promised to "look into it."

Around the time we learned that Bevilacqua had been appointed to the board, we also acquired a copy of the signed agreement between CTC and the University of Minnesota, which included the terms of the restrictions. The agreement went into effect in December 2013, seven months after the Minnesota Child Victims Act was made law, and was signed by Peter Brosius, who had been consistently telling us he had no information about the archive.

We sat with the information about the CTC board appointment and the archive agreement for many days, trying to decide how to respond to CTC as the board of CTA Wellness. I wanted to slam

CTC publicly but decided to wait. Our community was already reeling from the repercussions of the pandemic and the civil unrest. They didn't need more reasons to be upset.

We finally confronted Kim and Peter in a Zoom meeting. When we mentioned the thoughtless appointment of Bevilacqua, they appeared horrified, saying they didn't realize it would be so harmful to us.

"This is what institutional harm looks like," I replied. Their insensitivity after all the work we'd done with them was both disturbing and alarming. Their actions did not match their words.

When I asked Peter about his signature on the archive restriction agreement, he immediately knew what I was talking about. "I was surprised to see my signature on there myself," he said, for the first time admitting his participation in sealing its contents. "I don't remember signing it." He started to go on about the establishment of the archive, saying how important he thinks it is, when I interrupted him.

"Wait a minute, Peter," I said. "You were throwing things in dumpsters behind the theater. People in the neighborhood pulled things out that you were throwing away."

I had heard from a few people that in 2009, someone at the theater saw a bunch of papers being thrown out—boxes filled with thousands of pages, things like old programs, all from the Donahue era. The employee who saw these items in the dumpster informed people who might find value in what was being thrown out, and the tossed items were retrieved.

Peter ignored me and started talking about the value of preserving the history of the theater.

At this point, I stopped listening, knowing there was no point in arguing with someone who was trying to take credit for "preserving the history" when all I had seen him do since his arrival twenty years ago was try to bury it. If the history was so important to preserve, why had Peter sealed the archive for seventy-five years, long after the death of anyone who would find personal value in it?

In the end, they apologized and did the right thing. Bevilacqua was removed from their board, and they agreed to remove the restriction on the archive so alumni can have access to it. The board chair himself apologized, and he listened when we told him how painful the whole thing had been. We talked at length about the importance of having sexual assault survivor representation on their board. He promised they would make every effort to accomplish that in the next cycle of board recruitment.

At the time of publication, I'm not aware of any such appointments.

As for the archive, we succeeded in opening it to the public and alumni can now request access to it. We fought for this because we believe people have the right to that touchstone. For the survivors, having access to it might help in their healing process, to make it more real, so people can find themselves in its contents. When there are tangible items to hold, the body registers things in a different way. And it's symbolic—letting the light of day illuminate whatever is in there that reveals our past, and we have permission to excavate if we so choose.

It became clear that working so closely with CTC put me at risk of further harm from the institution. The impact of their actions was excruciating and can't be erased. I told them I wouldn't meet with them again. The sad thing is that CTC had an opportunity to do better, to set things right and be an example of how institutions can treat survivors of sexual violence. Instead, the institution became an excellent example of what not to do.

Institutions must do better for survivors of sexual violence. Stories come out almost weekly about histories of abuse at schools and other organized institutions for children. One of the largest recent lawsuits includes fifty-six plaintiffs who were former students at North Carolina School for the Arts who, in 2021, named twenty-nine offenders who abused students over four decades and nineteen complicit administrators. Their survivor stories are eerily familiar and sadly not surprising to me.

Where children gather, so do those who would take advantage of them. We must be more stringent in our vetting processes, vigilant in investigating rumors, and believing survivors when they come forward. Due diligence is vital, but it's up to institutions to also do the important work of taking care of those who are harmed on their watch.

An organization called The Center for Institutional Courage, led by founder Jennifer Freyd, PhD, is leading the conversation away from institutional denial and toward accountability and care. Even its name makes my heart leap. How I wish CTC had reached out to Dr. Freyd when the Minnesota Child Victims Act was written into law. I think the last few years would have looked very different. Maybe they would have taken up the mantle to advocate for survivors instead of continuing to deny their responsibility.

If you know of or work for an institution that has caused harm and would like them to move toward accountability, not away from it, please guide them to Institutionalcourage.org.

~ Complex Community Trauma ~

It's hard for me to live in the Twin Cities theater community—it's quite small with few degrees of separation. I can't even see a show without bumping up against the CTC legacy. Many have asked me how I was able to stay in this community or in theater at all. The simple answer—I shut down a part of myself. For a long time, I couldn't see how so many areas of my life had been touched, how the weeds of harm from my time at CTC had infiltrated my relationships and sense of self-worth. That is until I was able to unpack it with people able to accompany me through my journey of discovery. But that heightened awareness has also taken away my shield, the coping mechanism of numbness, which allowed me to "just keep swimming" in a scum-filled pond.

I was sitting outside a theater a few months after my trial, waiting for the theater to open for seating, when I heard a familiar female voice over my shoulder. "Eye spy with my little eye..." the voice said. I thought it was an odd thing to say, and then, into my peripheral vision, walked Wendy Lehr and her husband, Gary Briggle. Apparently, she had "spied" me as they approached the building but said nothing more; they just glared at me as they went in. I knew there was no way I could sit through a play knowing they were there, so I left.

As I walked across the parking lot, I ran into a friend who asked if I was going to see the show. I said, "No. I'll be back another night." I didn't explain.

My friend was with someone and turned to introduce me. "This is Laura Stearns," she said.

I recognized her companion as someone from the old CTC days.

The look on her face became harsh as my name sunk in. "Ooooh, Laura *Stearns*," she said, stretching out my last name with an I-know-who-you-are tone. And then she stared at me.

Most people in town have shown me gratitude and respect for my truth-telling. But not everyone. I quickly bid goodbye to them, got in my car and cried as I texted the friend I was supposed to be meeting to inform her I couldn't stay.

Our community fractured after Donahue did his time in 1984–85. Most of the theater community just kept on loving him, figuring he had "paid his dues" for his transgressions. He was still revered and continued to work in theater. The "magic" of what he created is still admired to this day.

In spring 2021, I saw a photograph on Facebook that sent me directly to the core of my trauma. It was an old CTC production photo from *Mr. Pickwick's Christmas* featuring the man who raped me when I was a kid. The person who shared the photo was celebrating the work of a different man, a set designer. Yet there was McLean—this despicable person, this sexual predator, this rapist who still hasn't been held accountable for his actions— beautifully lit on an exquisite set. These contradictions existing in the same photograph were jarring.

Thankfully, I was able to reach Rana by phone, and she provided accompaniment as I processed all the jumble of emotions rushing through me. This is what it's like for me to navigate this little theater town—emotional landmines are everywhere, and my fellow survivors continue to help me find my way.

Three years ago, a friend shared with me for the first time that he was a victim of Donahue. I had hoped he had escaped it. I was so devasted by the revelation I punched a punching bag with such force I almost broke my finger.

This friend also said to me, "We were complicit too, you know," meaning "we" as children. I understood why he felt that way. I knew my own silence had allowed others to be hurt, and this will always be a scar on my heart. But as my son so simply told me as I rode my tsunami of guilt after reading The Thread, "You were a child." There was little else we could do.

Here's what I know today: We did do the best we could with what we had in the midst of a culture that trained us to stay silent about our sexual abuse. McLean's words ring in my ears, "That was consensual, right?" *No, it wasn't consensual. You raped me. You tricked me into believing I mattered, and then you fucked me as if I were a blow-up doll. How dare you?*

"Right," I replied back then, because it was all I could say. Today, I'm a grown woman, and I have the courage to speak the truth and all the tools I need to do it. I didn't back then.

The damage of childhood sexual assault doesn't end at the edges of our minds and bodies. It infiltrates our relationships, our work, our art. Its residue is fertilizer that feeds destructive thinking, like a cancer that eats its host. The collateral damage is endless and its longevity limitless, working its way into different aspects of our lives, spilling into how we deal with everything from where we choose to live to our choice of having children or not.

Some of us couldn't bear to think of bringing a child into a world where such horrifying possibilities exist, so we didn't. Those who chose to have children found they had to navigate around parenting requirements, unaware of or ignoring the wounded child within. But how do we take care of a ten-year-old son or daughter when the child inside us is frozen in time? How can we attend to an adolescent learning about their sexual self and guide them healthily to claim their rightful human inheritance when our internal fifteen-year-old is lying paralyzed until the morning birds sing?

I cry for the children of the children who didn't have a complete parent available to them because their mother or father had been robbed of the elements necessary to do the job right. I mourn for the spouses trying to love away the wounds inside their partners when love can't erase the past or heal the wounds that lie deep within that assaulted partner. Lovers of victims didn't cause the harm, but they too live with the consequences of it. It's an unfair business, loving the survivor.

To the observer, the burden of abuse might look insignificant, like the size of a pebble, but for those who carry it, that pebble has the weight of a boulder. We've developed invisible mental muscles to bear it. Sometimes, friends and family try to help us carry that weight, but they don't have that invisible muscle, so the weight of it can drain them emotionally. It's possible to share the weight with other survivors, those who carry their own boulder—we both have that muscle and know how to use it. We hold each other up when our knees feel weak. It's our superpower.

Trauma survivors can struggle to make sense of their wounding. Harm stands on the edge of clarity, and our brains sometimes care for us too well by allowing us to forget. This mental fog leaves us struggling to pull together an incomplete picture. I weep for those who haven't been able to start this journey of healing, who try and dull the pain with drugs and alcohol, who accidentally overdose or take their own lives because they can't bear the weight of the abuse inflicted on them by selfish souls.

Silence makes the weight heavier. Speaking truth can provide some relief. We often don't understand how much weight we carry until some of it falls away. But this can also unlock a torrent of emotions, leaving a wounded person vulnerable if they don't have someone to catch them when the dam breaks.

My heart is broken by the recent discoveries. One of the kids who came forward in the 1980s had suffered a lifetime of chemical dependency. One of his friends encouraged him to file a lawsuit after my case went public. Even the thought of it sent him into a tailspin, and he ended up dead from an overdose. This is the reality of what's at stake and why we have dedicated so much of our time and hearts to CTA Wellness. We are trying to create a way to catch people as they face the inner demons invoked by sexual assault at the Children's Theatre Company.

Lies and secrets fester in the dark. There are many ways our society has allowed sexual abuse to happen. Ignoring or dismissing it deepens the wounds of the abused. But when we expose a wound to air and light, healing can happen. I think it's the same with community trauma—at least, that's been my experience. Informed care is necessary, and some of us are trying to figure out how to manage all the complexities with respect and create care for as many people in our community as possible.

There are people, of course, who were both victim and perpetrator. Abusing others after being abused is a trauma response, but it's not an excuse. Perhaps there's hope for some of these people too. It's complicated territory, and we must move cautiously. We don't want to cause more harm or be harmed in the process of trying to meet people where they are. *We move at the speed of trust, and trust is built with consistency over time.*

Just as scars of the flesh can be permanent, the hidden scars of an abused child don't disappear. Abuse survivors will always be able to trace their psychic finger along the rough edge of their splintered childhood. But it doesn't have to continue to hurt so badly. The scar can fade, and with it, the pain that burns under the surface reminding us of its presence.

Epilogue
~ The Evolving Tapestry ~

While working on this book, I decided to rent a house for a week in northern Minnesota to use as a writing retreat. I spent several days searching for the perfect place, wanting to find just the right spot. I happened upon a listing that fit all my requirements and then some, a beautiful place in the woods about two hours north of Minneapolis. The picture of the host, Derek, was friendly and familiar in a way I didn't understand. *Had I met this person before?* I booked the reservation.

I arrived to find that the house exceeded my expectations. Derek was generous and welcoming but clearly not someone I'd met before. I got a big enough place so friends and family could join me during the week to give me a soft place to land emotionally after my daytime writing as I was digging into some of the more difficult parts of my narrative. The decor was eclectic, with so much bric-a-brac it was impossible to absorb quickly. Every day I'd see something new. On the third morning, I started looking more closely at the pictures hanging on the wall in my bedroom. Over in the corner, partially hidden by a lamp, I found this framed poster:

Poster for the Loring Pasta Bar previously owned by McLean

My reaction was physical and immediate. The acids in my stomach roiled, my face got hot, my body started vibrating. I was horrified. The fact that I'd slept in that room and not seen it was unsettling. Then I got angry and started stomping around the room. *What the fuck. Is there nowhere I can go and escape him?* I grabbed the picture off the wall, wanting to break it into pieces, burn it, anything but have it near me. I decided that would be inappropriate, as the poster didn't belong to me, so I put it out in the garage instead.

The irony of this image appearing in this place I'd so carefully chosen was not lost on me, though I couldn't shake the distress of finding this poster in the room I'd been sleeping in. I decided to go for a walk in the field behind the house and meditate on the experience instead of going further into the emotions of it, walking being one of the ways I counteract dysregulation in my body when I'm triggered.

I believe there are no accidents, and the universe puts things in our path that can help us if we're willing to use them. What was it trying to say to me?

It had rained during the night, and my feet became wet from the grass. I was wearing moccasins, which I knew wouldn't keep the moisture away from my skin, so I decided to let myself be aware of the slow invasion of water. I began to do a thought processing I've developed to identify what's at the core of my upsets. It's a writing exercise,[85] but at that moment, I did it in my head, thinking as I walked:

Recognize the thought:

I'll never escape this. I guess I'm just doomed to keep reliving this horror. Why can't I just have a retreat without this shit being shoved in my face? McLean is in Mexico, not having to feel the consequences of his actions, and here I am, unable to escape the triggers of the harm he caused me even in the middle of the woods.

Identify the false core belief:

I don't deserve to be free of this pain. It will always haunt me no matter where I go.

Tell yourself the truth:

This is part of my history, and I can't change the past. But the emotions that surround it don't have to be in the driver's seat of my life. I deserve to be free of the pain that keeps me tethered to the harm, and one of the things I'm doing to free myself is writing my book.

---

85 RITE Thinking Process helps us find what's at the core of our personal belief system so we can make informed decisions, allowing us to choose a response instead of just reacting. I've developed this over many years and will explain it fully and provide exercises to learn how to do it in the companion book to this memoir called *Daring to Heal: Growing Beyond Trauma Through Awareness, Acceptance, and Action.*

Engage with a response:

I need to go write about this. Use the energy of the moment and focus on the task.

This exercise helped bring me into the present moment. My better self took the reins again, and I was able to think more clearly, to let it go and appreciate the irony of finding the poster, particularly on the day I planned to write about McLean. I saw the parallel between physically removing the picture and emotionally taking back the wheel to claim control of the situation.

To fuel my writing, I used the dichotomy of the poster being hidden by a light source and found strength in literally bringing it out into the open, allowing light to shine on it, and figuratively by using the juxtaposition of exposing something hidden behind a lamp.

As I talked about it with friends, I realized I didn't need to go into the darkest places of my mind and immerse myself in pain and emotions as I did on the witness stand. I was fully in control and could be present to what was happening in the moment without dissociating or falling into a well of painful memories. It was an incredibly helpful reclamation that might not have happened if I hadn't found the poster. Sometimes, if we're willing, a trigger can be a catalyst for the transformation of harm. We can turn around and face it head on and see it for what it is. In this case, I turned it into a metaphor.

I needed to talk to Derek about the poster. I'd felt a connection with him but didn't know how it would manifest. I realized this poster was what would bring us together. The next day, he came by to get something from the storage shed. I invited him into the house, gave him a short version of my history and told him about finding the poster. It turned out The Loring Pasta Bar was where he and his partner, Brandon, had met for their first date. The poster was a memento of the occasion.

I asked if I could borrow it, explaining that my editor wanted to scan it as a possible image in the book. I joked that I'd love to burn it but would happily return it when I was done. He said he was fine with me taking it.

Later that day, he texted me: "If the poster supports your healing, we want you to have it. We hear you and see you while supporting your survivorship journey." Then he and Brandon invited me to dinner at their home. These lovely men had given up a meaningful memento because they knew it brought me pain. And I'd only just met them.

I know it's only a poster, but their response was a far cry from the way people typically reacted to McLean and his restaurant. I know some people still gave him their money by eating at his restaurant while knowing he was a sexual predator. His value as a restauranteur and music venue owner was more important than the string of wounded people he'd left behind him or how he treated his employees—or his own family.

I'm grateful for Derek and Brandon and the spark of a new friendship. This interaction shows me that things are shifting—in me and the world around me. We're in a new era of reckoning with the way Rape Culture is seen and dealt with.

When I finally told my parents about what McLean had done to me, I described my life in two parts—my childhood and how the rape had affected my adulthood. After listening to my story, my father said, "It sounds like you're ready for act three." I love his perspective, and I'm grateful to him for pointing to it. This part is my third act.

The last two years have been difficult in a different way. I was dealing with the emotional fall-out of years of litigation, the death of my father, a global pandemic, and my mother's struggle with Alzheimer's. I was dedicated to caring for her because my brothers and I had decided to bring her home instead of letting her waste away alone in memory care. Mom and I became very close in the last years of her life. The barriers that had kept her from expressing herself wore down, and she often told me how proud she was of me, how pretty she thought I was. Her support was invaluable.

When she died, I was heartbroken though relieved she was no longer suffering. I took some time to sit with my sadness, and then something broke free, and I was able to pour out the more difficult sections of this book. There must have been part of me that was still protecting her from my story. It was a freedom I found, like her spirit was saying, "It's time to let it flow."

My mother lived in a generation of silence around claiming her personal autonomy and acceptance of the unacceptable. She passed some of that on to me. But it's the nature of generational healing to let go of the barriers handed down to us.

About six months before she died, sitting in her favorite rocking chair, Mom told me a story that broke my heart. It was from when she was a young woman before she met my father. She was in the car of a young man she was dating, and he tried to rape her right there. She described how she had fought him off and was able to get away. She had escaped something I hadn't been able to flee. At that moment, her earlier comment of "these things happen" made total sense. There's power in telling our stories because it gives others permission to tell their own. It connects us in ways we fear will make us sad if we let the words flow, but it can actually bring us closer.

My life has changed in dramatic ways because of the past few years and also from writing this book. But it hasn't been easy. It's been everything from the deepest despair to outright euphoria. I've lost both of my parents, left my marriage, embraced my authentic self, and came to fully understand just how deeply my life had been hijacked by childhood sexual violence. The healing I've experienced has surpassed all expectations.

During the pandemic, I had to put my ailing cat to sleep. He was twenty years old, and it was time. I was alone for months in my apartment, unable to hug my children and only able to see them at a distance or on a flat screen. The thought of going through the winter like that was unbearable, so I decided to step out of my fear and ask for what I needed, and what I needed was a dog.

My apartment had a policy that allowed cats but not dogs. I pled my case with the landlord. To my surprise, the response was fast and positive—yes, I could get a dog. I wouldn't have my beloved Wilbur today if I'd given into my fear. Others in the building now have dogs, and we find community through these beautiful beasties. Wilbur is a constant reminder to me to stand for what's important for my mental well-being.

Everyone is on their own journey, and I want to meet people where they are, not where I wish they would be. That means a mindful pace and full commitment to self-care because I can easily take on things that aren't mine.

The tapestry I've woven for you is incomplete. There are threads missing. Some of them I can't access, or they aren't mine to weave. Others sit waiting for me to pick up and incorporate into the bigger picture, an image that will continue to change as I move forward. I'm not sure how long the threads will last. I'll keep moving until it's clear there is nothing left for me to do but sit back and admire the final image finding beauty in its totality of harmony and dissonance.

Me and Wilbur by Lake Superior in Northern Minnesota.
Obligatory selfie

The Children's Theatre Alumni Wellness Fund went live in the Fall of 2021, and some CTC alumni are getting access to healing such as they've never encountered before.

To learn more about CTA Wellness, please visit CTAWellness.org. If you're able to donate to this Survivors' Fund, please do so in whatever way makes sense for you so the fund can help as many CTC alumni as possible get therapeutic help for years to come.

This is an ending... but more like a Peter Jackson movie ending—we're not done just yet. It feels horrible to read a book filled with uncomfortable content and then have to walk away and just hold it... like a bag of dog poop when there's no garbage can to throw it in. *I don't want to hold onto this!* Well, here's some good news; keep reading to gain some understanding of Rape Culture and you'll find action steps you can take to make the world around you a little bit better.

Bonus Chapter
Excerpts from *Daring to Heal: Growing Beyond Trauma Through Awareness, Acceptance, and Action*

~ What is Rape Culture? ~

Rape Culture is one of the most harmful and destructive social contracts that exists in our society. We've been fed a way of thinking and participating in the world around us that keeps us locked into the effects of trauma on multiple levels. Most people aren't aware of how they contribute to the problem, but we all do. If we can break free of this normalized way of being and put our efforts towards normalizing a Culture of Consent, it would change many of our problems at the root.

I wasn't familiar with the term Rape Culture until it became more commonly used after the rise of the #MeToo movement. It was coined back in the seventies by the second-wave feminists. It's important to understand Rape Culture because we need to dismantle it if we want to keep people safe. Knowing what it is will help the bystander, as well as the victim, understand the foundation that holds it in place. It's used to soften or dismiss the reality of sexual violence. The following description from Marshall U* provides an excellent definition:

Rape Culture is an environment in which rape is prevalent and in which sexual violence against women is normalized and excused in the media and popular culture. Rape Culture is perpetuated through the use of misogynistic language, the objectification of women's bodies, and the glamorization of sexual violence, thereby creating a society that disregards women's rights and safety.

Rape Culture affects every woman. The rape of one woman is a degradation, terror and limitation to all women. Most women and girls limit their behavior because of the existence of rape. Most women and girls live in fear of rape. Men, in general, do not. That's how rape functions as a powerful means by which the whole female population is held in a subordinate position to the whole male population, even though most men don't rape and many women are never victims of rape. This cycle of fear is the legacy of Rape Culture.

Examples of Rape Culture:

- Blaming the victim (She asked for it)
- Trivializing sexual assault (Boys will be boys)
- Sexually explicit jokes
- Tolerance of sexual harassment
- Inflating false rape report statistics
- Publicly scrutinizing a victim's dress, mental state, motives, and history
- Gratuitous gendered violence in movies and television
- Defining "manhood" as dominant and sexually aggressive
- Defining "womanhood" as submissive and sexually passive

- Pressure on men to "score"

- Pressure on women to not appear "cold"

- Assuming only promiscuous women get raped

- Assuming that men don't get raped or that only "weak" men get raped

- Refusing to take rape accusations seriously

- Teaching women to avoid getting raped instead of teaching men not to rape

As a woman, I recognize the historic harm that's been inflicted on women and those who identify as female or feminine. I feel it in my body, like an electrical current. It's not the same as the energy I carry as a sexual assault survivor, but it's born of the same generator because sexual violence isn't just about sex; it's about power—finding, claiming or utilizing power, whether physical or psychological. It's important that we understand the dynamics around sexual violence if we want to create change.

Cultural shift doesn't just happen. The evolution of society grows from the small ways we allow ourselves to be transformed, which then colors the way we are with each other. Ignorance allows us to hide from the realities of the prevalence of sexual harm in the world. Gaining awareness and understanding of Rape Culture and seeing how we participate in it is the key to pushing the cultural shift from complicity to accountability. The main barriers I see to changing Rape Culture are:

- Lack of understanding - Not enough information and dismissive attitudes

- Willful Ignorance - It's easier to look away than see what's true

- Power structures - Upholding male dominance and fearing the power of women

- Shock and disregard - Disbelief or discrediting victims when truth is spoken

- Language - Media misrepresentation, rape jokes, victim-blaming

Transforming Rape Culture requires:

- **Awareness** - Stop ignoring the truth about what's happening around you. See how you participate in Rape Culture—because we all do.

- **Acceptance** - Sexual violence is real, and it's not pretty. Allow yourself to really look at what's in the shadows. Not looking doesn't make it go away. It helps to keep it hidden, which helps support the system that holds Rape Culture in place. Accept the reality of what we're up against.

- **Action** - Be willing to be uncomfortable. Step outside of your comfort zone. Use your personal autonomy and your voice to affect change and encourage others to do so too. Insist on accountability.

The #MeToo movement, founded by Tarana Burke in 2006, was catapulted to national awareness in 2017 by the women in Hollywood who called out Harvey Weinstein, and it has changed the way we see Rape Culture. It set something in motion that has never before occurred—undeniable public awareness of the way women are widely treated and have been treated since the dawn of time.

The abusive and disrespectful treatment has been considered acceptable because of social norms. #MeToo cracked open something in society that was long overdue, and a tidal wave of truth-telling swept through our society. It called attention to the despicable and disgusting actions of Weinstein and his ilk, the people who enabled them, and the culture that normalizes this kind of oppressive, abusive and demeaning behavior.

Because of #MeToo, women, in general, are less willing now to accept unacceptable behavior. Men are reflecting on their own participation in cultivating this cultural blemish, discovering they've played a part in it by riding on the entitlement that goes with their gender. They're starting to see the ways they've trampled the physical barriers women have been trying to uphold for themselves, and women are seeing the ways they've continually moved the lines of personal safe space to conform or not make waves. It's a new era. But it's not enough.

#MeToo is one of the most important societal reckonings that has happened in our generation. It gave permission to half the population of our planet to take a breath and exhale truth in the form of a shared experience. Not all women choose to take advantage of that, but knowing that the definition of sexual violence includes not only rape or attempted rape but also unwanted or non-consensual sexual contact, sexual harassment and sexual exploitation, we all have some experience with it.

~The Part We All Play ~

Some women of my mother's generation roll their eyes at younger generations who speak out about sexual harassment because they tolerated so much of it throughout their lives. No one encouraged them to make a stink about it. They were told to deal with it because "you won't get far if you make a fuss." Harassment is everywhere, so why try?

Bystanders of harm stand slack-jawed at the boldness of people who perpetrate harm, from offenses such as rape jokes all the way to public demonstrations of physical abuse. Sometimes they stay silent because they're afraid to say something, but also because they're in shock and don't snap out of it. "Did I really see what I just saw?" They freeze. They forget. They move on.

Here's an ugly truth. A male friend told me he'd been sexually assaulted by a respected member of our community. I believed him, of course. He had no reason to lie to me. Despite that, one of my first thoughts was, "I wonder if it was just touching, or was he raped? We should find out if there were others so it will add legitimacy to his claim, otherwise, it's not as valid."

It pains me that these thoughts would ever enter my mind. I hated myself for it. This is how Rape Culture is embedded in me, a rape victim. I've been programmed to downgrade sex crimes. We all have. I hear about a gang rape and immediately wonder, "How many guys did it. Five? Ten?" As if the number matters. Isn't one enough? Honest to God, one rape is bad enough. One is one too many.

~ Shifting the Culture ~

Rape Culture is an implicit or unconscious cultural agreement that allows perpetrators of sexual violence to harm people without consequences. I don't know about you, but I don't remember ever agreeing to any contract that would allow such a thing. It's something that happened a long time ago and was passed on through the generations. Unfortunately, it continues to rule the way society responds to sexual violence and how it sees itself.

I renounce my participation in this contract. If there were a paper version, I'd burn it. I guess that's what women were doing back in the 1970s when they were burning their bras—they were flipping the bird to that social contract.

If the way I talk about Rape Culture sounds reminiscent of the ways people talk about white privilege and white supremacy, that's because it's the same structure that holds these destructive models in place. I'm drawing a parallel to illustrate the importance of dismantling both. It's up to each of us to shine the healing light of truth on these wounds of our society. We need to educate ourselves and each other to stand together and not shy away from the ugly truths. It's the only way to take down these hardened structures once and for all. The power in our collective voices is undeniable.

Allow me to take a moment to reach out to my Black and Brown-bodied female friends, all of those glorious BIPOC women who have endured the double jeopardy of these power structures. I see you. I love you. I believe you will change the world. You are inspiring.

We need to be willing to replace Rape Culture with Consent Culture in every area of our lives. We should stop in our tracks when we see that something is wrong and not uphold a system that relies on willful ignorance, even if it means inconveniencing ourselves—even if it means we walk away from something we've invested time and money in. Here are a few things that keep us from doing that:

- We don't want to accept how prevalent sexual violence is, largely because people don't want to talk about it or look at it because it's so ugly.

- We don't want to see that we allow this problem to flourish by ignoring it, which emboldens those who perpetrate the crimes because they know they can get away with it.

- We think it's not our problem to solve.

- We believe that victims of sexual violence are partly responsible for what happens to them.

It's hard to find the balance in this truth-telling. People become saturated by it after a while. I see it happening around the racial divisions in this country. "Can we please talk about something else?" Yes... and no. Yes, because people do need to take a break from the intensity—self-care is important. And no, because it isn't going to change unless we stay present to the truth and focused on change. Change doesn't happen by wishing something away; it happens through hard work and persistence.

How do we combat something that is so prevalent in our society? We speak the truth. We name it. We make space for others to speak their truth, and we listen. We encourage those who are afraid. We allow one voice to become ten, to become a hundred, to become a thousand, until the chorus of voices is so loud it can't be denied.

~ Ten Things You Can Do Right Now ~

There's no way we're going to get to the other side of Rape Culture without making mistakes. People will get hurt. Wrong words will be spoken. When it happens, be accountable for your actions. Recognize the fallibility of our humanness. Give yourself and others permission to stumble and fall. Create space and opportunity for accountability. But don't do it at the cost of your own wellbeing.

Here are ten things you can do right now to help dismantle Rape Culture:

1. Say what's true

Exercise your truth-speaking muscles by practicing speaking truth in every area of your life, especially *good* truth. Speaking truth gets easier the more you do it. Tell people you admire how awesome they are and do it often. Before you know it, you'll be an expert truth-teller.

2. Believe people

When someone says they were harmed, believe them without justification. It doesn't matter what the circumstances were. Your default should be to believe them. And don't do it quietly; say the words—*I believe you.*

3. Hold the line

If someone gets in your personal space without permission, hold your boundary line and ask them to back off. You have the right to do this; it's *your body.* You can be polite but be firm.

4. Empower children

Our children need to have agency over their own bodies. Ask permission to touch them. Help them understand they have a say in who touches them and teach them to respect the boundaries of others.

5. Name Rape Culture when you see it

Be an advocate for change. When you hear things that uphold Rape Culture, like rape jokes or derogatory terms for women and other underrepresented people, name it.

6. Don't just be a bystander, be an active upstander

When you see someone saying or doing something that isn't okay with you, say so.

7. Be accountable

When you do something wrong—and you will—be accountable for it. If you can't find the words at the moment, you can always go back later and make it right.

8. Demand institutional accountability

Don't allow employers to get away with not addressing power dynamics that uphold Rape Culture in their businesses. If they don't make strides toward change, take your business elsewhere.

9. Stop putting money toward upholding Rape Culture

You have a choice about the movies you see, the theaters you patronize, the music you listen to, the news you watch. Stop supporting social narratives that continue to uphold Rape Culture. Seek out artists, media and movements that are committed to shifting the culture and support them with your time and money.

10. Be a model of change

Encourage others by being a model. You never know who is watching you. BE LOUD.

Advocating for ourselves and others is a scary affair. It's time to be courageous, walk forward in spite of our fear and stop allowing it to keep us from doing what's right. Too often, I've been paralyzed by my fear, but when I take it by the hand and stay in motion, amazing things happen.

I don't like the word "fearless" when it comes to this work. Fearless is for gladiators and race car drivers. Courage is the stuff of advocates and survivors, those who walk forward anyway, not knowing how it will turn out, yet doing it because it's the next right thing to do. Courage has many faces. Sometimes it looks like testifying in a courtroom. Sometimes it looks like stepping in harm's way to advocate for the needs of someone unable to do it for themselves. It can also look like picking up the phone to ask for help when you're struggling. It's the same damn thing, and it all counts.

Walking forward in the face of fear causes us to become bigger than we were, to stretch beyond our boundaries and to find things we didn't know existed. Yes, sometimes the things I find in that unknown territory aren't so great. More often than not, though, I find something beautiful I didn't even know I needed. If I only pursue the things that are known to me, I'll never grow.

Acknowledgments

So many people have supported me emotionally through this journey, I fear that in writing down names I will forget someone. Nevertheless, I want to make sure that specific people are acknowledged. Here are the names of those who have shown up in ways that lifted me up, cheered me on, helped me realize I'm not alone, pointed to my strength when I thought I had none, helped me center myself when I was spinning emotionally.

In no particular order: Jen Maren, Peter Simmons, Marguerite Von Durkheim and Kory Johnson, Alyssa and Eric Breece, Sarah Super, Genevieve Bennett, Jo Holcomb, Wendy Goldberg, Ellen Fenster, Sophie Peyton, Eva Gemlo, T. Mychael Rambo, Jaydub, Yoke and Shawn Judge, Molly Glasgow, Laurie Beth Fitz, Lisa Steinberg, Shá Cage, Matthew Sciple, Rosy Simas, Scott Tracy, Victor Walter, Elizabeth Ellis, Sharon Gunther, Buffy Sedlachek, Tinia Moulder, Marty Ruben, EJ Subkoviak, Lorna Landvik, Ann Milligan Lees, Marshall Hambro, Anna Tift, Daved Thom, Erin Nanasi, Marin Kopper, Stacey and Michael Paul Dinner-Levin, Kate Wexler, Michelle Berg, Sue Scott, Ron Peluso, Meghan Kreidler, Laila Sahir, Lolly Foy, Roderic Culver, Yvonne Mont Martin, Sharalee Milligan, David and Renee Carey, Shari Baker, Sophine Saggau, Hope Funke, Jen Klink, Alessandra Bongiardina, Kayla McCaffrey, Chloé Bell, Carley Rosefelt, Annie Schiferl, Kat Rudman, Jesse Burgum, Leon and Shannon Hammer, Mike Warren, Alex Ritter, Andrea

Moriarity, Sulia Altenberg, Trevor Long, John Cutler, Jessie Lynn, Todd and Annette Hildebrandt, Jill Callander, Nina Grunseth, Max Mainwood, Ben Blackhawk, Warren Bowles, Aimeé Boyd, Emmeline Hall, Jeanie Jordan, Doug Anderson, Mark Bergren, Christian Bardin, Terry Lynn Carlson, Jeff Danovsky, Nathan Peterson, Wyatt McDill, John Gamoke, DJ Gramman, Kim Maguire, Amy Colón, Libby Starling and Kevin Dutcher, Jamie Coulter, Madilynn Garcia, Kim Mortenson, H. Adam Harris, Willie Weir, David Simmons, Rachel Adams, Mary Adams, Luke Diamond, Josette Antomarchi, Jamie Case, Nell Pierce, Sabra Thurber, Kevin McCormick, Chris and Angela Denton, Brenda Langton, Peter Colburn, Jody Wellumson, Ivy Loughborough, Jenny Gants, Debi and Ashley Adams, Quinton Skinner and Mo Perry, Josh Adams and Jon Barnes, Jean Heyer, Kristina Graber, Trisha Kirk, Erik Heger, Elizabeth Eilers Sullivan, Jolie Meshbesher, Colleen Barrett, Paul Toni, Loran Calvin, Beth Taylor Schott, Alison Edwards, Signe Harriday, Julie Warder, David Russell, Peter Thomson, Jann Garfano, Kristine Liemandt Bland, Patrick McDonald, Rebecca Noon, Tom Olson, Missy Yager, Emily Zimmer, Raye Birk and Candace Barrett Birk, Jolie Meshbesher, David Tufford, Clara Rusch, Jamie Case, Robert DuSold, Ellen Harvey, Ann Michels, Stacia Rice, Deal Seal, Ernie Sandidge, Nancy Seward, Michael John Pease, Heidi Fellner, Brandon Stahl, Jeremy Cohen, Peter Rothstein, Jacqueline Correa, Joy Langer, Adena Brumer, Kerstin Sjoquist, Zhauna Franks, Paul Reyburn, Angela Marie, Ryan Colbert, Greg Brown, Bonni Allen, Laura Zabel, Dan Rooney, Andrew Erskine Wheeler, Jeanette Simmonds, Crist Ballas, Joseph Haj, Travis Fine, Joel and Jen Liestman, Haley Finn, Ryan Melling, Sean Walters, Johanna Shapiro, Mark Millhone, C. Andrew Mayer, Danny Schmitz, TJ O'Donnell, Jim McDonough, David Pisa, Joanna Schnedler, Colleen Somerville Leeman, Elizabeth Efteland, Sam Bardwell, Hugh Kennedy, Lauren Keating, Kaia Lee, Kristen Froebel, Tony Anderson, Karen Bix, Peter Breitmayer and Michelle Pederson, Catherine Campbell, Yvonne Cournoyer,

Carolyn Denton, Gene and Val Larche, Leslee Jaeger, Mary Lisbeth Bartlett, Beth Desotelle, Robert Dorfman, Nicholas Adams, Nathan Ehrlich, Maija Garcia, Jody Goldie, Jana Goodermont, James Detmar, Chris Hewitt, John Humleker, Brian Kelly, Eden Alair, Jim Kurtzbein, Scott and Chris Stearns, Tracey Maloney, C. Amanda Maud, Tucker McCrady, Beth Hackman, Molly McManus, Lesley Moore, Bob and Susan Mortenson, Hope Nordquist, Brandon Eilers and Derek Nyberg, Domino Rosa, Amy Schmidt, Miriam Schwartz, Stacey Schwebach, Tricia Stogsdill, Sue Kotilla, Linda Tuma, Avi Aharoni, Meshach Weber, Aleksander Weirzbicki, Sally Wingert, Wini Froelich, Eric Webster, Jeremy Norton, Tasha Johnson, Maile Flanagan and Lese Hammet, Wendy Knox, Regina Williams, Emily Gunyou Halaas, Barbara Brooks, Nancy Lyons, Jessica Rau, Stacey Allen, Ellie Hyatt, Karen Horner, Melissa Beneke, Marta Keane, Aaron Fiskradatz, Mark Benninghofen, Jon Conte, Sharon Cooper, Patty Wetterling, Kenosha Davenport, Ashley Taylor-Gougé, The entire Adams Clan, The entire Stearns Clan, my Guthrie Family, my SVC family, and all the CTC alumni who have reached out to me in support over the years.

Very Special Thanks to:

How does one say thank you to a community? Everyone involved in Standing With CTC Survivors, The Artist Community Council, and CTA Wellness, you inspired me and kept me going, your support was invaluable. Kim and Griff for holding me together over vast miles and years. Jina, for being a bookend. Rana for opening your home and your heart, words are insufficient for my thanks. Alan, Shelly and Doug for giving me a beautiful space to finish this book. Dzendy for all of it. Shanan and Rainy for spa time, badass bitch time and SO much more. Marianne Combs for your tenacity. Elizabeth Larsen for bearing witness. Norah Shapiro for taking the deep dive. Don Goff for your support and your smile. Sally Wallach for being you. Rob Shapiro for creating a beautiful space and crying with me on the carpet. Jeffrey Hatcher for your support and most excellent feedback. Annie Enneking for bacon pancakes. Amber Brown for seeing me and knowing what to do. Medaria Arradando for keeping the music playing. Maria Asp for helping me keep my heart open. Elena Giannetti and Pogi Sumangil for your willingness to say what's true even when it's hard. DStew for Star Wars on a workday. Damon Runnals for raising the stakes. To the MNTAC Editors, Shelli Place, James Grace, Max Wojtanowicz, Aidan Gallivan, Kathy Kohl, Molly Fox, and Jenny Friend for staying with it. Ricardo Levins Morales for helping me stay grounded. Bridget Sullivan for your expert advice and long walks. The Badass Crones for the weekly lift and witnessing. Jeff Anderson for your guidance and willingness to allow the blemishes to be seen. To Molly, Stacey, Taylor, Mike, Michelle, Asja, Paul, Trusha, Darrow, and everyone at JAA for doing what you do. To the litigant group, you know who you are, for the bond that held me together when I was falling apart. To Ian Graham Leask, Gary Lindberg, Susan Thurston-Hamerski and everyone at Calumet for pushing me to make this book the best it could be. To Dawn McClelland for helping me rescue my littles. To Cordelia Anderson for your inspiration and encouragement. To Lee Adams for your years of support and sacrifices. To Bradley Dean for steaks cooked perfectly. To my parents for loving me so well. I miss you. And finally, to Tucker and Calvin for being the best children a mother could want, I'm so proud of you both for the men you have become.

Appendix

~ A Timeline of Events and Incomplete History of The Children's Theatre Company and School ~

This is my attempt to pull the pieces of this gigantic jigsaw puzzle together to make sense of it without a picture on the cover of the box. Some pieces will be missing, I'm sure. No single person holds all the pieces of this complicated story of the Children's Theatre Company (CTC). If you have already read the book, below you will find that more details are provided from what was shared in the history section earlier.

The sources for the information provided are cited and include evidence collected by Jeff Anderson and Associates for the civil cases filed in 2015–16, newspaper articles going back to 1961, public records, court documents, testimony given in depositions and in court, the PhD doctorate thesis of Martin John Costello and eyewitness accounts told directly to me. At times I share my thoughts, include world events for broader context, and events that happened in my own life.

This is a fraction of the evidence, things I'm able to share. Spoiler alert: If you haven't read the full book, this Appendix contains information from throughout the book and assembled here to place events and information into a timeline. Take the long road if you don't want to be overwhelmed with too much information at once.

1961

- In the spring of 1961, twenty-three-year-old John Clark Donahue graduated from the University of Minnesota with a theater degree.[86] Shortly after, he was hired as a teacher at Carl Sandburg Junior High. By October of that year, he was charged with the felony crime of sodomizing a student. Donahue was one of several men arrested during an investigation into what was described as a "homosexual ring" by the *Minneapolis Tribune* on October 24, 1961.[87] This ring was suspected of exchanging adolescent male victims—which we refer to today as child trafficking—and producing child sexual abuse images. He pled guilty to a lesser charge, was given a one-year suspended sentence and went to the workhouse for ninety days.[88]

- At the time of Martin John Costello's research and writing for his thesis, he reported the court records for Donahue's criminal activity in 1961 were "mysteriously missing," as he put it, from the Hennepin County District Court.[89]

- That same year, Beth Linnerson and John Davidson started a theater for children called The Moppet Players. This company would produce theatrical productions of classic children's literature and provide classes in theater performance and production to young people. Linnerson wanted to provide a way for young people to develop life skills through the study of theater arts. Classes were free to the neighborhood kids in the Cedar-Riverside

---

86 Costello Thesis, p. 133

87 *Minneapolis Tribune*, "Two Men Charged as Morals Case Probe Continues," October 24, 1961, p. 22

88 Stearns v. CTC No. 27-CV-15-20713, trial exhibit #69, Minnesota Department of Public Safety explanation of charges, SID# MN00166486.

89 Costello Thesis, p. 148

neighborhood where the theater was located at the time.[90] The Moppets are part of the CTC legacy.

1962–64

- Out of work and freshly out of jail, Donahue was hired by Linnerson as a set designer and painter for The Moppet Players. Linnerson was Donahue's classmate at the university and knew about his criminal history but felt sorry for him and believed she could "keep an eye on what was happening."[91] I didn't know her personally, but understand her to have been a kind woman, though completely misguided in her assumption that she could control a pedophile.

- The Moppets first performed in the back room of an Italian restaurant called Mama Rosa's. They moved to an abandoned police station, which was refurbished and turned into a performance space.[92]

- Donahue slowly gained more status, and by 1964 he was an instructor and associate artistic director alongside Linnerson. Davidson handled the business end of things. Donahue began to incorporate his teaching methods for producing Children's Theatre by and for children, believing that kids would rise to the challenge of higher levels of artistry if given the opportunity. Linnerson didn't share this philosophy. Donahue had the ambition to create something she was theoretically opposed to. Linnerson wanted to help

---

90 Costello Thesis pp. 131–134, and Deborah Caulfield, "The Scandal at the Children's Theatre," *LA Times Calendar*, July 22, 1984, p. 4

91 Deborah Caulfield, "The Scandal at the Children's Theatre," *LA Times Calendar*, July 22, 1984, p. 4

92 Stearns v. CTC No. 27-CV-15-20713, trial exhibit #53, CTC promotional materials, and Deborah Caulfield, "The Scandal at the Children's Theatre," *LA Times Calendar*, July 22, 1984, p. 4

kids find themselves through studying the arts. Donahue wanted to mold them and train actors for his plays.[93]

- During this period, Linnerson and Donahue's working relationship began to splinter. Why this happened is up for debate—it depends on which narrative you read. Costello's thesis refers to the tension between Linnerson and Donahue and the clear distinction in their theories of education of children in the arts. CTC literature makes it look like it was an amicable departure and natural progression to part ways. Regardless, Linnerson left the company in 1964, and Donahue was made artistic director for The Moppet Players. Davidson continued as administrator.[94]

1965

- Donahue was now in charge of the artistic side of the company, much to Linnerson's dismay, but only stayed with the Moppets for about a year. CTC literature says that Donahue decided to leave the Moppets in 1965 and founded Children's Theatre Company (CTC), bringing with him those artists from The Moppet Players who believed in his vision, including company members Wendy Lehr and Bain Boehlke. After Donahue departed the Moppets, the company continued to produce shows until at least 1968.[95] It appears there was a falling out between the two leaders, and the acting company and production teams chose sides.

- Apparently, Linnerson wasn't bitter because when she had the opportunity to tell the newly formed board of directors

93 Costello Thesis, p. 134
94 Costello Thesis, pp. 133 and 135, and Stearns v. CTC No. 27-CV-15-20713, Jeff Anderson and Associates Collected Evidence Archive, including notes from the board of directors and accounting records
95 Costello Thesis, p. 134

for CTC about Donahue's criminal past, she chose to remain silent. Though she said she felt "morally responsible" to say something because she was no longer in a position to keep an eye on him, she chose instead to give them a "vague warning" that none of them understood.[96] This choice is crucial to how Donahue would be able to build his legacy of harm, allowing a pedophile to have full and unquestioned access to children. Sadly, it was only one of scores of decisions made by people in a complicit community that allowed him to continue his reign of abuse.

- With Donahue as artistic director and Davidson as the managing director, the newly established Children's Theatre Company went into a partnership with the Minneapolis Society of Fine Arts (MSFA). CTC started performances in an auditorium at the Minneapolis Institute of Arts (MIA), which would be its home base for the better part of the next decade until construction of the current building was completed in 1975.[97] At some point, Davidson decided to leave the company and Donahue assumed administrative control, changing the power structure entirely, so he alone had artistic and administrative power of the organization.[98]

1965–69

- Donahue and his acting company began teaching theater arts performance and production classes to high school-aged kids using his educational methodology. In her deposition in 2018, core company member, Wendy Lehr, stated that

---

96 Deborah Caulfield, "The Scandal at the Children's Theatre," *LA Times Calendar*, July 22, 1984, p. 4

97 Stearns v. CTC No. 27-CV-15-20713, trial exhibit #53, CTC promotional materials

98 State v. Donahue DC85019-1, 20-1 and DC86175-1

Donahue had her and other company members start teaching classes without any previous teaching experience.[99] They learned to teach through trial and error and by observing and reflecting Donahue's vision.

- At no time did Donahue apply to be accredited as a teacher. The privilege of teaching and working with kids was simply given to him and never questioned. As Costello points out in his thesis, had Donahue applied for accreditation, his criminal past would have been exposed, disqualifying him.[100]

1967

- I was born.

- At least five male students at CTC report having been abused by Donahue in the late sixties.[101]

1969

- The first man landed on the moon. Richard Nixon was President of the United States.

- With endorsement from the Minnesota State Arts Board and the National Endowment for the Arts, Donahue established an official theater training program that was part of the Minneapolis Public School System's Urban Arts Program. Students would attend their regular public school classes in the mornings and then attend classes at the theater in the afternoon. Kids were awarded high school credits for

---

99 Video Deposition of Wendy Lehr, timestamp 12:13:31, given November 8, 2018
100 Costello Thesis, p. 139
101 Protected victim statements and depositions with Jeff Anderson and Associates

the classes they attended at the theater.[102] This was the basic structure when I first started attending. Thousands of kids participated in programs through the school and outreach programs between 1969 and 1986.

1970

- Donahue, having managed to obtain sole power over the institution, began surrounding himself with people who considered him a genius, praised his accomplishments and wouldn't question his authority, such as former students he had trained.[103]

- Donahue used fear and intimidation to keep people in line, adults and kids alike. No one wanted to be called out by him. If he were verbally berating a child, no one would challenge him, and in some cases, they would join in. Costello's thesis refers to notes from a Donahue court-ordered therapy session in 1984 conducted while he was incarcerated. It stated that Donahue said no one ever questioned him or told him he shouldn't be doing what he was doing, and he used that as an excuse for his abuse of children.[104]

- In the early seventies, rumors of Donahue's abuse of boys became more prevalent in the community, and reports started to surface in the staff.[105]

---

102 Stearns v. CTC No. 27-CV-15-20713, trial exhibit #53, CTC promotional materials, and Jeff Anderson and Associates Collected Evidence Archive, including student transcripts, schedules, and multiple statements taken by JAA
103 Costello Thesis, p. 133
104 Costello Thesis, p. 249
105 Furst and McEnroe, "Donahue Was Topic of Rumors for Many Years," *Minneapolis Tribune*, April 29, 1984, p. 10A

1971

- The school expanded to include a summer school program, outreach and residency training in public schools. The 1971 launch of a summer school program increased enrollment substantially.[106] Eventually, it grew to a five-week program called The Summer Institute, which included all-day classes attended by students from Minneapolis and around the country. Attendees worked on a production that was performed, crewed and presented by students at the end of the summer session.

1972

- The success of CTC regular season productions outshined anything the Moppets had ever done, and the growth of the school created national buzz and prestige. Donahue and company received national attention and many prestigious awards, including funding from the Rockefeller Foundation in 1972 and 1973, totaling three-quarters of a million dollars.[107] This put CTC into a category with the likes of the Lincoln and Kennedy Centers for the Performing Arts.

- These funds were crucial to the construction of a new building designed by the world-famous Japanese master architect Kenzo Tange who designed famous buildings worldwide, including the Tokyo Olympic Arena.[108]

- Donahue had been working with The Minneapolis Society of

---

106 Stearns v. CTC No. 27-CV-15-20713, trial exhibit #53, CTC promotional materials
107 Stearns v. CTC No. 27-CV-15-20713, trial exhibit #53, CTC promotional materials
108 Stearns v. CTC No. 27-CV-15-20713, trial exhibit #53, CTC promotional materials

Fine Arts (MSFA) since 1965, when CTC moved into MIA to perform its shows. During the construction of the new theater building, Donahue purchased a home owned by MSFA for one dollar. That home had been scheduled to be demolished in the area of the campus that would include the Minneapolis College of Art and Design. He had the home moved across the street to its current location.[109] Donahue paid for the house to be moved and renovated it.[110] I remember hearing stories about this as part of the CTC lore. The local paper wrote an article about it. This house had an upstairs where company member Wendy Lehr lived.[111] It's also the location of countless abuses of children.[112]

1973

- In addition to being both Artistic and Executive Director of CTC, Donahue was an associate director of the Minneapolis Society of Fine Arts and had solid connections with the most affluent people in the Twin Cities.[113]

- Donahue was fast becoming a darling of the community and CTC a gem of the city. The American Theater Association named Donahue "Arts Administrator of the Year," and he won the Jennie Helden Award for "excellence in professional Children's Theatre."[114]

---

109 Robert T. Smith column, *Minneapolis StarTribune* Other Editions feature, May 5, 1972
110 City of Minneapolis Block 6 Record, ADN 17090, GEO Galpin's Addition to Minneapolis, and State of Minnesota Department of Taxation Form 7-M, #3992242
111 Stearns v. CTC No. 27-CV-15-20713, testimony of Wendy Lehr, trial transcript, p. 1479
112 Protected victim statements and depositions with Jeff Anderson and Associates
113 Costello Thesis, p. 143
114 Stearns v. CTC No. 27-CV-15-20713, trial exhibit #53, CTC promotional materials, and Costello Thesis, p. 141

- Donahue was a charismatic figure who removed the boundaries between adults and children in the name of creating more authentic art. Kids loved him for this because he believed in what they were capable of, and that, in turn, made them believe in themselves. Most of his students credit him with making them into great artists, using phrases like "he saved my life" and "I wouldn't be the artist I am today without him." He was revered and admired because of how he was able to get the kids under his tutelage to blossom.[115]

1974

- The new building opened for the 1974–75 theater season. It is connected to the Minneapolis Institute of Arts and boasts a 736-seat auditorium with a 90' by 42' proscenium stage.

1977

- I was assaulted by Jeff Rusthoven.

1975–80

- In 1975, the MSFA was the governing body for MIA, CTC and the Minneapolis College of Art and Design (MCAD) and had contributed substantial funds for the construction of the new building.[116] By this time, Donahue was an associate director of MSFA, as well as artistic director of CTC.[117] His

---

115 Kay Miller, "A Story of Denial John Clark Donahue and the Children's Theatre— Parts 1, 2 and 3," for *Minneapolis StarTribune*, May 19, 20, 21, 1991
116 Stearns v. CTC No. 27-CV-15-20713, Jeff Anderson and Associates Collected Evidence Archive including Minneapolis Institute of Arts notes from the board of directors and accounting records
117 Costello Thesis, p. 143

position as "Associate Director" is described in the Costello thesis as a vice-president position.

- A dispute caused Donahue to break ties with MSFA. CTC incorporated as an independent nonprofit organization, signing a lease agreement with MSFA to stay in the building. Details of this decision are vague, and for someone who was so closely linked to the society, it must have been quite a conflict. It's clear that the relationship between Donahue and MFSA was complicated.[118]

- The Mandatory Reporting Law was passed in 1975, which requires anyone in a position of power over children, such as teachers, to report suspicion of child abuse to the authorities, stating that anyone who is a mandated reporter and "who has knowledge of or a reasonable cause to believe a child is being physically or sexually assaulted shall report." It goes on to say, "Any person required by this act to report suspected physical or sexual abuse, who willfully fails to do so, is guilty of a misdemeanor."[119]

- Throughout the seventies, Donahue continued to gain prominence in the community and established relationships with the most affluent and influential people in town. In the late seventies and early eighties, the theater received multiple national theater awards, and Donahue himself was lauded for his accomplishments and received multiple prestigious awards.[120]

- Donahue's professional behavior was becoming well known in the industry at large, even outside of Minneapolis.

118 Stearns v. CTC No. 27-CV-15-20713, trial exhibit #53, CTC promotional materials, and Costello Thesis, p. 143
119 Minn. Stat. § 626.556 (1975); Minn. Stat. § 260E.06 (2020)
120 Stearns v. CTC No. 27-CV-15-20713, trial exhibit #53, CTC promotional materials

- By the late seventies, the artistic staff of CTC was almost entirely made up of former students.[121]

- In approximately 1972, parent Jacqui Smith was told by two students, who were sixteen and seventeen, that they were "having sex relations" with Donahue. The students asked her not to tell anyone about it. Because the mandated reporting laws were not established yet, Smith honored that request and did not report to the authorities at that time.[122] However, by 1977–78, Jacqui Smith, now on the CTC Board, reported to Deborah Anderson, the Director of Sexual Assault Services for Hennepin County, information about students she was aware of who had been abused by Donahue.[123] Anderson, noting Donahue's prestige and connections to influential and wealthy people, recalled Smith's information as "the biggest bomb" that could hit Minneapolis if an investigation found any truth in the allegations.[124]

- MPD began investigating the rumors of sex abuse of children at the theater but was unable to get solid information. A former secretary at the theater called and told them that abuse was happening, though she was too afraid of the people at the theater to do more than inform them of the situation.[125]

- The police investigation stalled.

- The Hennepin County Attorney's Office began the Child Sexual Abuse Prevention Project in Minnesota.[126]

---

121 Protected victim statements and depositions with Jeff Anderson and Associates, and multiple eyewitness accounts

122 Furst and McEnroe, "Donahue Was Topic of Rumors for Many Years," *Minneapolis Tribune*, April 29, 1984, p. 10A

123 Stearns v. CTC No. 27-CV-15-20713, Testimony of Deborah Anderson, trial transcript, p. 1640

124 Grand Jury Transcript, testimony of Deborah Anderson, vol. 3, p. 1

125 Furst and McEnroe, "Donahue Was Topic of Rumors for Many Years," *Minneapolis Tribune*, April 29, 1984, p. 10A

126 https://www.ojp.gov/ncjrs/virtual-library/abstracts/child-sexual-abuse-

- Despite rumors of his abuse of male students, referred to as the "worst kept secret in Minneapolis" by one public school teacher, Donahue's popularity and reverence within the community grew because people were enamored with Donahue's vision of theater and the level of artistry being produced at CTC. Everyone around him chose to look the other way.[127]

- At least nine male students report being assaulted in the seventies by Donahue.[128]

- Donahue established working connections with such famous children's book illustrators and authors as Tomie dePaola and Dr. Seuss.[129]

- By 1980, CTC was highly acclaimed internationally and considered a premier theater for children in the United States with a budget of $2.7 million and an annual audience of more than a quarter-million people.[130]

1980

- By 1980, the teaching and artistic staff at CTC was almost entirely made up of people who believed Donahue was a genius and could do no wrong, and his former students, people who had grown up with no boundaries between adults and children, and for whom the sexualization of children was normalized.[131]

prevention-project-educational-program-children

127 Kay Miller, "A Story of Denial John Clark Donahue and the Children's Theatre— Part 1," *Minneapolis StarTribune*, May 19, 1991

128 Protected victim statements and depositions with Jeff Anderson and Associates

129 Stearns v. CTC No. 27-CV-15-20713, trial exhibit #53, CTC promotional materials, and Costello Thesis, p. 145

130 Costello Thesis, p. 124

131 Costello Thesis, pp. 118–123, Protected victim statements and depositions

- Drug and alcohol use by kids was common at CTC parties.[132]

- Awareness around child sexual assault was gaining ground in the United States.

- The National Center on Child Abuse and Neglect funded six prevention demonstration projects nationwide, including a play at the Illusion Theater in Minneapolis called TOUCH.

- Ronald Regan was elected president of the United States.

1981

- I started taking theater classes at CTC in January of 1981.

- In the fall, the fully accredited Conservatory School was established at CTC. Academic classes were scheduled during the morning, and theater education classes continued to be provided in the afternoon. Some theater school students continued to attend public schools for academics.

- A staff of ten teachers was hired to provide the academic education for the theater students. For the first year of the conservatory, there were around twenty-five students total. By 1984 there were over 120 enrolled students in grades three to twelve.

- Bureau of Criminal Apprehension (BCA) took over the investigation of sexual allegations at CTC.[133]

---

with Jeff Anderson and Associates, and multiple eyewitness accounts
132 Stearns v. CTC No. 27-CV-15-20713, testimony of Karen Hagen, trial transcript, pp. 85–87, and protected victim statements and depositions with Jeff Anderson and Associates
133 Stearns v. CTC No. 27-CV-15-20713, testimony of investigator Michael Campion, trial transcript, pp. 23–24

1982

- The BCA moved narcotics investigator Michael Campion to the CTC investigation, putting him in charge of it full time and removing him from his other cases so he could dedicate his full attention.[134]

- The BCA informed the CTC Board of Directors that Donahue was being investigated in 1982 and told them not to interfere with the investigation.[135] Instead of putting protections in place for the children, such as the "rule of three,"[136] which they could have done without interfering, executive director Sarah Lawless told Donahue he was being investigated. He denied any wrongdoing.[137]

- In August, *Smithsonian Magazine* featured the Children's Theatre Company as its cover story. McLean is pictured in the photograph as the character of the Caterpillar in *Alice in Wonderland.*[138]

- Wayne Jennings was hired as director of education for the Conservatory School.

- McLean started his grooming of me in the fall.

134 Stearns v. CTC No. 27-CV-15-20713, testimony of investigator Michael Campion, trial transcript, pp. 23–24.

135 Stearns v. CTC No. 27-CV-15-20713, testimonies of Michael Campion, trial transcript, pp. 23–24, and Winthrop Rockwell, trial transcript, pp. 1541–1545

136 Definition of "rule of three." This means no child will be left alone with an adult; there will always be at least two adults in the room with students at any given time if a student is alone.

137 Stearns v. CTC No. 27-CV-15-20713, testimony of Winthrop Rockwell, trial transcript, p. 1516

138 Costello Thesis, p. 145, and Randy Sue Coburn, "Children's Theatre Comes of Age in a Unique Minnesota Playhouse," *Smithsonian Magazine*, August 1982, pp. 53–54, featured on cover

1983

- Terri Hanson, a music teacher at South High School and director of the Urban Arts Program for public schools, was arrested for criminal sexual assault of a student and making child abuse images. He plea-bargained for a reduced sentence and yielded evidence of Donahue's participation in a homosexual pedophile ring that was using adolescent students to produce child sexual abuse images and child trafficking. Several victim statements describe parties they were brought to by Donahue, where children were being trafficked.

- In March, Jennings met with the BCA as part of promised cooperation with the investigation. He admitted he had heard rumors and that some parents had complained, but the complaints were "general complaints."[139] This is a direct contradiction to statements given by parents Ina Haugen and Mary Hallman.[140]

- Donahue received the John F. Sherman award for "Significant and Sustained Service" to American Theater.[141]

- A local restaurant had a lunch named after Donahue called the "John Donahue"—quiche du jour served with fresh fruit.[142]

- I was assaulted by Jason McLean in the spring at age fifteen.

---

139 Stearns v. CTC No. 27-CV-15-20713, trial exhibit #83, BCA Case #82000421, Continuation of Investigation Report, Agent Patrick Shannon, March 1, 1983

140 Stearns v. CTC No. 27-CV-15-20713, testimonies of Mary Hallman, trial transcript, pp. 57–60 and Ina Haugen, trial transcript, pp. 63–71

141 CTC application for Ongoing Ensembles Narrative Proposal, submitted to the National Endowment for the Arts and MN State Arts Board, March 28, 1984

142 Deborah Caulfield, "The Scandal at the Children's Theatre," *LA Times Calendar*, July 22, 1984, p. 4

1984

- Minnesota's Statutory Rape law changed.[143] The age of consent was sixteen, but a new limitation was added—when the perpetrator was in a position of power, such as a teacher, boy scout leader, or a priest or rabbi, the age of consent went up to eighteen. This was an important shift in the law and should have happened long before 1984.

- The National Center for Missing and Exploited Children was established this year.

- Awareness of child sexual abuse and the prevention of it had been building since the late seventies/early eighties and was now gaining momentum locally and nationally. These kinds of child protection efforts were crucial to shifting culture and educating people about the prevalence of the problem, which laid the foundation for the work done by *The Boston Globe* exposing the Catholic Archdiocese's coverup of predator priests in the early 2000s.

- Bancroft Elementary schoolteacher Dennis Lambert gave the BCA names of students he knew to be having "continuous sexual relationships" with Donahue.[144] One of the students had been abused by him for years, starting when he was twelve years old. It was later revealed that Lambert himself was raping one of these boys and in his statement, referred to this child as "extremely seductive."[145]

- CTC student T. J. O'Donnell knew Donahue was being investigated and contacted BCA investigator Michael Campion to report an incident he had witnessed at Donahue's home between Donahue and a pre-teen student.

143 Age of Consent, Minn. Stat. § 609.345
144 Costello Thesis, p. 157
145 Costello Thesis, p. 160

T. J. had been sexually assaulted by Donahue many times, but it was seeing him do something to another child that prompted him to finally act. Children want the abusive behavior to go away, not necessarily the abuser themselves. T. J. told me he admired Donahue as a teacher and mentor and didn't want all that to end. He wanted Donahue to stop abusing him and other boys. T. J.'s phone call is what broke the case open and led to Donahue's arrest.[146]

- Donahue was arrested on April 18, 1984. After the press conference announcing Donahue's arrest, the police hotline received almost two hundred phone calls with supporting information.[147] Donahue pled guilty to seven counts of first- and second-degree criminal sexual conduct[148] but bargained it down to three counts in the end. Eventually, he admitted to sixteen victims,[149] and by 2019, twenty-three victims had been officially identified.[150]

- Sentencing guidelines offered the possibility for Donahue to go to federal prison for several years. His plea bargain allowed him to avoid going to federal prison. Instead, he was sentenced to one year in the workhouse and fifteen years of probation. He was placed in the work release program after ten months.[151]

- Jason McLean was suspended for suspicion of "having relationships" with female students. He managed to convince

146 Kay Miller, "A Story of Denial John Clark Donahue and the Children's Theatre— Parts 1, 2 and 3," *Minneapolis StarTribune*, May 19, 20, 21, 1991, and eyewitness testimony, T. J. O'Donnell

147 Costello Thesis, p. 160

148 Costello Thesis, p. 165

149 Kay Miller, "A Story of Denial John Clark Donahue and the Children's Theatre— Part 1," May 19, 1991, p. 3E

150 Protected victim statements and depositions with Jeff Anderson and Associates

151 Costello Thesis, p. 250, and Peter Vaughan, "Donahue to Direct Play at Mixed Blood," *Minneapolis StarTribune*, November 8, 1985, p. 2C

all of his victims that their "relationship" was consensual and told them not to talk to the BCA if they called.[152] They all agreed. McLean was reinstated to the acting company in the fall and went back to work.[153] He also went right back to abusing teenage girls.[154]

- Sarah Lawless resigned as executive director of CTC, denying that her decision had anything to do with what was happening at the theater.[155]

- Donahue's legal fees were paid by affluent CTC board member Mrs. Stanley Brooks Gregory.[156] In her deposition in 2018, stage manager Mary Winchell referred to attending a party at Gregory's home and that she had a large Chagall painting on the wall. This is an example of the echelon of people in the community who surrounded Donahue.

- After his arrest, city records show that Donahue transferred the deed of his home to MSFA, the entity that had sold him the home for one dollar in 1972 and owned the property that CTC was built on. The house was transferred back to Donahue in 1986.[157]

- CTC director of outreach Tony Steblay was suspended for suspicion of abusing female students. Steblay had been hired

---

152 Stearns v. CTC No. 27-CV-15-20713, testimonies of Jina Penn-Tracy, trial transcript, pp. 36–37, and Melissa Beneke, trial transcript, pp. 92–93, and multiple eyewitness accounts

153 Stearns v. CTC No. 27-CV-15-20713, trial exhibit #136, Memorandum of Understanding between McLean and interim Executive Director, John B. Davis, signed October 22, 1984

154 Protected victim statements and depositions with Jeff Anderson and Associates

155 Kay Miller, "A Story of Denial John Clark Donahue and the Children's Theatre—2," *Minneapolis StarTribune*, May 19, 1991, p. 2E

156 Stearns v. CTC No. 27-CV-15-20713, Jeff Anderson and Associates Collected Evidence Archive

157 City of Minneapolis Block 6 Record, ADN 17090, GEO Galpin's Addition to Minneapolis

at CTC despite the fact that he had been fired a couple of years earlier from Hopkins-Eisenhower High School for inappropriate behavior with girls in the theater program.[158]

- In the fall, a Grand Jury was convened to investigate the rumors involving several CTC staff members. Twenty-six students were subpoenaed. Several staff members were investigated, some of them were charged with criminal sexual conduct or failure to report suspected abuse. The result of the poorly run investigation and the lack of cooperation on behalf of students and staff was that only five other people were charged with either sexually assaulting students or failing to report abuse.[159]

- Sean McNellis was charged with two counts of third-degree criminal sexual conduct and was given a continuance of his case without a trial. A year later, his case was dismissed.[160]

- One of the perpetrators, Steven Adamczak, convinced the girls who had bravely come forward to report him, saying that if he went to jail, he'd be raped by other prisoners. In order to save him from that fate, the girls all recanted on the stand, saying they weren't really abused. He was acquitted, and the judge shook his finger at the girls telling them they were horrible children for lying about being assaulted.[161] The re-wounding of what their abuser did, the victim-blaming, and the way the judge treated them deeply affected them for their entire lives.

- Don Fogelberg, teacher and director of academic education for the Conservatory School, was fired in the early spring of

---

158 Costello Thesis, p. 141
159 Stearns v. CTC No. 27-CV-15-20713, Jeff Anderson and Associates Collected Evidence Archive
160 Costello Thesis, p. 189
161 Costello Thesis, pp. 180–184, and protected victim statements and depositions with Jeff Anderson and Associates

1985 for being in a "sexual relationship" with a sixteen-year-old student from out of state who was living with him and his family. He wasn't reported. There were no legal consequences for his offense. Fogelberg was part of the team promoting the Conservatory School to out-of-town students in the summer of 1984. He assured students and parents it was now safe for kids at CTC—all the "bad apples" were gone.[162]

- Jennings and Conservatory School teacher Scott Creeger were indicted by a grand jury for failure to report suspected sexual abuse of CTC students, which was required by the Minnesota Mandatory Reporting and Maltreatment of Minors Act. Because of the abuses that happened at CTC and the outcome of the Creeger and Jennings cases, prosecutors turned their attention to getting the language in the law amended instead of appealing the rulings. Their efforts were successful, and the State Legislature amended the Mandatory Reporting law, changing the vague wording and closing the loopholes that allowed Jennings' lawyer to get the charges dropped.[163]

1985

- November, Donahue was put on the work release program and hired at Mixed Blood Theater in Minneapolis to direct a show. He was welcomed back into the theater community and was still loved and respected by many.[164] The parole

---

162 Karren Mills, "Theater Staff Member Fired After Admitting Sex With Female Student," *Associated Press*, March 1, 1985

163 Margaret Zack, "County Won't Appeal Dismissal of Charges Against CTC Officials," *Minneapolis StarTribune*, November 28, 1984, p. 4B, and Editorial, "For Better Reporting of Child Abuse," *Minneapolis StarTribune*, November 30, 1984, p. 24A

164 Kay Miller, "After Workhouse, Time in Wings, Donahue Ready for Bigger Roll," *Minneapolis StarTribune*, May 21, 1991, p. 3E

agreement that was part of his sentencing was never enforced.[165]

- I graduated from High School.

1986

- McLean, who had stayed on staff at CTC after his reinstatement in the fall of 1984, continued to abuse several girls at the school. The new CTC artistic director, Jon Cranney, who claimed he found out McLean was "breaking the rules" with students and fired him, admitted under oath that he didn't report him as was required by the Mandated Reporting law.[166]

- McLean claims he wasn't fired but chose to resign. In his resignation letter to Cranney on January 15, 1986, McLean cited his reasons for leaving were rumors and innuendo about his "easy rapport" with students, and he requested a severance package that included: the theater to pay off any fines to Actors Equity, continuation of his salary and benefits through the end of the season, agreement not to contest his unemployment insurance claim, erasure of any and all negative citations regarding the "ethics of my behavior with students that may appear on my employment record with CTC," and "the striking of any and all negative remarks which may appear on the records of students appertaining to me." The theater's general manager, Jay Bush, agreed to all of it in writing. McLean wasn't reported for his behavior.[167]

---

165 Costello Thesis, p. 239
166 Stearns v. CTC No. 27-CV-15-20713, testimony of John Cranney, trial transcript, pp. 1623–1633
167 Stearns v. CTC No. 27-CV-15-20713, trial exhibit #139, resignation letter of McLean, dated January 15, 1986

- McLean started a new restaurant called The Loring Café.

- Donahue, after a stint working and doing theater in Arizona, returned to the Twin Cities and was welcomed back into the theater community with the exception of CTC, where he was forbidden to set foot in.[168]

- Donahue went to work for McLean at his restaurant and theater, The Loring Café and The Loring Playhouse.

1987

- Lawyer Martin John Costello wrote a thesis called "Hating the Sin, Loving the Sinner: The Minneapolis Children's Theatre Company Adolescent Sexual Abuse Prosecutions" for his doctorate in philosophy, which was granted in November 1987. In his thesis, as well as in interviews, Costello categorized the CTC prosecution as a complete failure.[169]

- Three of Donahue's victims sued him and CTC for the abuse they endured. The cases were settled out of court.[170]

1991

- Seven years after the arrest of Donahue, after the statute of limitations had expired, *Minneapolis StarTribune* journalist Kay Miller did an in-depth, three-part investigative story about what had happened at CTC.[171]

---

168 Kay Miller, "After Workhouse, Time in Wings, Donahue Ready for Bigger Roll," *Minneapolis StarTribune*, May 21, 1991, p. 3E

169 Kay Miller, "Lawyer Costello's Book indicts Courts, Handling of Sex Abuse Cases," *Minneapolis StarTribune*, May 20, 1991, p. 3E

170 Stearns v. CTC No. 27-CV-15-20713, Jeff Anderson and Associates Collected Evidence Archive

171 Kay Miller, "A Story of Denial John Clark Donahue and the Children's Theatre—Parts 1, 2 and 3," *Minneapolis StarTribune*, May 19, 20, 21, 1991

2015–19

- Jeff Anderson and Associates received more than two hundred phone calls providing information after the first lawsuits were announced on December 1, 2015.

- Once the investigation for litigation was complete, a total of twenty-eight perpetrators were identified on staff at CTC through testimonials of survivors.

- Based on what I know, I would estimate the number of children who were abused by Donahue alone is in the high hundreds. It's impossible to know how many children were sexually abused by the dozens of abusers at CTC over the two decades Donahue was in charge.

- The body of evidence collected by Jeff Anderson and Associates could have put The Children's Theatre Company out of business.[172]

---

172 Stearns v. CTC No. 27-CV-15-20713, Jeff Anderson and Associates Collected
    Evidence Archive

About the Author

Laura Stearns is a theater maker, writer, community activist, consultant, Victim Support Advocate, co-founder of the Minnesota Theater Accountability Coalition, and founding board member of CTA Wellness. Laura's experience as a civil litigant against the Children's Theatre Company in Minneapolis for institutional neglect helped inform training for the field of Civil Litigant Advocacy, and her experience has amplified the need for more stringent policies to protect children in performing arts production and education around the globe. Her testimony at the state legislature supported the removal of the criminal Statute of Limitations for rape victims in the state of Minnesota. Laura is an accomplished actor and has worked in theater both on and off stage for more than three decades. As a survivor of childhood sexual abuse, she uses her diverse skill set as an entertainer to bring lightness and accessiblity to the challenging subject of sexual violence. Her book *Daring to Heal: Growing Beyond Trauma Through Awareness, Acceptance, and Action* focuses on the universal effects of trauma as a natural response to traumatic events, and how we can transform our core belief system to shift society away from rape culture towards a culture of accountability and consent. It will be available in spring 2023.